CW01631024

UNDER ... H

UNDERSTANDING *Maqāṣid al-Sharīʿah*

A Contemporary Perspective

Musfir bin Ali al-Qahtani

INTERNATIONAL INSTITUTE OF ISLAMIC THOUGHT

P.O. BOX 669, HERNDON, VA 20172, USA
www.iiit.org

LONDON OFFICE
P.O. BOX 126, RICHMOND, SURREY TW9 2UD, UK
www.iiituk.com

978-1-56564-666-7 *Limp*
978-1-56564-668-1 *Cased*

Printed in Malta by Gutenberg Press

Layout and Design
Shiraz Khan

Contents

Foreword

MUSFIR BIN ALI AL-QAHTANI contributes in this work to the ever growing body of scholarly literature in the field of *maqāṣid al-sharīʿah* (higher objectives of Islamic law). *Understanding Maqāṣid al-Sharīʿah: A Contemporary Perspective* calls for the development of a juridical sense that is finely tuned to the higher objectives and purposes of Islamic rulings, the aims of which are the formulation of a new methodology in understanding the revealed texts and the reform of Muslim thought and its application. The author draws our attention to the importance of understanding various levels of *maqāṣid*, including distinguishing between primary aims (*al-maqāṣid al-aṣliyyah*) and secondary aims (*al-maqāṣid al-tābiʿah*).

Al-Qahtani asserts that a positive understanding of the objectives of the Shariʿah should produce affirmative human and cultural development in Muslim societies. The real strength of this work, however, is in the author's application of higher objectives and aims to different areas of jurisprudence, such as in deriving and issuing religious rulings (*iftā'*), and to important social issues and problems present in Muslim societies, such as extremism, jihad, commanding right and forbidding wrong, social change, crisis of Muslim thought, countering religious excessiveness, the need for recreation and leisure, citizenship and nation-belonging, spreading beauty and harmony in Islam, and the role of Muslim women in society. For these reasons, the book should appeal both to the general reader and specialist alike.

Where dates are cited according to the Islamic calendar (hijrah) they are labelled AH. Otherwise they follow the Gregorian calendar and labelled CE where necessary. Arabic words are italicized except for those which have entered common usage. Diacritical marks have been added only to Arabic names not considered modern. English translations taken from Arabic references are those of the author.

The IIIT, established in 1981, has served as a major center to facilitate serious scholarly efforts based on Islamic vision, values and principles. The Institute's programs of research, seminars and conferences during the last thirty years have resulted in the publication of more than four hundred titles in English and Arabic, many of which have been translated into other major languages.

We express our thanks and gratitude to the author for his cooperation and all those directly or indirectly involved in the completion of this book.

IIIT
1436 AH / May 2015 CE

Preface

All praise be to God (SWT),[1] and blessings and peace be upon His trustworthy Prophet Muhammad (ṢAAS)[2], his household and his Companions.

The aims of Islamic law, or the Shariʿah, constitute a general framework for existent and anticipated Islamic rulings. They are the comprehensive goals to which a Muslim refers whenever he or she is uncertain, particularly when partisanship, blind imitation, and preoccupation with the details of controversial issues are the order of the day. They are also a refuge for someone who seeks a way out of a crisis or seeks an Islamic solution to a particular *nāzilah* (a novel case that was unknown in the history of Islamic jurisprudence and for which Islamic rules are needed). In any of these situations, the aims of Islamic law, or *maqāṣid al-sharīʿah*, are there to offer guidance. Many Muslim reformers have taken *maqāṣid al-sharīʿah* as their primary reference point. Imam al-Shāfiʿī, for example, brought the Muslim community together after they had been divided into two groups, *Ahl al-Ra'y*[3] and *Ahl al-Ḥadīth*,[4] via a focus on *maqāṣid al-sharīʿah* in his famous work, *al-Risālah*; in a similar spirit, Shaykh al-Islam Ibn Taymiyyah explained the way of the righteous predecessors after division had eaten deep into the fabric of the Muslim community concerning belief and law. Imam al-Shāṭibī did the same in his famous work, *al-Muwāfaqāt*, in which he clarified matters relating to acts of worship and other fundamental issues in light of *maqāṣid al-sharīʿah*.

Therefore, selecting a working methodology to clarify the aims and general principles of Islamic law in times of crisis and division is beneficial to Muslims both individually and collectively. Such crises might involve, for example, excessive preoccupation with disagreements over peripheral matters; blind imitation of fallible human beings as opposed to following the infallible revelation; giving preference to means over ends, and stressing avoidance of harm over achievement of benefit. Such phenomena have brought division to the Muslim community and, consequently, weakness and degeneration.

The present work is an attempt to apply the science of *maqāṣid al-sharīʿah* to contemporary needs, particularly the need to formulate new Islamic methodologies, and to reform and diversify Islamic action. I refer to such an approach as "goals awareness" given the need to understand the goals of Islamic law lest we come to hasty conclusions concerning their means of application. In this way we can bring about guided change and lucid reform, being cognizant of and attentive to the realities before us.

This work consists of a preface, introduction, and five chapters. The preface presents the science of *maqāṣid al-sharīʿah*. Chapter One examines the impact of goals awareness on contemporary methods of arriving at fatwas, or Islamic legal rulings. Chapter Two deals with the need to be aware of cultural constructions. Chapter Three discusses goals awareness as it relates to the crisis of religious extremism. Chapter Four examines the impact of goals awareness on Muslims' way of thinking. Finally, Chapter Five highlights the urgent need for goals awareness in social action.

May God grant me sincere intention and correct action and let this work be pleasing to Him. Whatever I have written that is correct is from God alone, and whatever is mistaken is from me and from Satan. God knows best, and is the best of all judges. Blessings and peace be upon our beloved Prophet Muhammad, members of his household, and his Companions.

Dr. Musfir bin Ali al-Qahtani

INTRODUCTION

OVERVIEW OF THE INTRODUCTION

To introduce and discuss the meaning of *Maqāṣid al-Sharīʿah*, its definition, how it is understood, and its differing categories.

THE aims of Islamic law are the purposes for which this law was ordained, and which are considered in all or most of its rulings. Islamic law has been ordained exclusively for the benefit of humankind in this world and in the Hereafter.[1]

A thorough study of Islamic law will show that its rulings exist either to bring benefit or to ward off harm. Examples of this in the Qur'an include the following statements:

> [We have sent all these] apostles as heralds of good tidings and as warners, so that men might have no excuse before God after the coming of these apostles. (*Sūrah al-Nisā'* 4:165)

> We have sent thee [O Prophet] as an evidence of our grace towards all the worlds. (*Sūrah al-Anbiyā'* 21:107)

A close study of the rationales behind known rulings will show clearly that such rationales, taken together, are the very goals of the Shariʿah and the pivot around which its rulings revolve. This is illustrated by the following statement of God, which follows a command to perform ritual ablutions: "God does not want to impose any hardship on you" (*Sūrah al-Mā'idah* 5:6). The same principle is evident in God's statement ordaining fasting: "Fasting is ordained for you as it was ordained for those before you, so that you might remain conscious of God" (*Sūrah al-Baqarah* 2:183), and His statement about prayer: "Prayer restrains [us] from loathsome deeds and from all that runs counter to reason" (*Sūrah al-ʿAnkabūt* 29:45).

Other verses also explain the wise purposes behind Islamic rulings. Imam al-Shāṭibī writes, "Since it has been established by thorough study that this is the case [i.e., that the law of Islam aims to serve people's best interests] and that it benefits knowledge, we can, therefore, say with all certainty that this is the general characteristic of all the details of Islamic law."[2]

Thus, three things are found in every ruling of the Shariʿah: (1) a clear and easily defined cause (*ʿillah*), (2) the benefit (*maṣāliḥ*) the action concerned will bring, that is, the wisdom (*ḥikmah*) behind the legislation concerned, and (3) the benefit to be attained or the harm to be prevented by the ruling in question, also known as the purpose or intent (*maqṣad*).[3]

These are permanent features of all Islamic rulings. There is no Islamic ruling or legislation but that it aims to actualize a benefit, prevent some harm, or free the world from some evil or transgression. In short, the Shariʿah aims at actualization of the general goals of making individuals and societies happy, preserving law and order, and bringing humankind to the pinnacle of perfection, goodness, and civilization. Everything in Islamic legislation is about ensuring benefits. Whatever it demands is for the purpose of actualization of benefit, immediate or long-term; and all its prohibitions are for the purpose of preventing harm and evil.

Since the goals of the Shariʿah are so intimately connected to Islamic laws in their every detail, it follows that being acquainted with them is a matter of necessity for all people. Moreover, since the goals and purposes of Islamic law enable us to see the wisdom behind each Islamic command or prohibition, they serve to strengthen our faith, certainty, and commitment to right action. As for Muslim jurists, they consider the goals of Islamic law when investigating existing rulings, studying texts, and deducting new rulings. In order to know the ruling that applies to a given case, one needs first to understand the relevant texts. When seeking to reconcile seemingly contradictory proofs or texts, one may seek help through the goals of the Shariʿah. If there is a need to explain God's ruling on a case through methodologies such as analogical deduction or *istiḥsān*, the goals of Islamic law will help to clarify matters.[4]

It is precisely this situation which prompted Shaykh Ibn Ashur to write his invaluable book, *Maqāṣid al-Sharīʿah al-Islāmiyyah*. In his introduction he wrote:

> In this book I discuss important aspects of the goals of Shariʿah, citing examples of the same, and providing proofs of their genuineness. Such goals can serve as a light by which those seeking understanding of the religion can minimize differences of opinions among themselves, and by means of which budding scholars can learn to weigh divergent opinions in a manner that is fair and just. It is hoped that this method will enable us to overcome partisanship and base our views solely on the truth. My intention is to help Muslims who, when faced with new events and situations, can discern the most appropriate Islamic rulings in the face of numerous divergent views.[5]

Similarly, eminent scholars before Shaykh Ibn Ashur pointed out the importance of this field of knowledge and stressed jurists' need for it. Among these scholars were Imam al-Juwaynī,[6] al-Ghazālī,[7] al-ʿIzz ibn ʿAbd al-Salām[8] and his student, Imam al-Qarrāfī,[9] Shaykh al-Islam Ibn Taymiyyah[10] and his student Ibn al-Qayyim.[11]

However, it was Imam al-Shāṭibī who brought this knowledge to light, stressing its principles, and played a major role in establishing its foundations and explaining its rules. His book, *Al-Muwāfaqāt*, in which he includes a groundbreaking discussion of the goals of Islamic law, is thus an indispensable reference for scholars of jurisprudence.[12]

In view of the foregoing, the present work deals with methods which introduce the jurist to rulings on contemporary juristic issues in light of the goals and purposes of Islamic law. We stress the importance of maintaining consistency with these goals and purposes while taking into consideration all relevant evidences, principles, and the opinions of the leaders of the various schools of jurisprudence. Imam al-Shāṭibī asserted:

> It is the Lawgiver's purpose that a morally accountable Muslim's intention when acting should be consistent with the Lawgiver's intention when legislating. The proof for this may be clearly observed in the establishment of Islamic law .... What is, therefore, required from a morally accountable Muslim is to ensure that his actions are in concordance with the intent of the Lawgiver.[13]

Shaykh Abdullah Darraz states that, "As for the *mujtahid* particularly, it is important for him or her to identify the goal of Shariʿah in its ruling on each matter in order to determine the validity or accuracy of categorizing such a ruling under the general goals which Islamic law seeks to achieve, since specific rulings are considered to be expressions of more general principles."[14]

This goal-oriented perspective on the part of the *mujtahid* is the guiding rule for deducing all types of rulings. The following points shed light on the role played by the aims of Islamic law in acquainting the *mujtahid* with rulings on newly arising issues and questions.

(1) The Meaning of *Maqāṣid al-Shariʿah*

The linguistic definition: The term *maqāṣid* is the plural of *maqṣad*, a word that conveys a number of meanings, including: (1) to aim at something, to come to it, to head towards it; (2) straightness of a path; an example of this is God's statement, "It rests with God alone to show you the right path (*wa ʿalā Allāhi qaṣd al-sabīl*), yet there is [many a one] who swerves from it" (*Sūrah al-Naḥl* 17:9); and (3) justice, moderation and avoidance of excess. This is shown in God's statement: "Be modest in thy bearing (*waqṣid fī mashyika*) (*Sūrah Luqmān* 31:19)." We also have the Prophet's statement: "Be just, and you will attain the goal,"[15] which means, "Be balanced and moderate."[16]

Perhaps the first meaning is the most inclusive and the closest to what we need. We can then say that *maqāṣid* are things that the

Shariʿah aims at in its rulings, and toward which it strives on a path which is balanced and moderate.

As for the literal meaning of the word *sharīʿah* or *sharʿ*, it denotes clearness and exposition. It also denotes a source of water. Therefore, *sharīʿah* is a means of complying with the requirements of servitude to God; it is also said that it is the path of religion.[17]

The technical definition of *maqāṣid al-sharīʿah*: The term *maqāṣid al-sharīʿah* is widely used among both earlier and later scholars. However, neither I nor other researchers before me have found a precise definition for the word *maqāṣid* in the works of such scholars. Even the pioneering al-Shāṭibī did not define this term precisely, perhaps because he wrote almost exclusively to other scholars rather than to laymen. This may be seen in the statement that:

> No one should expect to benefit from this book until he is fully acquainted with the science of the Shariʿah, both its fundamentals and its subsidiaries, its texts and its logical foundations, and is not given to imitating other scholars or favoring a particular school of thought.[18]

It should be borne in mind that this term had been in use for centuries before al-Shāṭibī's time, and that al-Shāṭibī did not believe in being too preoccupied with detailed definitions. He believed, rather, that terms can be defined by making them more tangible and accessible to those seeking to understand them.[19]

Though earlier scholars did not define *maqāṣid al-sharīʿah*, there have been attempts by some contemporary scholars and jurists to do so. Eminent scholar al-Tahir ibn Ashur writes, "The general goals of Shariʿah are the meanings and wise purposes to which the Lawgiver gives consideration in all or most pieces of legislation, and which are not restricted to a particular kind of Islamic ruling."[20] This definition is peculiar to the general goals of Shariʿah. There are, in addition, specific goals and wise purposes pertaining to matters of this world and the afterlife that are not covered in this definition.

Allal al-Fasi defines the goals of the Shariʿah as, "the ends the Shariʿah seeks to achieve, and the mysteries the Lawgiver has embedded within each of its rulings."[21] This definition covers the general and the specific goals of the Shariʿah. Therefore, it is, overall, an acceptable definition.

For his part, Ahmad al-Raysuni defines *maqāṣid al-sharīʿah* as, "The objectives for whose actualization Islamic law was established for the benefit of humankind."[22] This definition is close to that of Allal al-Fasi, though it excludes the latter's reference to "specific goals". Hence, al-Raysuni appears to believe that "the benefit of humankind" includes both general and specific benefits.

Yusuf Hamid al-Alim defines *maqāṣid al-sharīʿah* as, "the aims which legislation strives to achieve, and the underlying purposes which the All-Wise Lawgiver has placed in each ruling of the Shariʿah."[23] This definition covers the two types of goals, although it is somewhat redundant, being a combination of the definitions offered by the two previously mentioned scholars.

Wahbah al-Zuhayli defines *maqāṣid al-sharīʿah* as "the objectives and wise purposes which the Lawgiver embeds in each of its [the Shariʿah's] rulings."[24] It will be noted that this definition resembles those provided by Ibn Ashur and al-Fāsī, while other contemporary scholars have offered definitions similar to those related above.[25]

Based on the foregoing, the term *maqāṣid al-sharīʿah* refers to the meanings and wise purposes, generally and specifically considered by the Lawgiver, to bring about benefits for humankind in this world and the Hereafter.

The Definition Explained

"Meanings" (*al-maʿānī*, plural of *maʿnā*): This word, common among many scholars, particularly earlier ones, is used in the sense of "causes" (*ʿilal*). Imam al-Shāfiʿī said:

> If there is a ruling by God or His Messenger and the wisdom behind that ruling is explained, and if we then encounter a case upon which there is no explicit text (from either the Book of God or the

> Sunnah of His Prophet but which shares the same cause (*maʿnā*) as that upon which there is a textual ruling, then that ruling is applicable to the new case.[26]

In his explanatory notes on *Uṣūl al-Bazdawī*, Abd al-Aziz al-Bukhari comments that in the phrase "knowing the texts with their meanings" (*maʿrifat al-nuṣūṣi bi maʿānīhā*)", the word translated as "meanings" (*al-maʿānī*) refers to "linguistic and legal meanings now referred to as causes (*ʿilal*)," since earlier scholars used the word *maʿnā* in place of the word *ʿillah*.[27]

Wise purposes (*ḥikam*, plural of *ḥikmah*): Al-Qarrāfī explains that in the parlance of *uṣūl al-fiqh* scholars, a *ḥikmah* is "that on account of which an effective cause (*al-wasf*), that is, a cause which reflects the universal aims of the law, becomes a specific cause (*al-ʿillah*).[28] The goals of Islamic law are manifested through the causes of legal rulings and the wisdom which underlies them.

"Considered by the Lawgiver": It is understood from this phrase that the basic characteristic of God's rulings is that they are premised on causes that lead to benefits that are the very objectives of the Lawgiver.[29]

"To bring about benefits for mankind": This clause explains the general objective behind promulgation of Islamic rulings, which is to bring about what is good and beneficial for human beings at large.

"In this world and the Hereafter": This clause indicates that the objectives of the Shariʿah are to bring about what is good and beneficial for humankind in this world and the next. Many of those who study the objectives of the Shariʿah do not explain the benefits that someone will receive in the afterlife from the rulings of Islamic law. However, Imam al-Shāṭibī states, "Laws are promulgated for the benefit of humankind in both this world and the Hereafter."[30]

Other terms similar in meaning to *maqāṣid al-sharīʿah*: There are numerous terms used to refer to the objectives of the Shariʿah. This is to be expected given the broad range of meanings encompassed by this concept, including legislative rules, basic principles, and aims which can all be categorized generally under the rubric of objectives or goals of the Shariʿah. Another reason for this plethora of terms revolving around a single theme may be the gradual historical development of the science and the maturation of its terminology.[31] The following are some of the terms to which we are referring:

Al-Maṣlaḥah: In its general Islamic connotation among *uṣūl al-fiqh* scholars, this term is more or less synonymous with the term "legal intent" (*al-maqṣad al-sharʿī*), or one of the objectives of Islamic law. Imam al-Rāzī writes:

> The term 'legal interest' or 'legitimate interest' (*maṣlaḥah sharʿiyyah*) is a description that directly or indirectly includes attainment of one of the goals of Islamic law, whether that goal is religious or worldly. What we mean by the goals of Shariʿah are those entities whose attainment and preservation are required by the texts of Islamic law, such as life, reason, chastity, property and honor.[32]

Imam al-Ghazālī touched upon the theme of *maqāṣid al-sharīʿah* through his discussion of the topics of *maṣlahah* and *istiṣlāḥ* due to these terms' close connection to one another. He writes:

> As for *maṣlaḥah*, it originally means efforts made to bring about a benefit or to prevent harm. But this is not what we mean by this term, because the achievement of benefit and prevention of harm are merely human goals whose actualization brings about people's well-being. Rather, what we mean by this term is preservation of the goals of the Shariʿah, which aims at the preservation of five entities: people's religion, their souls, their reason, their progeny and their wealth. Anything that entails preservation of these fundamentals is a *maṣlaḥah*.[33]

Many *uṣūl al-fiqh* scholars have made similar statements in this regard. The recognized goals of the Shariʿah are those which are consistent with the Lawgiver's intentions. When the pursuit of a given *maṣlaḥah* involves a potential harm to society, such a *maṣlaḥah* should not be recognized because it conflicts with the clear and the defined purpose of the Lawgiver, which is not is subject to human wishes and desires.[34]

Al-Ḥikmah **(wise purpose)** is a term used as a synonym for "the purpose of the Lawgiver." For instance, they say, "the purpose of this is such and such, or the *ḥikmah* behind this is such and such," although jurists use the word *ḥikmah* (wisdom) more often than the word *maqṣad* (goal), and their writings are filled with references to the wise purposes behind various Islamic precepts.[35]

In his study of the use of the word *ḥikmah* by Muslim juristic scholars, Abd al-Aziz al-Rabiah notes that it is used in two senses: (1) the intended purpose for a given legal ruling, that is, the human interest to be achieved or maximized, or the harm to be prevented or minimized by means of such a ruling, and (2) the cause or occasion that necessitates the promulgation of a law, such as hardship.[36] It will be noted that these two definitions are almost identical, and that both signify the actualization of the Lawgiver's true purpose.

Al-ʿIllah: Different usages of this term have caused significant controversy. However, our concern here is to identify how it is used to express the purpose of the Lawgiver, which in this context is synonymous with *ḥikmah*. Over time it has come to be used primarily to refer to the apparent effective cause around which rulings of the Shariʿah revolve.

Mustafa Shalabi has identified the following three uses of the word *ʿillah*: (1) the benefit or harm that results from an action, (2) the benefit derived from or the harm prevented by promulgation of a ruling, and (2) the visible occasion for promulgation of a ruling in which there is a benefit for humankind.[37] He states:

> It is correct to call these three things *al-ʿillah* (cause)... Later, however, they referred to effective causes (*awṣāf*) with the word *ʿillah*. In such cases, the word *ʿillah* was used figuratively because it is through these effective causes that the *ʿillah* is defined. Similarly, they refer to any benefit or harm that may result from an action as a wise purpose (*ḥikmah*), while acknowledging that it is actually the *ʿillah*.[38]

Hence, Imam al-Shāṭibī defines *ʿillah* as a *ḥikmah*, i.e., the wise purpose or benefit associated with something that has been commanded or permitted, and the harm associated with something that is forbidden. For instance, hardship is the *ʿillah* for allowing a traveler to shorten prayers and not to fast; therefore, being on a journey is the justification for this concession. In general, the *ʿillah* is the benefit or the harm itself, not its presumed source.[39] The way in which Imam al-Shāṭibī interprets *ʿillah* is the most suitable in the study of the objectives of Shariʿah, since the connection between the *ʿillah* and the benefit to be sought and/or the harm to be avoided is necessary for making analogical deductions and deriving rulings.

Scholars of Islamic jurisprudence also use the term "appropriate" (*munāsib*) in describing the goals of the Shariʿah, where the concept of appropriateness is a means of identifying the justification for a ruling. Imam al-Bayḍāwī said, "What is meant by 'appropriate' is that which brings benefit and prevents harm."[40]

> In explaining the meaning of the word "appropriate", Imam Shams al-Dīn al-Iṣfahānī states, "Appropriateness means that the effective cause calls for a ruling whose intention is to bring benefit or prevent harm in the particular situation concerned."[41]

In his annotation on *Jamʿ al-Jawāmiʿ*, Imam al-ʿAṭṭār states that "the word 'appropriate' refers to the wisdom reflected in the *ʿillah* referred to above as the purpose of the Lawgiver."[42]

Imam al-Ghazālī defined appropriateness in terms of the relationship between a given ruling and the human interests it helps to achieve. He wrote:

> What is meant by 'appropriate' is the way in which benefits are achieved as a result of a given ruling. For example, alcohol is forbidden because it robs a person of his reasoning capacity, which is the very basis for a person's being morally accountable. This ruling may thus be described as 'appropriate.'[43]

These, in sum, are some terms that are close in meaning to *al-maqāṣid al-sharʿiyyah*, or the goals of Islamic law. We have mentioned only the most widely used ones while omitting those that occur less frequently.[44]

(2) Proofs Supporting Recognition of *Maqāṣid al-Shariʿah*

In what follows, we shall cite textual and logical proofs which support the recognition of *maqāṣid al-sharīʿah.*

Textual Proofs

Recognition of the goals of Islamic law is not supported by a single specific text. Rather, it is supported by all the texts of the Shariʿah taken together. Indeed, every text in the Qur'an and the Sunnah tends to confirm the general principles and goals of the Shariʿah.

Imam al-Shāṭibī writes that,

> ... in affirming the intent of the Lawgiver as embodied in these principles,[45] scholars do not rely on a particular text or interpretation. Rather, based on the clear sense of countless passages, including texts with universal applicability and those applicable only to specific situations, and details pertaining to cases in every area and type of jurisprudence, they have discovered that the law taken as a whole... gravitates toward support for these principles.[46]

According to Imam al-Shāṭibī, the process of establishing the validity of *maqāṣid al-sharīʿah* requires clear evidence and proofs for the claims being made.[47] After considering the kinds of proofs that establish the authenticity of *maqāṣid al-sharīʿah*, al-Shāṭibī continues:

> The proof sought could be established through another dimension: the spirit of the law... A careful study of the Shariʿah, looking at its general and detailed proofs, will show that the goals of the Shariʿah cannot be demonstrated through one specific text, but, rather, only by examining a variety of texts with diverse purposes.[48]

A thorough, inductive study of the Shariʿah and the bases for its rulings makes its clear that it affirms goals which promote human beings' welfare both in this world and the Hereafter. Imam Ibn al-

Qayyim wrote:

> The Qur'an and the Sunnah of God's Messenger contain many texts in which the rulings of the law are explained or justified based on the wise purposes and benefits that serve as its foundation. If the texts to which we refer came to only 100 or 200, we would cite them here. However, there are more than 1,000 texts in the Qur'an and the Sunnah which address these issues in a variety of ways.[49]

Clearly, it would be difficult to establish the validity of *maqāṣid al-sharīʿah* by citing such a large number of texts. Nevertheless, it can also be established on the basis of the various principles affirmed by these texts. Some of these principles are as follows:

First: God informs us in many places in the Qur'an that He is *al-Ḥakīm* (the All-Wise).[50] This attribute necessitates that His rulings be ordained purposefully. It is the wise who put things in their proper places, and God's rulings do precisely this, having been ordained for people's benefit in this world and in the Hereafter. Ibn Al-Qayyim wrote:

> A statement cannot be regarded as wise unless it leads to praiseworthy goals and fulfills useful purposes. When a statement becomes a guide to beneficial knowledge and righteous deeds, the desired goal is achieved. But if the speaker, by his speech, does not intend to benefit the audience, provide them with guidance, lead them to happiness, or warn them against things that could impede its attainment, and if he fails to speak of this ultimate goal, send messengers and revelation concerning it, or lay down rewards and punishments toward its fulfillment, then he cannot be wise, nor can his speech be considered a source of wisdom.[51]

But highly exalted is God above such a description!

Second: God informs us in numerous places in the Qur'an that He is the Most Merciful.[52] The following verses are illustrative: "Our Lord, we have believed, so forgive us and have mercy upon us, and You are the best of the merciful" (*Sūrah al-Mu'minūn* 23:109); and, "But My mercy encompasses all things" (*Sūrah al-Aʿrāf* 7:156).

However, God can only be described as "Most Merciful" if He intends to show kindness to His servants by what He has created for them, commanded them to do, and legislated for them. Had His commands not been intended as kindness to His servants, then such commands could not be rightly called compassionate even if the servants actually experienced compassion through them. Therefore, as concluded by Ibn al-Qayyim, "Denying that there is any wisdom behind or any purpose for whatever God does is, in essence, a denial of His mercifulness."[53]

Third: There are numerous Qur'anic verses in which God informs us that He has done "such and such" for "such and such a reason", or in which He explains His actions in some other terms. Such passages, which serve as a basis for formulation of the general and specific goals of the Shariʿah, include:

> And thus have We willed you to be a community of the middle way, so that with your lives you might bear witness to the truth before all mankind, and that the Apostle might bear witness to it before you. And it is only to the end that we might make a clear distinction between those who follow the Apostle and those who turn about on their heels that We have appointed [for this community] the direction of prayer which thou [O Prophet] hast formerly observed. (*Sūrah al-Baqarah* 2:143)

> God wills that you shall have ease, and does not will you to suffer hardship; but He desires that you complete the number [of fasting days required], and that you extol God for having guided you aright, and that you render your thanks [unto Him]. (*Sūrah al-Baqarah* 2:185)

> Because of this did We ordain unto the children of Israel that if anyone slays a human being – unless it be in punishment for murder or for spreading corruption on earth – it shall be as though he had slain all mankind; whereas, if anyone saves a life, it shall be as though he had saved the lives of all mankind. (*Sūrah al-Mā'idah* 5:32)

And after giving instructions concerning the distribution of war booty, God explains the wisdom behind His instructions with the words, "so that it may not be [a benefit] going round and round among such of you as may [already] be rich" (*Sūrah al-Ḥashr* 59:7).

Similarly, the Messenger of God explained the injunction to ask permission before entering someone else's home, saying, "Verily! The command to request permission to enter [another's household] has been given lest one see what others would not want him to see."[54] There are, in addition, numerous other Qur'anic verses and sayings of the Prophet which either make explicit mention of the reasons for this or that ruling, or from which such reasons may be inferred, and which in this way affirm the goals of the Shariʿah.[55]

Fourth: A number of texts from the Qur'an and the Prophetic Sunnah explain certain general and specific purposes of the Shariʿah. One of these general purposes is to spare people undue hardship. We read, for example, that God "has laid no hardship on you in [anything that pertains to] religion" (*Sūrah al-Ḥajj* 22:78); "God wills that you shall have ease, and does not will you to suffer hardship" (*Sūrah al-Baqarah* 2:185); and, "God does not want to impose any hardship on you" (*Sūrah al-Mā'idah* 5:6).[56] As for specific goals relating to people's well-being, a number of these are mentioned in connection with jihad, zakah, and fasting.[57]

Fifth: There are general texts that encompass the actualization of all benefits. We read, for example, "Behold, God enjoins justice, and the doing of good, and generosity towards [one's] fellow-men; and He forbids all that is shameful and all that runs counter to reason, as well as envy; and He exhorts you [repeatedly] so that you might bear all of this in mind" (*Sūrah al-Naḥl* 16:90). In this connection, Imam al-ʿIzz ibn ʿAbd al-Salām said, "The most comprehensive Qur'anic injunction of all that is beneficial and warning against all that is harmful is God's statement: 'Behold, God enjoins justice, and the doing of good...'"[58]

In response to the claim that Islamic rulings do not cater to the interests of humans, Shaykh Muhammad al-Amin al-Shanqiti would refer often to God's statement, "Verily, this Qur'an shows the way to all that is most upright" (*Sūrah al-Isrā'* 17:9).[59] And similarly, the Prophet's statement that "no one should harm another, or reciprocate harm"[60] makes clear that the Shariʿah does not allow one to harm another, nor does it condone harming anyone in return.[61]

The foregoing are only a few of the many textual proofs that the Shariʿah was revealed to fulfill lofty goals of great benefit to the entire creation.[62]

Logical Proofs

Although the textual proofs cited thus far are sufficiently compelling in and of themselves, I would like now to cite a number of logical arguments to show that there is no contradiction between human reason and the texts of the Qur'an and the Sunnah. In so doing, I hope to disprove the doubts raised by rationalists. Therefore, what follows are rational proofs that the Lawgiver has goals, and that His ordainments aim at bringing about benefits and preventing harm:

First: Rulings devoid of wisdom and desirable goals can only be made by someone who is either ignorant of what he is doing – which, of course, is not applicable to the One Who possesses knowledge of all things – or unable to achieve such goals, which is impossible in the case of the One Who has power over all things. Furthermore, rulings devoid of wisdom and worthy goals can only be made by someone unwilling to bring benefit to others, which is equally inapplicable in the case of the One Who is the Most Merciful and Whose kindness is an integral part of His being. Indeed, such a Being could be nothing but a Benefactor, the Bestower of favor and blessing. If it were suggested that some factor might prevent this Being from willing and intending those goals, this also is impossible in the case of the One in Whose way nothing can stand, for He is the Doer of whatever He wills. Nor could these goals be assumed to be defective; indeed, such an assumption would turn the facts on their heads and be contrary to logic. After all, one who acts in wisdom and for a desired purpose is more praiseworthy than one who acts without a purpose. Likewise, one who creates is more perfect than one who does not; one who knows is more perfect than one who does not know; one who speaks is more perfect than one who does not speak; one who has the ability to will is more perfect than one who lacks this ability. And all these facts are logically unimpeachable. Therefore, denying the Lawgiver's wisdom and purposefulness is tantamount to attributing to Him the very opposite and most demeaning qualities.[63]

Second: It only reasonable to assert that God cares for the welfare of His servants throughout the span of their existence. After all, it is He who created us out of nothing and granted us His favor by making His other creatures subservient to us. As we are reminded in the Qur'an, "And He has made subservient to you, [as a gift] from Himself, all that is in the heavens and on earth. In this, behold, there are messages for people who think!" (*Sūrah al-Jāthiyah* 45:13).

It is impossible that God would care for the welfare of His servants both in this world and in the Hereafter while neglecting our interests in matters relating to the rulings of His own law. Indeed, it is these rulings that preserve our possessions our lives and our honor, without which we could not exist. Hence, it must be acknowledged that God takes our interests and welfare into consideration while ordaining the rulings of the Shariʿah.[64]

Third: God Almighty has bestowed honor on the human race. He says, "Now, indeed, We have conferred dignity on the children of Adam" (*Sūrah al-Isrā'* 17:70). Human dignity requires that people have the capacity to achieve personal well-being in its highest forms.[65]

Fourth: It is generally recognized that unless a system aims to bring about benefit or prevent harm, it is a failed system that deserves to be neither implemented nor emulated. No sane person would allow his (or her) system or method of doing things to be described as faulty and devoid of benefit. If even human beings, in all their imperfection and ignorance, would reject such a system, then how more unacceptable would it be to the Supreme Lawgiver?[66]

(3) Categories of *Maqāṣid al-Sharīʿah*

As we have noted, God has sent messengers with His revelations to benefit His servants both in this life and in the life to come.[67] This overall aim of the divine law has been manifested to varying degrees from one society to another depending on a variety of factors, some of which have negatively impacted the Law's benefits to humankind. A *mujtahid* who observes such disparities among societies and circumstances will be better able to compare one situation with another, arrive at sound analogical deductions, and recognize the ways in which to apply the divine law's precepts to this question or that.

In what follows we will examine three of the various approaches to categorizing *maqāṣid al-sharīʿah*.[68]

APPROACH NO. 1 is based on the types of interests or benefits the law of Islam is intended to preserve. This approach divides *maqāṣid al-sharīʿah* into three types: (1) essentials (*maqāṣid ḍarūriyyah*) (2) exigencies (*maqāṣid ḥājiyyah*), and (3) enhancements (*maqāṣid taḥsīniyyah*).

1) *Essentials*

Al-Shāṭibī defined essentials (*maqāṣid ḍarūriyyah*) as,

> things that are vital to actualizing benefits in matters of religion and earthly affairs, and the absence of which would render such actualization impossible. Their absence will lead to corruption and loss of life, and in the Hereafter, a failure to attain salvation and bliss.[69]

As for al-Fattūḥī, he defined them as, "that which yields benefits that are of an essential nature."[70] It will be clear from the aforementioned definition of essentials (*maqāṣid ḍarūriyyah*) that they are entities without which an upright life – indeed, life itself – would be impossible. Imam al-Ghazālī, Ibn ʿAbd al-Shakūr, Ibn al-Subkī, al-Fattūḥī (Ibn al-Najjār), and others identified these aims, in descending order of priority, as: religion (*al-dīn*), life (*al-nafs*), reason (*al-ʿaql*), progeny (*al-nasl*), and property (*al-māl*).[71]

Imam al-Shāṭibī placed these essentials in a different order,[72] namely, religion, life, progeny, property, and reason,[73] while al-Ṭūfī and Ibn al-Subkī added a sixth essential, that of honor (*al-aʿrāḍ*). They argued that sensible people would most often be willing to sacrifice their lives and wealth in defense of their honor. Therefore, anything that is defended with something that is essential should also be viewed as an essential.[74]

Proof that the law of Islam came to preserve these essentials is derived from an inductive study of firmly authenticated texts that promote the preservation and protection of these five entities. Imam al-Shāṭibī wrote:

> Not only the Muslim community, but other religious communities as well, would agree that Islamic law was ordained for the preservation of five essentials: religion, life, progeny, property, and reason. The Muslim community recognizes this fact even though there is no particular text which states this explicitly, nor is there a specific principle to which these essentials can be traced. Rather, their concordance with the Shariʿah may be inferred from a body of textual evidence so diverse that it cannot be limited to a single theme or category.[75]

Ibn Amīr al-Ḥājj stated, "The fact that the essentials of the Shariʿah consist in the preservation of these five entities may be induced from a study of reality and of the various religions' customs and laws."[76]

The laws of all religions recognize these benefits in various ways; however, the law of Islam, which is the last of all the divinely revealed laws, gives them the clearest recognition, having ordained ways both to bring them into existence, and to preserve them.[77] The existence of religion is ensured through faith and its pillars, and through the principles and protocols governing acts of worship. By virtue of these things the religion is enlivened, people's affairs are put right, and the society is kept on a strong and solid foundation. As for preservation of the religion, Islam accomplishes this by encouraging believers to invite others to faith, by warding off aggression against the religion, by fighting against whoever may seek to destroy it and obliterate its symbols and landmarks, by stopping those who attempt to cast doubts on its doctrines, and by preventing incorrect or distorted legal rulings.

Islam works to preserve life through the ordainment of marriage, by commanding us to consume what is necessary to for our survival, and by prescribing punishments for those who perpetrate actions that may pose danger to life. Regarding reason, with which God has endowed all human beings, Islam preserves it by forbidding intoxicants and carrying out the divinely ordained punishment against those who imbibe alcohol or other intoxicants. Progeny is preserved by Islam through the institution of marriage. Adultery, fornication, and wrongfully accusing others of committing them are forbidden, and punishments are prescribed for perpetrators. Similarly, abortion is forbidden except in cases of clear necessity. As for material property, Islam encourages its lawful acquisition by permitting various transactions and by enjoining efforts to earn it by legitimate means, and it works to preserve it by prohibiting theft and prescribing a punishment for this crime. Islam forbids us to cause damage to other people's property, and provides for compensation to be paid in the event that such damage occurs. To the same end, Islam forbids those who are mentally incompetent to exercise control over wealth, whether theirs or other people's.[78] In sum, Imam al-Shāṭibī wrote:

> Fundamental acts of worship and belief, such as testifying that 'there is no god but God and Muhammad is His Messenger', ritual prayer, zakah, fasting, and pilgrimage, are meant to preserve the very existence of the religion. Customs involving food and drink, clothing and shelter are meant to preserve the existence of life and the mind. Numerous transactions have been instituted to preserve the existence and subsistence of progeny, wealth, life and reason, while criminal laws are meant to preserve the very existence of all the above.[79]

2) *Exigencies (Maqāṣid Ḥājiyyah)*

In explaining exigencies (*maqāṣid ḥājiyyah*), Imam al-Shāṭibī tells us that they, are a necessary means to avoid discomfort and undue hardship. If these aims are not fulfilled, the morally accountable Muslim will face some hardship, though not to a degree that would threaten the interests of the Muslim community as a whole.[80]

Therefore, exigencies are comprised of things the need for which is not so dire that their absence would cause a disruption in life's flow, obstruct benefits, or deprive one of absolute necessities.[81] Rather, they are things whose absence would only cause some inconvenience, disrupt people's acts of worship, or cause some disturbance to their otherwise untroubled lives. What are termed "exigencies" (*al-maqāṣid al-ḥājiyyah*) are meant to relieve people of hardship, since the law of Islam is founded upon ease and the prevention of discomfort and hardship, be it in relation to worship, daily customs, social and monetary transactions, or criminal procedures. Imam al-Shāṭibī stated:

> In connection with acts of worship, special concessions are granted when there is a possibility of hardship, such as when a Muslim is ill or on a journey. Similarly, hunting, partaking of enjoyable food and drink, clothing, shelter, and means of transportation are all permitted for the purpose of alleviating hardship. This permissibility is also accorded to transactions such as loaning, sharecropping contracts, forward buying, and surrendering subsidiary items along with the principal goods being purchased, such as the fruits of a tree one is buying or the belongings of a slave who has been sold. This principle is likewise applicable in criminal matters such as *al-ḥukm bi al-lawth*, that is, handing down a guilty verdict against someone accused of murder based on circumstantial evidence, *al-tadmiyah,* a declaration by a wounded person before he dies that "so-and-so killed me," *al-qasāmah*, which is the declaration, under oath, by family members of someone who has been murdered that a particular individual killed their clansman, and *ḍarb al-diyyah ʿalā al-ʿāqilah*, that is, distributing the burden of paying blood money among consanguine relatives, the size of their shares being proportionate to their closeness to the accused, and the like.[82]

These and other legal rulings whose purpose is to relieve morally accountable Muslims of undue hardship help to achieve two significant objectives of the Shariʿah: (1) they remove an incentive to abandon the right path while reducing the risk of someone's developing an aversion to acts of worship and other Islamic obligations; and (2) they make it less likely that a Muslim will neglect his or her religious obligations due to a feeling of being overwhelmed by excessive religious duties. Muslims should avoid being overzealous in some actions lest they be negligent in others. In other words, they should carry out their religious obligations in such a way that none of them is fulfilled at the expense of any other.[83]

It goes without saying that exigencies (*al-maqāṣid al-ḥājiyyah*) are of a lesser degree of importance than essentials (*al-maqāṣid al-ḍarūriyyah*). This is why Imam al-Āmidī said, "Laws can be diverse in connection with exigencies (*al-maqāṣid al-ḥājiyyah*), but not in connection with essentials (*al-maqāṣid al-ḍarūriyyah*)."[84]

3) *Enhancements (Maqāṣid Taḥsīniyyah)*

Enhancements are entities that, while they are not necessary for a person's survival, nevertheless serve to make life easier and more enjoyable. According to Imam al-Shāṭibī, this category of *maqāṣid al-sharīʿah* encompasses,

> the adoption of fitting, praiseworthy practices while shunning filthy habits that would be abhorrent to a person of reasonable sensibilities. As such, these aims fall under the rubric of refined manners and noble morals.[85]

Individuals' and societies' adoption of refined manners and noble morals is an attempt to pursue the highest possible path in life, a path through which people seek to improve both their inward characters and their actions. Nevertheless, no one will be harmed or endure hardship if enhancements are not pursued.[86]

Imam al-Qarrāfī described enhancements as entities that can be regarded as "extras"[87] given the complementary role they play. Commenting on enhancements, Ibn Ashur wrote:

> As I see it, enhancements are things that help to perfect the Muslim

community in such a way that Muslims can live safe, tranquil lives, and their society can earn the respect of other nations. As a result of Muslims' commitment to exemplary habits, such as modest dress and growing a beard – in short, practices that reflect refined human sensibilities – the people of other nations will want to become part of the Muslim community, or, at least, to develop close relations with it ... The pursuit of *al-maqāṣid al-taḥsīniyyah* also includes avoidance of those things that might lead to corruption, which is preferable to waiting until corruption actually occurs.[88]

Enhancements, like exigencies and essentials, are reflected in all types of Islamic rulings. In this connection al-Shāṭibī states:

[Enhancements include] acts of worship such as the removal of impurities, attention to ritual purity overall, concealing one's private parts, wearing adornments, seeking nearness to God through supererogatory acts of worship such as voluntary alms giving; and in commendable customs such as the observance of rules of etiquette relating to eating and drinking, abstaining from unclean and unwholesome foods and drinks, and avoiding both excess or over abstemiousness in relation to food and drink. [Enhancements are likewise applicable] to things such as prohibiting the sale of ritually unclean substances, surplus water, and grazing fields; making it unlawful to deprive slaves of the opportunity to serve as witnesses and imams, or to deprive women of the right to be rulers and offer their hand in marriage; allowing a slave to seek liberation, as through a writ of manumission (*kitābah*), or through an agreement whereby he or she will be emancipated upon the death of his/her owner (*tadbīr*)...[89]

At this juncture, mention should be made of some important matters relating to essentials, exigencies, and enhancements. With every ruling God has issued to fulfill different kinds of aims, He has ordained what might be termed complementary rulings known as *mukammilāt*, *tatimmāt*, or *tawābiʿ*.[90] Al-Fattūḥī writes:

The reason they are referred to as being complementary is that they cannot stand by themselves. For although they have an impact, they do so only in conjunction with the primary ruling with which they are associated, and should not be given more consideration than they warrant.[91]

We can define a complementary ruling as something by virtue of which the wise purpose underlying an essential, an exigency or an enhancement may be achieved, whether by blocking something that might prevent the wise purpose from being fulfilled, or by adding something that manifests this wise purpose all the more perfectly and powerfully.

For each type of complementary ruling, Imam al-Shāṭibī cites examples that illustrate the role they play in preserving *maqāṣid al-sharīʿah*. In the category of essentials, the principle of parity in retribution can be cited as an example. In this case, al-Shāṭibī tells us, parity in retribution is not essential; rather, it is of a complementary nature.[92] Other examples illustrating the category of essentials include equal sustenance, equal wages, prohibiting the act of looking at a woman who is neither one's wife nor a woman who is not marriageable to the person looking for reasons of consanguinity; and prohibiting the consumption of even a small amount of an intoxicant.

The second category, that of exigencies, may be represented by examples such as considerations of compatibility in marriage.[93] Also, if we classify business transactions as exigencies, then calling on others to witness a transaction, mortgages, and guarantees are of a complementary nature to such transactions.

The third category, that of enhancements, is related to matters such as rules of conduct for dealing with ritual impurity, actions recommended for maintaining ritual purity, spending out of one's lawful earnings, and making choices concerning animals to be slaughtered for ritual purposes, including those slaughtered for the Feast of Sacrifice (*al-uḍḥiyah*) and following the birth of a child (*al-ʿaqīqah*), and concerning which slave to manumit.[94] However, enhancements should under no circumstances be allowed to override essentials. For example, jihad (against evil, wrongdoing and oppression) is an essential, while carrying it out in fairness is an enhancement. If an enhancement which is complementary to an essential threatens to invalidate the essential, then it should not be reckoned with, since the absence of something which is merely complementary should not be allowed to invalidate something which is more fundamental.[95]

The essentials (*al-maqāṣid al-ḍarūriyyah*) of Islamic law form the basis for its exigencies (*al-maqāṣīd al-ḥājiyyah*) and enhancements (*al-maqāṣid al-taḥsīniyyah*). If an essential is absolutely defective, the exigency and the enhancement would likewise be absolutely defective. However, if one or both of the latter two (the exigency and the enhancement) were defective, the essential would not necessarily be rendered defective in an absolute sense. However, absolute defectiveness in the enhancement or the exigency might cause a defect in the essential in one respect or another.[96]

APPROACH NO. 2 to categorizing *maqāṣid al-sharīʿah* is based on their level of importance or urgency. When *maqāṣid al-sharīʿah* are categorized in this manner, they divide themselves into two types. The first type consists of what we might term primary aims (*al-maqāṣid al-aṣliyyah*), that is, aims which embody the Lawgiver's most fundamental purposes. A more fundamental or primary aim will undoubtedly embody an interest more paramount than an aim which is less fundamental. Imam al-Shāṭibī states, "Fundamental aims are those which the morally accountable Muslim has no say in, and which are recognized as essential in every religion."[97]

The reason such matters are not subject to human input lies in the fact that they are necessary to safeguard inalienable public interests which are not specific to a particular situation, condition, or period of time. Imam al-Shāṭibī sought to explain the unquestionable nature of the essentials of Islamic law by dividing them into two groups. The first group was that of individual essentials (*ḍarūriyyāt ʿayniyyah*), which are duties required of each individual Muslim. Each individual Muslim is commanded to preserve his religion on the level of doctrine and practice, and to protect and preserve his own soul, life, and mind.[98]

The second group is termed collective essentials (*ḍarūriyyāt kifā'iyyah*), which include actions that protect Islamic society's public interests and preserve social order. Collective essentials are achieved through, for example, the work of those who hold positions of authority, and who help to protect and preserve the religion and people's rights in both the private and public spheres. Those assigned responsibility for protecting the public interest are forbidden to receive benefits in return for what they do. No ruler or holder of a position of authority must receive any remuneration from those he serves. Likewise, no judge should receive any gift from either of the contending parties to a litigation over which he presides. Hence, bribes and gifts given on account of the position someone occupies are prohibited.[99]

The second type into which *maqāṣid al-sharīʿah* are divided based on this categorization is that of secondary aims (*al-maqāṣid al-tābiʿah*), which are subsidiary to primary aims. Secondary aims help to actualize primary aims; they may be associated with them or annexed to them, either based on an injunction of the Shariʿah, or based on the morally accountable Muslim's intention in the context of his/her practices and customs. According to Imam al-Shāṭibī, morally accountable Muslims have some say with respect to secondary aims.[100]

Secondary aims are divided into three types based on the degree to which they affirm and support primary aims. Type 1 includes those that reinforce primary aims by making them attractive. An example is marriage (a secondary aim), which was ordained for the sake of procreation (a primary aim). The primary aim of procreation is associated with secondary aims such as the quest for shelter, spousal support, and cooperation toward securing the benefits of this world and the world to come. These secondary aims clearly reinforce marriage by fostering harmony and affection between spouses – a condition that furthers procreation, which is the primary objective of marriage in the Shariʿah.

Type 2 includes secondary aims which cancel out primary aims, and which, for this reason, are invalid. These include marriages which are entered into in order to allow a woman to remarry her first husband (*nikāḥ al-taḥlīl*), and temporary marriage (*nikāḥ al-mutʿah*), each of which works against the primary aim of marriage, which is procreation and a lasting conjugal bond. This sort of secondary aim should not be pursued, since it defeats the purpose of the Lawgiver.

As for Type 3, it is comprised of secondary aims that neither reinforce a primary aim nor cancel it out as in the case of Type 2 above. This type of secondary aim would include the case of marrying someone with the express intention of harming her/him, usurping her/his wealth, or some other motive which, although it might threaten the marriage's continuance, does not guarantee its discontinuance. This is because the intention to harm one's spouse does not necessarily mean that such harm will actually take place; neither does it mean that the occurrence of harm would necessarily lead to divorce due to the possibility of reconciliation, obtaining a legal injunction against the offending spouse, and the like.

This third type lies somewhere between Type 1 (secondary aims that reinforce a primary aim) and Type 2 (aims that are unequivocally contrary to the Lawgiver's purpose in ordaining marriage).[101]

APPROACH NO. 3 to categorizing *maqāṣid al-sharīʿah* is based on the extent to which they encompass the various rulings of Islamic law. This categorization yields three divisions: (1) general aims (*al-maqāṣid al-ʿāmmah*), (2) specific aims (*al-maqāṣid al-khāṣṣah*), and (3) partial aims (*al-maqāṣid al-juz'iyyah*).

1) *General Aims*

General aims are the goals and objectives which are reflected in all or most areas of Islamic legislation. According to Ibn Ashur, they are,

> ...the wise purposes that can be discerned in all or most areas of Islamic legislation; hence, they are not restricted to one type of ruling to the exclusion of others. As such, they go to make up the global attributes and aims of Islamic law as a whole. These include wise purposes that are observable in many, though not all, types of Islamic legal rulings...[102]

Preservation of the five essentials spoken of earlier – religion (*al-dīn*), life (*al-nafs*), reason (*al-ʿaql*), progeny (*al-nasl*), and property (*al-māl*) – is included among the general objectives of the Shariʿah, the most comprehensive, fundamental and sublime of which is achievement of benefit and prevention of harm. In fact, this is the pivot around which all aims of Islamic law – *maqāṣid al-sharīʿah* – revolve.[103]

As we have seen, one of the overall aims of Islamic law is the elimination or mitigation of hardship. As al-Shāṭibi puts it:

> Elimination of hardship is a universal goal of the Shariʿah. Hence, you will not find a general obligation in the Shariʿah that is characterized by hardship to more than a small degree. This is the implication of God's statement that He "has laid no hardship on you in [anything that pertains to] religion" (*Sūrah al-Ḥajj* 22:78)."[104]

Other universal aims of the Shariʿah are justice, concordance, and harmony.

2) *Specific Aims*

Specific aims are goals and objectives that are peculiar to a particular type of ruling or a set of closely related rulings, such as the objectives of acts of worship (*maqāṣid al-ʿibādāt*), the objectives of social or financial transactions (*maqāṣid al-muʿāmalāt*), or the objectives of criminal laws (*maqāṣid al-jināyāt*). Similarly, they may be the objectives of a certain area of Islamic law, such as ritual purity (*al-ṭahārah*), sales (*al-buyūʿ*), and so on.[105]

3) *Partial Aims*

Partial aims are objectives that relate to a particular question or issue. The categories of general aims and specific aims apply either to the Shariʿah in its entirety, or to all cases relating to a particular area (such as ritual impurity, penal law, etc.), whereas what we are terming partial aims (*al-maqāṣid al-juz'iyyah*) pertain exclusively to a particular question or issue, or to a particular proof from which the larger purpose of Islamic law can deduced.The clearest explanation of such partial aims can be found in the works of Shaykh al-Islam Ibn Taymiyyah and his student, Ibn al-Qayyim.[106]

I

Awareness of *Maqāṣid al-Sharīʿah* and Its Importance for Contemporary Methods of Deriving Legal Rulings (*al-Iftā'*)

OVERVIEW OF THIS CHAPTER

This chapter discusses growing numbers of unqualified individuals now issuing fatwas and the ease with which such so-called muftis are accessed. Importantly it discusses the issue of rulings which are based on ignorance or misinformation and critiques current practice, especially in connection with contemporary issues.
It aims to:

1. Offer clarifications with respect to *maqāṣid* as they relate to the issuance of fatwas on newly emerging events and situations on the individual and communal levels.
2. Call for a balanced approach avoiding extremism and excessive laxity.
3. Explain ways in which Islamic law promotes ease for morally accountable Muslims and the principles that guide this aim.
4. Explain how rulings should be derived. Juristic scholars have specified a number of guidelines for ensuring that one realizes legitimate, Islamically recognized human interests when engaged in ijtihad and issuing legal rulings. These are explored including the following principles: (i) to include human interests among the aims of Islamic law. (ii) to ensure that the interest in question does not conflict with any legal text. (iii) to verify that the interest in question is indisputable or, at the very least, that there is convincing evidence of its validity. (iv) to ascertain that the interest in question is universal in nature. (v) to ensure that consideration of the interest in question will not threaten some other interest of greater or equal importance.

Introduction

GIVEN the need to root Islamic practice in sound, authentic Islamic principles, it is of the utmost importance that we study Islamic rulings on contemporary issues and events. Muslim thinkers on all levels have made significant contributions to this field. Indeed, there is hardly a Muslim scholar of note but that he has written at least one work on the subject of contemporary issues and *iftā'*, that is, the process of issuing Islamic legal rulings. *Iftā'* is one of the basic foundations of the Islamic legislative system, and serves to manifest the applicability of the Shariʿah to all times and places.

In view of the constantly changing circumstances facing the Muslim community, there is an ongoing need for muftis, that is, individuals qualified to issue fatwas, or Islamic legal rulings. Moreover, given the growing numbers of unqualified individuals now issuing fatwas and the ease with which such so-called muftis are accessed, I here offer some needed clarifications with respect to *maqāṣid al-sharīʿah* as they relate to the issuance of fatwas on newly emerging events and situations on the individual and communal levels. Together with a careful reading of the changing circumstances that call for new legal rulings, the aims of Islamic law – *maqāṣid al-sharīʿah* – are the foundation for all sound fatwas.

Maqāṣid al-sharīʿah are linked at all times with what will benefit people as beings answerable to God's law, and bring them out of bondage to self-centered whims and caprices. This liberating effect of *maqāṣid al-sharīʿah* enables people to become God's servants voluntarily, out of free choice, and not simply because they are forced to obey the divine law. However, there is a growing lack of clarity concerning what is truly to people's benefit as individuals answerable to God's law, while people's personal inclinations further interfere with a proper understanding of what is in their real best interest. This situation is exacerbated by the fact that while some muftis tend to focus excessively on lenient interpretations of the Shariʿah that provide greater ease and freedom, others consider this trend to be a departure from true Islam.

As I see it, the purpose of Islamic law is neither to impose hardship and undue restrictions on people, nor to leave them free to satisfy their every desire, subservient to their every whim. Hence, my purpose in this chapter is to explain the ways in which Islamic law promotes ease for morally accountable Muslims and the principles that guide this noble aim. In this way, I hope to maximize the benefits the Shariʿah offers to God's servants both in this life and the next.

I have divided my discussion into four main subtopics: (1) the importance of *iftā'* and its place in Islamic law; (2) the meaning of facilitation (*taysīr*) in Islamic law; (3) a balanced approach to *iftā'* (striking a balance between lenience and austerity); and (4) guidelines for applying the principle of facilitation (*ḍawābīṭ al-taysīr*) in *iftā'*, or the issuance of Islamic legal rulings.

(1) The Importance of *Iftā'* and its Place in Islamic Law

The process of issuing fatwas plays a significant role in helping people understand the religion of Islam. God, the Mighty and Most Sublime has mentioned this fact in a number of verses in the Qur'an:

> And they will ask thee to enlighten them about the laws concerning women. Say: "God Himself enlightens you about the laws concerning them" – or [His will is shown] in what is being conveyed unto you through this divine writ about orphan women [in your charge]. (*Sūrah al-Nisā'* 4:127)

> They will ask thee to enlighten them. Say: "God enlightens you [thus] about the laws concerning [inheritance from] those who leave no heir in the direct line: If a man dies childless and has a sister, she shall inherit one-half of what he has left, just as he shall inherit from her if she dies childless..." (*Sūrah al-Nisā'* 4:176)

The centrality of this process is demonstrated by the fact that God Himself has assumed the role of mufti in responding to people's changing circumstances.[1] The importance of this kind of legal explanation is further highlighted by the fact that the Prophet, too, undertook the challenge of issuing fatwas. In fact, much of his time was spent answering people's questions about how to respond to various situations that arose in their lives.[2]

Imam Ibn al-Qayyim devoted a section of his valuable work, *Iʿlām al-Muwaqqiʿīn ʿan Rabb al-ʿĀlamīn* to the subject of fatwas and the circumstances on which the Prophet ruled.[3] The Companions, their successors, and the imams and scholars who followed in their footsteps continued emulating the example of the Prophet through their teachings and explanations, which likewise underscores the vital role played by fatwas in Islamic life and practice. Hence it has been said, "*Iftā'* might be likened to recording a signature on God's behalf."[4]

Given the impact fatwas are bound to have on Muslims' lives and the guidance they provide on both the material and spiritual levels, whoever wishes to issue fatwas on newly emerging situations must be properly qualified for the task. It is scholars that people seek out in the face of unfamiliar or frightening events, unresolved disputes, or difficult problems, especially in this contemporary age of ours with its peculiar confusions, complications, and rapid changes. Thus, in order to protect Islamic law's lofty status from ignorant and false claims, there is a clear need for rules and regulations to guide the process of ruling on new situations.

The Prophet warned of the danger of allowing ignorant individuals to rule on new cases or to offer their own interpretations of the Qur'an due to the grave harm this might inflict on both the religion and its adherents. He said:

> Indeed, God does not wrest knowledge away from people all of a sudden. Rather, He removes it gradually through the deaths of their scholars until, when not a single scholar remains, people take one another as their leaders, though they are all equally ignorant. Then, when asked questions [about religion], they issue rulings without knowledge, thereby revealing how they have strayed from the truth and led others astray.[5]

In explanation of this saying of the Prophet, Ibn Ḥajar wrote saying, "This hadith is an exhortation to preserve knowledge and a warning against allowing the ignorant to assume positions of leadership. It also indicates that issuing fatwas is an act of true leadership, and condemns those who undertake this action without knowledge."[6]

Imam al-Shāṭibī explains the greatness of this kind of leadership, saying:

> A mufti relates knowledge on God's behalf just as the Prophet did,

> he "signs" people's actions in light of his knowledge of God's law just as the Prophet did, and he is the enforcer of God's commands in his capacity as vicegerent, just as the Prophet was. This is why those who fulfill these functions are referred to as "those from among you who have been entrusted with authority" (*ūlī al-amr*), obedience to whom is associated with obedience to God and His Messenger. As God Almighty has said, "O you who have attained to faith! Pay heed unto God, and pay heed unto the Apostle and unto those from among you who have been entrusted with authority. . ." (*Sūrah al-Nisā'* 4:59).[7]

Given the critical nature of the functions performed by muftis, it is essential that the work they do be subject to strict regulation and that it not be entrusted to people who would take it lightly and who fail to fulfill the conditions for carrying it out in proper fashion.

(2) Understanding the Principle of Facilitation in the Shariᶜah

It is clear from innumerable statements in the Qur'an that the religion of Islam is founded upon ease and the removal of difficulties. God, the Mighty Judge, has made this religion a mercy to all mankind, while His Apostle came to remove the shackles and chains that had bound the nations who came before us. Hence, God Almighty declares, "Indeed, there has come unto you [O mankind] an Apostle from among yourselves: heavily weighs upon him the thought that you might suffer; full of concern for you is he, and full of compassion and mercy towards the believers" (*Sūrah al-Tawbah* 9:128), and "[thus, O Prophet,] We have sent thee as an evidence of Our grace towards all the worlds" (*Sūrah al-Anbiyā'* 21:107). In a similar vein, the Prophet said, "God did not send me to cause hardship for others, or to suffer hardship myself; rather, He has sent me as a teacher, and as one who brings ease,"[8] while one of the clearest descriptions God has given for the Prophet is that he will "make lawful to them the good things of life, and forbid them the bad things, and lift from them the burdens and the shackles that were upon them aforetime" (*Sūrah al-Aᶜrāf* 7:157).

It is for this reason that the Messenger of God, knowing that his followers would want to emulate him in all that he did, would refrain from performing certain actions lest they become burdens to the Muslim community. For example, he said, "If I weren't afraid it would become a burden to the Muslim community, I would have commanded them to use the *siwāk* (tooth-stick)..."[9] There are numerous other statements to the same effect in the traditions handed down from the Prophet, who used to command his Companions to be gentle with people and not to impose hardships on them. When he sent Muʿādh ibn Jabal and Abū Mūsā al-Ashʿarī to Yemen, he said to them, "Make things easy rather than difficult, give glad tidings, and do not alienate [people from Islam]."[10]

However, there has emerged an approach to contemporary issues which places undue stress on lenience and facilitation. This school of thought on *iftā'* is currently widespread on both the individual and institutional levels, especially given the fact that society in our day and age has developed a tendency toward materialism as opposed to spirituality, self-centeredness in opposition to selflessness, and opportunism rather than ethics. Temptations to evil are as ubiquitous as are obstacles to righteousness, and the task of clinging faithfully to one's religion might be likened to trying to hold a hot ember in one's hand. Muslims today are being inundated from all directions by torrents of unbelief that seek to distance them from their religious practices and beliefs, and they often feel they have no one to support them in their struggles. In the face of this reality, many jurists call for the greatest lenience possible in Islamic legal rulings in the hope of making the religion more attractive to those who come to them with questions, and of helping them be more steadfast on the right path.[11]

This endeavor, which is founded upon the lofty goal of relieving believers of undue hardship, benefiting them and protecting them both in this world and the world to come, undoubtedly arises from pure motives. However, we have begun to witness certain excesses in the emphasis on facilitation (*taysīr*) and the allowance of concessions (*al-akhdh bi al-tarakhkhuṣ*) which have led some jurists of this school to reject certain Islamic texts, or to interpret them in ways that are not linguistically and legally sound.

Pressures arising from the current state of affairs and people's alienation from religion do not justify us in sacrificing principles or doctrines that should be treated as bedrock fundamentals. For no matter how much societies change and develop, the texts of the Shari^cah continue to be applicable to all times and places. In addressing this issue, Shaykh Muhammad al-Tahir ibn Ashur has the following to say:

> Muslims agree unanimously on the general applicability of the Shariʿah to all humankind in all generations, times and places, although the precise manner of this applicability needs to be clearly explained. As I see it, there are two ways to conceive of this general applicability: (1) to say that, with its various universal principles, the precepts of the Shariʿah can be applied to numerous situations and circumstances without causing any discomfort, hardship or difficulty. (2) To say that the conditions and circumstances that obtain in various ages and nations are such that they can adapt to the precepts of Islam without causing any discomfort, hardship or difficulty. For example, Islam was able to change some of the conditions that obtained among the Arabs, Persians, Copts, Berbers, Byzantines, Tatars, Indians, Chinese, and Turks in such a way that they abandoned the futile practices and beliefs of their forebears without discomfort, hardship, or difficulty.[12]

It is both erroneous and perilous to justify the status quo by exceeding the proper limits in applying the principle of facilitation and indiscriminately adopting any statement, or applying any independent judgment, without recourse to the relevant arguments and proofs. Yusuf al-Qaradawi analyzes this trend as follows:

> This school's adherents attempt to confer legitimacy on the status quo by looking for interpretations of the Shariʿah which form a basis for preserving it. Their task may be to institute or justify laws, decisions, and procedures supported by those in power. Some of them undertake this mission in all sincerity and with firm conviction. They are not seeking to win anyone's favor or to satisfy those in power. However, they suffer the effects of a defeatist mentality in the face of Western civilization's philosophies and presuppositions.

Others do so out of a craving for the worldly advantages enjoyed by those in power or those who control the world's affairs from behind the scenes, out of a desire for recognition and fame, or for any number of related motives, including the fear and greed that have the power to move even those known for their piety and scholarship.[13]

The adverse impacts of this kind of ijtihad can be clearly seen by anyone. Through some of their fatwas, adherents of this trend have erased the distinctions between Muslim and non-Muslim societies on the pretext of taking into consideration the differences between the circumstances faced by contemporary Muslims and those of earlier generations.[14]

(3) A Balanced Approach to *Iftā'* (Toward a balance between lenience and austerity)

In the area of contemporary *iftā'* one finds two contrasting approaches, one of which is marked by unwarranted rigor and austerity, and one of which is characterized by an excessive focus on facilitation and ease. In what follows I will summarize the principle features of these two approaches:

THE FIRST APPROACH: EXCESSIVE RIGOR AND CAUTION. This approach is marked by three main features: (1) uncompromising bias in favor of a particular theological school of thought, or in favor of specific views or individual scholars, (2) sole adherence to the superficial, literal meanings of religious texts, and (3) excessive insistence on the principle of *sadd al-dharā'iʿ*, that is, prohibiting anything that has the potential of leading to a forbidden act.

(1) *Uncompromising bias in favor of a particular school of thought, view or scholar*. Religious fanaticism grows out of the erroneous belief that one possesses the one and only incontrovertible truth in matters of religious interpretation. This belief engenders closed-mindedness, an unrealistically high opinion of oneself, and hostility to anyone who holds opposing or competing views. A jurist or mufti who holds such a belief will adopt an extremist methodology and seek to impose his views on others while banning views or schools of thought other than his own. In so doing, he causes

inconvenience and hardship for both himself and others by holding blindly to this opinion or that without any consideration for other opinions, even if they have good evidence in their favor.

Imam Aḥmad said, "When a scholar issues a fatwa to people, he should not impose his school of thought on them or cause them hardship."[15] It should also be noted that according to a majority of Muslim scholars, one should not follow any one particular school of thought in all the views one adopts.[16] Shaykh al-Islam Ibn Taymiyyah states in a similar vein:

> A Muslim who faces an unfamiliar situation should seek a fatwa from someone he [or she] believes will tell him God's and His Messenger's ruling on it regardless of what school of thought the mufti represents. No Muslim should imitate a particular scholar in all that he says, nor is there anyone, apart from the Messenger of God himself, whose commands and sayings a Muslim should always adhere to. Rather, one can either accept or reject the statements of anyone on earth with the exception of the Prophet.[17]

In the course of analyzing the impact of fanatic adherence to a particular school of thought on the process of thought and research, Yusuf al-Qaradawi notes:

> Some schools of thought still hold that it is incumbent upon Muslims to follow a particular theological school of thought, and that rulings on new issues should only be issued within the framework of this single school of thought and the statements of its proponents, particularly the earlier ones among them... When those who hold this view are asked about a new development, they only look for similar cases in the writings of their particular school of thought, and if they find none, they rule that the new development is forbidden. It is as if the default ruling on an action is that it is forbidden unless the school of thought's earlier scholars declared it permissible.[18]

The same can be said about blind support for the views and interpretations of a particular sect or imam regardless of whether they correspond to the truth or conflict with it.

The unprecedented changes, developments and complexities being witnessed by modern society require us to rethink numerous juristic rulings based on specific occasions, human interests or prevailing customs. Such rulings might have to do with modern practices such as various types of sales, forward buying, guaranties, bills of exchange, and others. When one adheres exclusively to the writings of certain jurists, writings which may not contain any explicit text or scholarly consensus on the issue of concern, these earlier rulings may be so restrictive and harsh that they fly in the face of the ease and magnanimity of Islam, especially in view of the fact that people may urgently need to engage in such practices.

People living in this day and age need to be familiar with Islamic rulings on transactions that form an integral part of their lives, and concerning which the basic Islamic ruling is permissibility. However, in some situations, such transactions might border on the prohibited, in which case a jurist could be tempted to declare them impermissible even though the basic stance of Islamic law on them is that they are permissible and valid, just as[19] the basic ruling concerning things that are beneficial is that they are allowed.[20]

As a result, people would either seek out anomalous or weakly attested views, of which there are an abundance, or refuse to be restricted by any Islamic legal injunctions whatsoever in their day-to-day transactions, which was even more disastrous. Had the jurists been more lenient in their rulings, specifying which transactions were permissible and which were not while offering legally acceptable alternatives, this would have been far better than burdening people with untenable blanket prohibitions.[21]

A case in point is the question of how to deal with the steadily increasing numbers of pilgrims to Makkah and the resultant overcrowding, discomfort and occasional deadly stampedes. This situation has led many scholars to modify their views on numerous issues and go against the prevailing teachings of their respective schools of thought in hopes of sparing people hardship and inconvenience. Only God knows how much more strained and miserable people would be had these scholars adhered to traditional positions, issuing their fatwas without regard for changing circumstances!

For instance, the rite of pebble throwing during the three days following the Feast of Sacrifice (ʿId al-Adha), which correspond to the 11th, 12th and 13th of Dhu al-Hijjah, begins at high noon and extends until sunset. The majority of jurists hold that throwing the pebbles after sunset is not valid.[22] Nevertheless, a number of perceptive jurists and fatwa authorities are of the view that it is permissible to throw them after nightfall, which spares pilgrims discomfort from the overcrowding that occurs during the daylight hours.[23]

In view of the hardship, strain and inconvenience caused in recent years by the requirement that the pebble throwing only be performed after high noon, there may also be good reason to consider the possibility of allowing this rite to be completed before noon, especially for pilgrims with time constraints who need to leave Mina on the 12th of Dhu al-Hijjah. It should be borne in mind that the rituals of the pilgrimage, while based on emulation of the Prophet, are also intended to provide to the extent possible for pilgrims' ease and comfort. In fact, some leading scholars from among the Successors to the Prophets' Companions ruled in support of allowing pebble throwing before noon, and this is the ruling adopted by the Ḥanafī school of juristic thought.[24]

(2) *Sole adherence to the superficial, literal meaning of religious texts*. Proper reverence for authoritative religious texts is fundamental to Islam, and a requirement of anyone who offers new or original interpretations based on his or her independent judgment. However, when one clings solely to the apparent meaning of such texts without a deeper understanding of message and their underlying aims, the result will be error and distortion. The existence of this superficial approach is evidenced in the following statement by Salih al-Mazid: "In our day and age there are those who say that 'all one needs in order to engage in ijtihad is a Qur'an, a copy of *Sunan Abī Dāwūd*, and a dictionary!'"[25]

Such would-be scholars know nothing about jurisprudence, still less about the proper practice of ijtihad. Yusuf al-Qaradawi refers to them as 'neo-Ẓahirīs'[26] – though, in my view, they differ somewhat from the original Ẓahirīs. According to al-Qaradawi:

> Most of those to whom I refer as "neo-Ẓahirīs" specialize exclusively

> in the study of Hadith. They lack experience in dealing with the principles of jurisprudence, and they are unfamiliar with the differences that exist among jurists and their methods for deriving rulings from Islamic legal texts. Moreover, they show almost no concern for either *maqāṣid al-sharīʿah* or the process of adapting legal rulings to changing places, times, and circumstances.[27]

The statement closest to these people's lips and pens is, "This is forbidden", without regard for the gravity of these words, and without presenting sufficient proof from Islamic legal texts or principles. As a consequence, they impose the harshest possible rigors on those who adhere to their rulings, and this despite God Almighty's explicit warning: "...do not utter falsehoods by letting your tongues determine [at your own discretion], 'This is lawful and that is forbidden,' thus attributing your own lying inventions to God. For, behold, those who attribute their own lying inventions to God will never attain to a happy state!" (*Sūrah al-Naḥl* 16:116).

Based on this method of handling Islamic legal texts, many a lawful action has been forbidden, many a means of attaining knowledge has been blocked, and many an individual has been forced out of Islam on the pretext that they had violated clear-cut texts. However, scholars well-established in knowledge take a different view. According to Imam Ibn al-Qayyim al-Jawziyyah:

> No mufti should assert that God or His Messenger declared such and such to be lawful, forbidden, obligatory or objectionable without clear knowledge of the matter based on explicit statements by God and His Messenger. A number of our righteous predecessors warned that one should beware of stating that "God has declared such and such lawful" or "God has declared such and such forbidden", lest God say to him, "You have lied. I did not declare such and such lawful, neither did I declare such and such forbidden!"[28]

The practice of issuing definitive rulings on new situations without founding them upon indisputable knowledge is bound to cause people inconvenience and hardship, which is in clear violation of Islamic law's magnanimity and the mercy it demonstrates toward human beings.

In recent times certain individuals have gone so far as to declare governments and entire societies as unbelievers; they have revolted against their rulers, dissociated themselves from the Muslim community, and declared enmity against whoever goes against their views based on a warped understanding of Islamic texts, and ignorance of sound methods for extracting rulings from such texts. Indeed, one of the strangest teachings they have come out with is that commission of sins (not including that of *shirk*, or associating partners with God) excludes one from the fold of Islam. Mahir al-Bakri, a member of Takfīr wa al-Hijrah (the "Excommunication and Exodus Group") has declared that "the word 'sinner' (*ʿāṣin*) is synonymous with the word 'unbeliever' (*kāfir*)...It has to do with the issue of names and appellations, since in God's religion, you can't call someone a Muslim and an unbeliever at the same time."[29]

This superficial approach to religious texts, which has caused the Muslim community severe hardship with its twisted interpretations and views, might be seen as an extension of the Kharijite movement, which made things difficult both for its followers and for others, and that of the Ẓahirīs.

(3) *Excessive insistence on the principle of sadd al-dharāʾiʿ, that is, prohibiting anything that has the potential of leading to a forbidden act.* Many texts indicate that the principle of preventing lawful acts that might lead to unlawful acts is a valid means of preserving *maqāṣid al-sharīʿah*, since it is consistent with the general principle of "bringing about benefit and preventing harm" upon which the Shariʿah is founded. Ibn al-Qayyim gives eloquent expression to this notion when he states:

> Whenever the Lord Almighty declares something forbidden, and when there are ways and means that lead to the forbidden act, He likewise forbids these ways and means. In this manner He renders His prohibition effective by preventing His servants from approaching what He has prohibited. If God permitted the means leading to a forbidden thing, this would render the prohibition defective, and people would be tempted to commit wrongdoing.[30]

However, a problem arises when excessive use of the principle leads to an imaginary source of harm being considered at the expense of preponderant benefits. In such a situation, a jurist may close the door to a benefit and, as a result, inadvertently violate the aims of the Shariʿah. Examples of this phenomenon would include prohibiting the cultivation of grapes for fear that they might be used to produce alcohol, or forbidding neighbors to live close to each other for fear of people entering into illicit sexual relationships. There is a consensus among Muslim scholars that such activities should not be forbidden, since their benefits outweigh any potential or hypothetical harm or disadvantage.[31]

Some contemporary self-styled jurists go to extremes by refusing to benefit from the systems, sciences, knowledge and inventions of other nations, regarding such openness as a form of unacceptable innovation in matters of religion and a contravention of the guidance brought by the Messenger of God.[32] However, it will be clear to the keen observer that most new developments in the fields of economics and medicine originated in non-Muslim countries, and that to reject them all simply because of where they came from represents a needlessly restrictive approach. People are continuously becoming acquainted with new customs and systems as a result of their contact with other nations. Hence, if Muslim scholars consistently issue harsh rulings in rejection of what other nations have to offer without offering convincing proof in support of their hard-line stance, people are liable to abandon the religion and begin indulging in whatever they see fit, convinced that there is no use in seeking out Islamic rulings on them, since they are bound to be restrictive and based on the principle of *sadd al-dharā'iʿ*. Hence, the only customs and developments that should be definitively rejected on Islamic grounds are those that would be likely to lead to palpable harm, while those that may open the way to new forms of worship and obedience should be allowed and affirmed.[33]

This stern, uncompromising approach to fatwas on newly arising situations might manifest itself in numerous ways. For example, a mufti might take a deliberately cautious stance on every controversial issue by declaring an action forbidden (or obligatory, depending on the nature of the action in question) for fear of being lax in enforcing Islamic rulings, or to spare morally accountable

Muslims ambiguous situations that they might not be prepared to handle. Cautious rulings of this nature might then be applied across the board to all people, and under all circumstances. A second, more concrete example of this tendency would be a mufti's ruling that women are forbidden to work outside the home even when they abide by all Islamic standards of conduct, and in spite of the clear need for women to enter the work force.[34] Further examples include declaring all banking unlawful for fear that it might involve usury; or prohibiting all kinds of photography or motion pictures in spite of the dire need for them in this day and age,[35] and even when all relevant Islamic protocols are observed.

It bears noting that it is every individual Muslim's right to exercise caution in relation to moral decisions given the spiritual consciousness and peace of mind this may engender. But to impose the same restrictions on the Muslim populace at large, or to apply the same caution to the fatwas one issues, could cause other Muslims undue hardship.[36]

Although it is sometimes desirable to avoid controversy,[37] this principle should not be taken as an absolute rule. Rather, scholars have stipulated that it is only desirable to apply it given the following conditions: (1) The avoidance of controversy should not lead to some contravention of Islamic law, such as neglecting an action that constitutes part of the firmly attested example left by the Prophet, commission of an undesirable act, or failure to act upon an established principle; (2) The proof cited by one's opponent should not be clearly weak, since in such a case, the controversy is not worth reckoning with in the first place; (3) Avoidance of the controversy should not lead to some other controversy; (4) The one who acts upon the principle should be below the level of a qualified *mujtahid*. If he is a qualified *mujtahid*, then he should bypass the principle of 'being on the safe side', go on to exercise ijtihad, and issue a fatwa based on what he believes to be the best attested view in light of the evidences and proofs available to him.[38]

In discussing the effects of attempting to 'be on the safe side' in connection with every situation one encounters, Yaqub al-Buhusayn states:

This principle is inconsistent with the aim of alleviating hardship (which is a fundamental principle of Islamic legislation), since it requires one to do everything he or she perceives as being mandatory, and abstaining from everything he or she perceives as being forbidden, which would be burdensome to the morally accountable Muslim. In fact some scholars state that, "if a morally accountable Muslim were to abide strictly by the principle of 'being on the safe side', even for a single day, in all of matters concerning which there is source of indisputable evidence, he would suffer significant hardship. Imagine, then, what situation would arise if he adopted this approach at all times, and asked the general Muslim populace, including women, villagers and Bedouins, to do the same. It would undoubtedly disturb the order of people's lives, and be detrimental to people's ability to earn their livelihoods."[39]

THE SECOND APPROACH: EXCESSIVE FOCUS ON FACILITATION AND EASE. This approach is distinguished by the following features: (1) unwarranted reliance on the notion of human interest (*maṣlaḥah*), even when this means going against established Islamic legal texts; (2) overuse of concessions (*rukhaṣ*), and combining one juristic school of thought with another; and (3) juristic evasion of the injunctions of Islamic law.

(1) *Unwarranted reliance on the notion of human interest (maṣlaḥah)*. The human interest recognized in the Shariʿah is not a self-contained or independent piece of textual evidence. Rather, it is deduced from an aggregate of particular, detailed pieces of evidence derived from the Qur'an and the Sunnah having to do with preservation of the five essentials discussed above – religion (*al-dīn*), life (*al-nafs*), reason (*al-ʿaql*), progeny (*al-nasl*), and property (*al-māl*). Since the validity of human interest has been established based on this aggregate of textual details, it would be logically impossible for any given human interest to contradict the purport of such texts.[40]

Hence, Muslim scholars and jurists are generally agreed that *maṣlaḥah* is that which corresponds with the objectives of the Shariʿah and does not contradict any Islamic legal text or consensus. Moreover, the overall benefits of a given human interest should be recognizable with a fair degree of certainty; otherwise, it is not to be reckoned with. However, Imam al-Ṭūfī is quoted as having said that when there is a contradiction between *maṣlaḥah* on one hand, and textual proofs and consensus on the other, greater weight should be given to *maṣlaḥah*.[41]

Some contemporary jurists and muftis tend towards excessive reliance on *maṣlaḥah* even this results in fatwas that conflict with recognized textual evidence. An example of this is a statement by Shaykh Muhammad al-Ghazali concerning the permissibility of women holding the highest political offices. He wrote:

> To the people of Makkah, the Prophet recited *Sūrah al-Naml*, which tells us how the Queen of Sheba led her people to prosperity and security through her wisdom and intelligence. How, then, could he have issued a judgment that contradicted what had been revealed to him? Indeed, what nation, led by a woman of her caliber, could possibly be lost?[42]

Shaykh al-Ghazali posed this rhetorical question in opposition to the statement attributed to the Prophet according to which, "No nation that submits to a woman's rule will ever prosper."[43]

Another example is the fatwa issued by the former mufti of the Arab Republic of Egypt on the permissibility of receiving interest from a bank even though such interest is known to be usurious, and even though such a fatwa flies in the face of clear textual proofs and a consensus among Muslim scholars that usury is forbidden however much or little it may be.[44]

Other recent fatwas have stated, for example, that the sale of alcohol is permissible in the interest of helping the state to attract tourism; that it is permissible for people not to fast the month of Ramadan lest their fasting have a negative impact on business; that usury (*al-ribā*) is permissible in the interests of promoting commerce; and that the mingling of the sexes in public places is permissible as a means of promoting refined manners and making men and women less sexually attracted to each other![45] Other fatwas indicate that male and female children should be given equal shares of inheritance.[46] Some have even gone so far as to approve women's appearance fully adorned on immoral programs in the media on the pretext of adapting to modern developments with a new jurisprudence and a new understanding.[47]

All this is being done under the guise of acting in keeping with human interests and adapting the Shariʿah to the requirements of modern life.

(2) *Overuse of concessions (rukhaṣ), and combining one juristic school of thought with another.* There is nothing wrong with availing oneself of the legal concessions provided for in the Qur'an and the Sunnah. Indeed, it was the Prophet who said, "It pleases God for us to avail ourselves of His concessions, just as it pleases Him for us to obey His commands."[48]

As for needlessly pursuing concessions based on particular interpretations, and adopting an eclectic approach that involves borrowing sometimes from one juristic school of thought, sometimes from another, or sometimes from one scholar, sometimes from another depending on which of them offers the most lenient ruling, a number of scholars have issued stern warnings against it. In so doing they follow the lead of the Prophet himself, who said, "There are three things I fear for you, though they are bound to occur: a scholar who lapses into error, a hypocrite who disputes concerning the Qur'an, and worldly treasures that will be opened to you."[49] A scholar's lapse into error is a dangerous thing, since it may cause others to lapse into error as well. So, it is potentially the cause of great evil.

Some contemporary scholars have reported a controversy among scholars over whether it is permissible for a mufti or others who look into unprecedented legal cases to adopt concessions declared by other scholars.[50] However, this report needs to be taken with some reservations for the following three reasons.

First, the disagreement has to do with whether it is permissible for a layperson to adopt the opinion of whichever qualified *mujtahid* he prefers, there being no essential difference between one *mujtahid* and another. However, although scholars have differed on this issue, they agree unanimously that if the position taken by one *mujtahid* is shown to be better attested than that taken by others, then this position should be adopted, and it is not permissible for people to adopt other scholars' concessions without clear justification and regulation.[51] Therefore, it is invalid to draw an analogy between a debate among scholars on one issue and another unrelated issue that differs from the first in both meaning and context. In sum, while a layperson may be entitled to adopt concessions declared permissible by a mufti or *mujtahid* of his or her choice, the *mujtahid* or mufti himself/herself must issue his or her own fatwa based on his or her own research and ijtihad.[52]

Second, some scholars have ruled that one may adopt the opinion of any scholar one chooses. However, as has been mentioned, this applies only to laypeople, only when one is under duress, and only if one is not driven by selfish whims or desires. Imam al-Zarkashī states:

> It is clearly stated in the fatwas of Imam al-Nawawī that it is not permissible to go in search of concessions. When asked whether, when necessity requires, a follower of one juristic school of thought may avail himself of a concession allowed by a different juristic school of thought, al-Nawawī replied that one may act upon the fatwa of anyone qualified to issue fatwas. However, he stipulated that one must not deliberately seek out a scholar who is known to issue concessions on the point in question, nor a scholar whose juristic school of thought one knows to allow for such concessions.[53]

Therefore, scholars only allow one to seek out concessions in special cases justified by need, and no mufti should make it a practice to approve concessions for everyone who requests a legal ruling, or in every situation on which he rules.[54]

Third, some scholars, including Ibn Ḥazm[55] and Ibn al-Ṣalāḥ,[56] forbid the pursuit of concessions even on the part of laypeople. Similarly, Ibn ʿAbd al-Barr wrote, "There is a consensus among scholars that a layperson should not seek out concessions."[57] Imam al-Shāṭibī spoke at length on the pernicious effects of pursuing concessions from one juristic school of thought after another and the havoc it wreaks on the process of *iftāʾ*.[58] Eminent scholars are not known for their excessive lenience. In fact, al-Samʿānī posits that one of the qualities that define competent *mujtahids* is that they avoid laxity and fatwas that approve concessions. He then mentions two categories of overly lenient scholars:

> (1) those who are lax in looking for proofs and ways of making rulings, and who are satisfied with the results of initial research and thought. Such scholars are negligent in their ijtihad and are, therefore, not qualified to issue fatwas; and (2) those who are given to seeking concessions and have a penchant for misinterpreting the Sunnah; such scholars take their religion for granted, and they are more sinful than those in the first category.[59]

A methodology of lenience based on seeking out concessions leads to a tendency to submit to one's desires, and violates the order which the Shariʿah was intended to preserve. On this point al-Zarkashī stated:

> If a layperson asks a mufti for a ruling on a situation he is not certain how to respond to, he/she is saying, in effect, "Rescue me from my self-centered desires and show me how to follow the truth." In such a situation, it would be unacceptable for the mufti to tell him/her: "There are two opinions concerning your problem. So choose whichever suits your fancy!"[60] Or, "I will look for a scholarly opinion that will work for you!" Imam Aḥmad said, "If someone acted upon every concession he/she heard, for example, the position taken by the Kufan school concerning wine, the position taken by the Madinan school on listening to music, and the Makkan school's view on temporary marriage, he would turn into a libertine."[61]

Al-Qāḍī Ismāʿīl al-Mālikī (d. 282 AH/895 CE) is reported to have said:

> I once went in to see al-Muʿtaḍid and he gave me a book. When I looked at it, I discovered that it was a collection of concessions some scholars had erroneously approved, and the evidence each of them had cited in their favor. "Whoever compiled this book is an atheist!" I declared. Al-Muʿtaḍid asked, "Are the hadiths it cites not authentic?" "They are correct," I said, "but a scholar who declares intoxicants permissible will not approve temporary marriage, and a scholar who approves temporary marriage will not approve intoxicants. There isn't a scholar on earth who has never erred. But whoever compiles the errors of all the scholars put together and acts

upon them will lose his religion." Al-Muʿtaḍid then ordered the book burned.[62]

The modern world has witnessed laxity on the part of numerous scholars in the form of eclectic approaches to juristic questions and the tendency to approve needless concessions. As for situations in which a person is compelled to make use of a concession, each case should be judged on its own merits.

(3) *Juristic evasion of the injunctions of Islamic law.* This is another feature of the school of laxity and excessive facilitation. The Prophet forbade this kind of evasion.[63] Consequently, most scholars agree that it is disallowed.[64] In this connection Imam al-Qarrāfī states:

> When there are two possible rulings on an issue, one rigorous and the other lenient, a mufti is not permitted to issue the rigorous ruling to laypeople, and the lenient ruling to rulers and those of high station. Such a practice is sinful and a betrayal of the religion, since it makes light of Muslims' best interests. It is a sign that the heart lacks seriousness and reverence for God Almighty, and is filled instead with a craving for worldly power and the desire to draw near to the creature as opposed to the Creator. May God protect us from the wiles of the heedless![65]

Abū al-Walīd al-Bājī reported one of his contemporaries as saying that he had brought a case before a group of muftis who, in his absence, issued him a fatwa that was unfavorable to him. When they saw him, they said, "We did not know that the fatwa was meant for you!" whereupon they issued him a more favorable fatwa premised on a different narration. Al-Bājī commented, "All scholars of good repute agree that this kind of conduct is impermissible."[66]

In detailing which types of juristic artifices are permissible and which are not, Imam Ibn al-Qayyim states:

> A mufti is not permitted to avail himself of forbidden and reprehensible artifices. Neither is he allowed to seek out concessions in the interest of someone to whom he wants to grant a favor. Doing so is sinful, and such a mufti should not be consulted for fatwas. If, on the

other hand, he is well-intentioned in resorting to a permissible artifice which is neither suspicious nor harmful in order to help the person seeking the fatwa out of a difficult situation, then it is permissible; in fact, it is commendable. God Almighty directed His prophet Job (peace be upon him) to release himself from a vow he had made by taking a bunch [of grass] and striking his wife with it a single time.[67] Similarly, the Prophet guided Bilāl ibn Rabāḥ to use some dirhams to buy dates, after which he could sell them and buy other dates, thereby avoiding the practice of usury (*al-ribā*). Therefore, the best way out of a difficult situation is one that enables one to avoid sin; while the worst is one that causes one to fall into sin by committing an act that is prohibited, or which exempts one from a duty that God and His Messenger have imposed. And God alone guides to the right path.[68]

Many contemporary muftis have fallen into the error of approving actions that are prohibited under the Shariʿah; such actions include modern forms of sale on credit (*bayʿ al-ʿīnah*),[69] banking transactions that involve usury; deceptive means of exempting people from the payment of zakah or justifying failure to repay debts; permitting common law marriage, as some countries do, as a way of justifying fornication; or allowing a woman to go back to her husband after he has divorced her irrevocably. All these are examples of legal artifices that are condemned by the Shariʿah.[70]

(4) Guidelines for Facilitation (*Ḍawābiṭ al-Taysīr*) in *Iftā'*, or the Issuance of Islamic Legal Rulings

The law of Islam embodies quintessentially a path of moderation and ease. Hence, those who engage in ijtihad pertaining to situations that call for new fatwas are expected to strike a balance between excessive strictness and excessive indulgence. Imam al-Shāṭibī states:

> The mufti who has mastered the art of issuing fatwas is one who possesses the ability to keep people on the path of moderation, which is most fitting for the general public. Such a mufti would never lead people along a path of extremism or laxity. The proof for

> the correctness of this view is the fact that the Straight Path which the Shariʿah has brought involves the pursuit of moderation and avoidance of both over-strictness or permissiveness. It follows, then, that if a mufti fails to help those who seek his rulings to achieve such moderation, he has failed to fulfill the Lawgiver's purpose in giving us the Shariʿah. Whatever entails a deviation from the path of moderation is considered blameworthy by well-grounded scholars. Extremism is by definition opposed to justice and fairness; and that, of course, is not in people's best interests.
>
> Both extremism and laxity are destructive. For if a person seeking a fatwa is taken along the path of austerity and hardship, he/she will be alienated from the religion, which will in turn cause him/her to abandon the pursuit of felicity in the Hereafter. Such cases have actually been witnessed. Conversely, if someone is led along a path of laxity, he/she is likely to follow his/her whims and desires, which is contrary to the aims of the Shariʿah, since following one's desires is perilous. There are many proofs of this.[71]

By identifying the features of approaches that are either too extreme or too lax, we may be better able to identify what constitutes a moderate approach. Some scholars hold that a mufti may be stern in his fatwas if he is dealing with someone who is a flagrant sinner who takes disobedience to the Shariʿah lightly, and that, so long as he remains within the bounds of the textual evidence, he may be lenient towards those who tend to be very stern with themselves or others. In this way, the mufti will help restore those who seek his fatwas to a path of moderation.[72]

Therefore, the mufti must always take account of the condition and circumstances of the person seeking him out for a fatwa, allowing his ruling to be determined by the principles of the Shariʿah and the evidence at hand. Imam Sufyān al-Thawrī said rightly, "Knowledge, in our view, is the ability to discern appropriate concessions based on trust; as for austerity, anyone can master it."[73]

What Sufyān al-Thawrī appears to mean is that true knowledge entails adhering to the Lawgiver's intent by making use of what is supported by the Shariʿah and which, at the same time, is most beneficial and conducive to ease. This is undoubtedly the view of scholars marked by uprightness, piety and moderation, all of which – particularly in this generation – are required of those who wish to issue religious rulings and speak in the name of the Shariʿah. Knowledge protects a mufti from issuing rulings out of ignorance, piety protects him from issuing rulings on impulse, and moderation shields him from both extremism and laxity. This should be the prevailing approach; it is the most correct manner in which to engage in independent reasoning; and it is the method advocated by leading scholars.[74]

In order to realize the Lawgiver's purpose of holding human beings accountable for the pursuit of what is best for them both in this world and the next, there is an urgent need to regulate the ways in which the principle of facilitation (*al-taysīr*) is applied in *iftā'*, or the process of issuing fatwas. Hence, in what follows I will discuss nine guidelines which Muslim scholars have laid down for the application of this important principle to rulings on contemporary issues. These are:

1. Make certain that the ruling is based on knowledge and fairness.
2. Undertake a precise, thorough investigation of the case before issuing a legal ruling in which the principle of *taysīr* is to be applied.
3. Cite all relevant textual evidence and applicable rules when ruling in favor of a weakly attested lenient view.
4. Provide a permissible alternative when judging a given action to be forbidden.
5. Ensure that, when applying the principle of *taysīr*, the interests explicitly recognized in Islamic law are being properly realized.
6. When considering a more lenient ruling, recognize the principle of relief from hardship (*rafʿ al-ḥaraj*).
7. Give due consideration to the anticipated consequences of issuing a lenient ruling.
8. Gain a solid understanding of the circumstances surrounding the case in question before issuing a ruling that involves application of the principle of *taysīr*.
9. Investigate the commonly accepted customs of relevance to the application of a more lenient ruling.

1: *Make certain that the ruling is based on knowledge and fairness.* Numerous conditions apply to the process of ruling on unprecedented cases, among which are knowledge and justice. The condition of knowledge includes the requirement that the legal verdict be well-informed and clearly pronounced once the case has been considered from all angles. As for the condition of justice, it involves the requirement that one not be unduly lax in the fatwa issued, and that one avoid all favoritism. One must give due consideration to what the truth requires, while approaching people's problems with the compassion called for in the law of Islam, and issuing rulings that steer people toward moderation in all they do.

Numerous factors have distanced those ruling on modern situations from the path of knowledge and justice. However, this situation is not new. On the contrary, scholars from earlier generations have also expressed distress over those who depart from the path of integrity and understanding. Imam Mālik (d. 179 AH/795 CE) testified to this when he said:

> Nothing taxes me more severely than to be asked about a matter of *ḥalāl* and *ḥarām* (what is permitted and what is forbidden), since it requires me to make a clear-cut judgment regarding the Law of God. Indeed, I have met some scholars and jurists who would rather die than be asked to rule on such matters! At the same time, some people of our generation seem ever so anxious to speak about these things and issue fatwas on them. If they could see the retribution they will receive in return, they would be far more reticent to speak. Whenever matters were brought to ʿUmar ibn al-Khaṭṭāb, ʿAlī ibn Abī Ṭālib and ʿAlqamah, the best of the Companions,[75] they would gather all of the Prophet's Companions and consult with them before issuing a verdict. As for the people of our own time, they take pride in passing their own verdicts, and as a consequence, little knowledge is opened to them.[76]

Imam Mālik's statement describes the methodology which was adhered to by our God-fearing forebears who, when preparing to rule on newly arising situations, avoided hasty, ill-thought-out verdicts and inadequate research and investigation. Instead, they would consult together on the matter and look into it with the proper care. By contrast, modern-day muftis often rush to conclusions and fail to consult with others before issuing a ruling. As a result, the approach to issuing legal rulings has become flawed, and the fatwas issued reflect a clear disregard for the lofty position that ought to be accorded to the Shariʿah.[77]

Jurists are clearly in need of guiding principles, especially when ruling on contemporary issues in relation to which it is all too easy to fall into error given the cultural conflicts, intellectual and doctrinal trends, and powerful psychological, social and political influences at work in modern society. Moreover, flawed and extremist interpretations and viewpoints are rendered all the more dangerous by the ease with which they are spread by the modern media, be it written or audio-visual in nature.

2: *Undertake a precise, thorough investigation of the case before issuing a legal ruling in which the principle of taysīr is to be applied.* The modern world presents Islamic jurisprudence with some of the most arduous challenges it has ever faced, since it confronts us with situations that earlier generations of Muslims not only did not face, but could never have imagined. The new situations that arise reflect the nature of the times in which we live, and which are marked by the free exchange of ideas and the development of scientific and technological solutions designed to address a variety of problems, both old and new.

Therefore, the jurist must have a precise understanding of the situation on which he has been asked to rule. The judgment we make about something grows out of the way in which we conceptualize or perceive it. Hence, many a mufti has exposed his ignorance through the fatwas he has issued! Alas, it often happens that people will experience something in one way, while the scholar asked to rule on the situation will perceive it in a different way. A situation must always be examined from all angles before a ruling on it is issued.[78]

In a letter he sent to Abū Mūsā al-Ashʿarī, ʿUmar ibn al-Khaṭṭāb spoke of the need for a thorough understanding of cases on which a mufti is required to rule. He said:

> Ruling on legal cases is an indisputable obligation and a means of emulating the example of the Prophet... Understand well whatever

> evidence is presented to you from sources other than the Qur'an or the Sunnah. Then draw analogies between the rulings found in the Qur'an and the Sunnah, and the situation presently before you. Acquaint yourself with the points of similarity between them; then adopt whatever view you think will be most pleasing to God, or what you think is closest to the truth.[79]

When faced with unprecedented issues, a mufti should be careful to make certain of his facts, and not be hasty to pass judgment, since something might happen to change the situation in one way or another and, as a consequence, the way he should respond to it. Should he issue a ruling based on a faulty understanding, he will miss the mark and fall into error that might cause many others to fall into error as well.[80]

In this connection, the Prophet is reported to have said, "If someone is issued a fatwa the basis for which is uncertain [and acts thereon], his sin will be upon the person who issued the fatwa."[81] He also said, "The quickest of you to issue fatwas will be the quickest to enter hell."[82] Similarly, Ibn Masʿūd is reported to have said, "Whoever answers every question he is asked is out of his mind."[83] Whenever Ibn Masʿūd was asked about a legal matter, he would spend an entire month thinking about how to answer it. Then he would say, "Oh, God! If I answer correctly, it will be by Your grace, and if not, it will be the fault of Ibn Masʿūd!"[84] Imam Mālik is quoted as having said, "I've been pondering a certain legal question for more than ten years, and to this day I haven't arrived at an answer to it,"[85] and, "Sometimes when a question is posed to me, I think about it for nights on end."[86]

The aforementioned quotes point clearly to the necessity of seeking true certainty before issuing a religious ruling, and of not being hasty to answer those who have requested such a ruling. If, when a mufti is considering a question posed to him, he keeps sight of the importance of the function he performs, he will dedicate himself all the more sincerely to his honorable task, which will in turn guarantee his success in carrying out his weighty responsibility.[87] Imam Ibn al-Qayyim comments in this connection:

> Whoever is appointed to the position of mufti must prepare himself well for it, realizing the loftiness of the station he now occupies. Moreover, he should have no compunctions about declaring the truth and submitting thereto. After all, God is his Upholder and his Guide. How could he fail to have confidence when he knows that the function of mufti is one that God himself – the Lord of the Worlds – once took upon Himself?[88]

When researching a contemporary situation with a view to issuing a fatwa on it, one should always consult people with specialized knowledge in whatever fields are pertinent to the case, including those of medicine, economics, astronomy, and the like. In so doing, the mufti is acting on the words of God Almighty who, speaking to the skeptics of the Prophet's time who doubted whether he was bringing a message consistent with that of earlier prophets, said to them, "If you do not know this, ask the followers of earlier revelation" (*Sūrah al-Anbiyā'* 21:7).

If the issue of concern has to do with medicine, for instance, it should be brought before health professionals who can explain whatever needs to be clarified. If it has to do with economics and financial matters, economists should be consulted. After all, someone who knows nothing about modern currencies might rule that no zakah is due on them, or that it would be impossible to engage in usury (*al-ribā*) with them since they are not gold or silver![89] Similarly, someone with no knowledge of artificial insemination will be unable to pass a valid fatwa on the matter of in vitro fertilization, or test-tube babies.[90]

By adhering to the Prophet's counsel regarding the importance of consultation, muftis can guard against issuing rulings based on ignorance or misinformation, especially in connection with contemporary issues. Present-day collective scholastic efforts in the form of juristic academies, fatwa-issuing bodies, and academic research centers are helping to broaden the circle of knowledge and consultation, a process that will help to ensure that juristic research is carried out with competence and caution.

In this connection al-Khaṭīb al-Baghdādī wrote:

> Then the mufti should consult qualified, knowledgeable individuals concerning what ruling he should issue on the matter at hand. He should ask each of them for his or her opinion. This practice brings a blessing, since it is a way of emulating the righteous earlier generations of Muslims. God Almighty [commanded the Prophet], saying, "And take counsel with them [the believing community]..." (*Sūrah Āl ʿImrān* 3:159). And in fact, the Prophet consulted with others about a variety of concerns, and instructed his followers to do the same. His Companions would thus consult together before issuing legal rulings.[91]

3: *Cite all relevant textual evidence and applicable rules when ruling in favor of a weakly attested lenient view.*
This guideline will help the mufti to bolster each religious ruling with its textual proofs and to acquaint the person who requested the ruling with the basis for the fatwa he has been given. The citation of textual proofs will silence those who might otherwise have found fault with the ruling, and rob negligent, irresponsible people of any excuse for ignoring the ruling and letting their whims and desires govern their behavior. In this regard, Imam Ibn al-Qayyim wrote:

> A mufti should seek, to the best of his ability, to mention the proofs for whatever ruling he issues, as well as the source from which he drew them. He should not simply give his questioner a fatwa devoid of evidence, or with no mention of its source. Should he do so, this merely reveals his own lack of understanding and knowledge. Whoever ponders the rulings given by the Prophet, whose words themselves are a source of proof, will find that they include a reference to the wisdom underlying the ruling, similar rulings relating to other situations, and their legal basis.[92]

Elsewhere Ibn al-Qayyim stated:

> Some people have decried the mention of proofs in verdicts; this decrial is itself worthy of being decried! Indeed, the beauty and soul of any verdict is its proof. How can the mention of God's word and the words of His Messenger, the consensus of the believing community and the sayings of the Prophet's Companions, and the drawing

of valid analogies between later and earlier rulings possibly be viewed as blameworthy?[93]

Describing what happened to the process of issuing fatwas after the time of the Prophet's Companions and their successors, Ibn al-Qayyim wrote:

> Then a long time passed, and people drifted away from knowledge. Scholars' zeal for issuing correct rulings dwindled to the point where, when they were asked for a ruling on this or that action, they would reply with nothing but "Yes" or "No", without citing any proof or source for their verdicts. Such scholars recognized neither their own negligence nor the merit of those who supported their rulings with textual proofs. Then things deteriorated even further until those who issued fatwas with proofs were criticized and condemned. Perhaps the time will come when people no longer see fatwas themselves as being of any value![94]

4: *Provide a permissible alternative when judging a given action to be forbidden.*

This rule is of great importance for the times in which we live. The reason for this is that most new developments in Muslim societies have their origins in non-Muslim, and modern decadent societies that do not observe an Islamic ethos, and which invade our communities with powerful, seductive influences in the form of financial and economic practices, trends of thought, and the media, among others. In the face of such influences, a mufti must be equipped to recognize and affirm what is Islamically lawful and acceptable, and to reject and forbid what is unlawful and objectionable. The mufti should also be prepared to explain the wise purpose behind whatever prohibitions he issues while showing the way toward appropriate lawful alternatives, since in this manner he serves to protect the religion and reform people's ways. Such an approach demonstrates true understanding of God's ways, and a desire to provide people with prudent counsel. Imam Ibn al-Qayyim states:

> When a mufti with solid understanding and the ability to provide

> wise counsel is asked for a legal opinion and forbids the inquirer to engage in the action concerned even though the inquirer needs to engage in said action (or something similar thereto), he will direct the inquirer to an appropriate alternative. In this way, the mufti will help to prevent the inquirer from pursuing what is forbidden and encourage him to pursue what is permissible. However, such an approach will only be followed by a compassionate, well-informed scholar who seeks closeness to God and who relates to others based on the knowledge he has been endowed with. Such a scholar might be likened to an experienced physician who seeks to protect his/her patients from whatever would harm them and prescribe for them whatever would be to their benefit. Hence, just as the physician strives to heal the body, the religious scholar strives to heal the soul.[95]

There is a well-attested saying of the Prophet according to which, "Whoever is sent by God as a messenger is duty-bound to direct his people to the best he can possibly teach them, and to direct them away from what he knows to be bad for them."[96] This is the way of God's apostles, and of those who have inherited from them the task of communicating God's truth to others.[97]

5: *Ensure that, when applying the principle of taysīr, the interests explicitly recognized in Islamic law are being properly realized.* When examining a case, a mufti must consider whether the interests recognized in Islamic law are being actualized, bearing in mind that the law of Islam aims to preserve what is of benefit, and to remove whatever causes harm. The scholar investigating a new case will frequently base his or her ruling on a consideration of what are termed unrestricted interests (*al-maṣāliḥ al-mursalāh*), that is, interests that are not mentioned explicitly in either the Qur'an or the Sunnah but which are, nevertheless, viewed by the majority of Muslim jurists as being valid human interests recognized under Islamic law.[98] This is why Imam al-Āmidī has stated:

> If unrestricted interests were not a valid legal consideration, it would be impossible to issue fatwas on new situations due to the fact they receive no specific mention in the Qur'an or the Sunnah, there is

no existing consensus on them among Muslim scholars, and there are no analogous precedents that could be cited.[99]

The validity of the practice of taking unrestricted interests into account is made evident by the many new phenomena with which we are now confronted, including administrative systems on the metropolitan, national and international levels, and the various types of documentation required for monetary transactions, marital agreements, and other types of contracts. Thus, if a jurist lacks a proper understanding of the aims and objectives of the Shariʿah and the imperative to preserve the five essentials recognized by Islamic law (religion, life, human reason, material property, and progeny), he or she might well close the door to numerous legitimate actions that ought to be permitted, or open the door wide to many an evil that ought to be prohibited.

Consequently, juristic scholars have specified a number of guidelines for ensuring that one realizes legitimate, Islamically recognized human interests when engaged in ijtihad and issuing legal rulings. These guidelines dictate that a mufti should:

(i) Include human interests among the aims of Islamic law.
(ii) Ensure that the interest in question does not conflict with any Islamic legal text.
(iii) Verify that the interest in question is indisputable or, at the very least, that there is convincing evidence of its validity.
(iv) Ascertain that the interest in question is universal in nature.
(v) Ensure that consideration of the interest in question will not threaten some other interest of greater or equal importance.[100]

It should be borne in mind that if a jurist has issued a fatwa on a given situation based on a valid human interest, he/she will need to modify the fatwa if the human interest on which it was based undergoes some change. It will be clear that the change in the fatwa here reflects a change in the circumstances surrounding the ruling, not in the Shariʿah.

6: When considering a more lenient ruling, recognize the principle of relief from hardship/harm (rafʿ al-ḥaraj).

The term "harm" as used here refers to "anything that would lead to undue hardship either in body, soul, or property, whether immediately, or at a later time."[101] Therefore what is meant by *rafʿ al-ḥaraj*, or alleviation of harm, is "sparing morally accountable persons hardship in relation to the Islamic law's requirements of them."[102]

There is so much support for *rafʿ al-ḥaraj* in the Qur'an and the Sunnah that it has become a firmly established principle of Islamic law. God Almighty declares that He "does not want to impose any hardship on you" (*Sūrah al-Mā'idah* 5:6), and that He "has laid no hardship on you in [anything that pertains to] religion" (*Sūrah al-Ḥajj* 22:78). Similarly, the Prophet declared, "This religion is one of ease."[103]

Given the categorical support for *rafʿ al-ḥaraj* in the Qur'an and the Sunnah, jurists are obliged to observe this principle in relation to all situations on which they are called upon to rule by not issuing any fatwa whose implementation would impose undue hardship on the person concerned. Similarly, they must permit concessions, either by allowing that which would not normally be allowed or by providing an exemption from that which would normally be required in the cases of individuals with legitimate justifications for availing themselves of such concessions.[104]

The following conditions must be met in order for a jurist to apply the principle of *rafʿ al-ḥaraj* when ruling on unprecedented situations:

- The harm involved must be real and have a specific, known cause, such as illness or travel, whose presence will result in extraordinary hardship. Thus, no consideration may be accorded to imaginary harm on account of which there is no real reason to grant a concession, since it is invalid to base one's ruling on a nonexistent cause, just as it is invalid to base it on mere conjecture, speculation, or illusion.

- Alleviation of the harm in question must not conflict with an

Islamic legal text. Harm and hardship may be taken into account in situations not addressed by a specific text. However, if their alleviation comes into conflict with an explicit text of the Shariʿah, they may not be considered.[105]

- The harm in question should be widely occurring. Ibn al-ʿArabī said, "If the harm in question is related to a situation that occurs commonly among people, it must be alleviated. However, if it is specific to a particular person, we give it no consideration. According to some principles presented by al-Shāfiʿī in a discussion of matters of disagreement, hardship of a widespread nature should be recognized and alleviated."[106]

7: *Give due consideration to the anticipated consequences of issuing a lenient ruling.*

A mufti must consider the question of whether a given application of a text will realize the desired aim or not. Someone investigating a new situation must not issue a ruling on said situation until he/she has thought carefully about what results this ruling will yield. The practice of considering end results is a well-founded principle with plentiful textual support in Islamic law.[107] God has said, "And devour not one another's possessions wrongfully, and neither employ legal artifices with a view to devouring sinfully, and knowingly, anything that by right belongs to others" (*Sūrah al-Baqarah* 2:188); and "do not revile those [beings] whom they invoke instead of God, lest they revile God out of spite, and in ignorance" (*Sūrah al-Anʿām* 6:108).

This principle is likewise supported by the example of the Prophet, who, when he was told to kill a person whose hypocrisy had become public knowledge, said, "I fear lest people should say that Muhammad murders his friends."[108] In another context the Prophet said to ʿĀ'ishah, "Had your people not just emerged from a life of unbelief, I would have rebuilt the Kaʿbah upon the foundations laid by Abraham."[109] There are, in addition, numerous other texts supporting this principle.[110]

On the importance of considering future consequences of a legal ruling, Imam al-Shāṭibī stated:

> The question of what long-term consequences an action will lead to is an important consideration when preparing to issue an Islamic legal ruling, be the action in question in keeping with the Shariʿah, or in conflict with it. A *mujtahid* should not rule for or against a given action until he has investigated the long-term consequences of undertaking, or refraining from, said action. The action in question might be permissible due to a benefit it is expected to achieve, or harm it is expected to prevent. However, this same action might involve long-term consequences that work against its intended outcome. Alternatively, the action might be impermissible due to a harm it is expected to cause, or a benefit it is expected to thwart; however, this same action might bring long-term consequences that are the reverse of what it causes in the short-term. Hence, if a jurist rules that the former action is unconditionally permissible, the short-term benefit it brings might be negated by some harm of equal or greater magnitude in the long run. Conversely, if the latter action is judged to be unconditionally impermissible, the harm prevented in the short-term by its prohibition might be outweighed by some even greater harm caused by this same prohibition. This is a very difficult area for those involved in interpreting the Shariʿah. However, it is a praiseworthy undertaking with great rewards, since one knows one is acting in keeping with the aims and objectives of the law of Islam.[111]

How many a door to evil has been opened by fatwas that failed to take into account the harm and corruption that might result from them? Telling examples include the permission given to women in some Islamic countries to be employed in all specializations and to participate in all areas of life alongside men without considering the harm that might come to them as a result of their unsuitability for some of these areas; short-sighted fatwas on jihad; and anomalous perceptions that have brought destruction and carnage to many Muslim lands.

The benefits to be achieved by taking future consequences into account may be seen, for example, in fatwas that criminalize trafficking in drugs and intoxicants and legitimize the use of the death penalty for those convicted of such crimes to serve as a deterrent. Such rulings close the door to evil and protect people from harm.

8: *Gain a solid understanding of the circumstances surrounding the case in question before issuing a ruling that involves application of the principle of taysīr.*

When investigating a case that calls for a legal ruling, the jurist should allow his/her legal interpretation and the resultant fatwa to reflect changes in time, place, and social, political, and economic conditions. Islamic legal rulings are intended to achieve justice, bring benefit, and prevent harm; this being the case, they are closely bound to prevailing social and moral conditions at any given time. Thus, many rulings which, at the time they were issued, successfully addressed a particular problem in a particular environment, may become useless or, worse still, positively harmful in subsequent generations due to people's changing circumstances.

Many later jurists have issued fatwas that differ from those issued by predecessors who represented the same schools of juristic thought as their own. These later jurists have made plain that the reason for the difference between their fatwas and those of their forebears lies in changing times and circumstances and deteriorating morals. Therefore, such later jurists are not in disagreement with earlier jurists. In fact, if earlier jurists could have witnessed the altered circumstances of later societies, they would have issued the same rulings that their successors did.[112] Herein lies the basis for the juristic principle that says, "Changing rulings are an acceptable outcome of changing times."[113] The following examples illustrate the application of this principle:

- Imam Abū Ḥanīfah was of the opinion that there is no need to have someone vouch for a witness's trustworthiness unless it has been challenged by an opponent, and that one may content oneself with an appearance of honesty. As for his two companions, Abū Yūsuf and Muḥammad, they held that a judge must have someone vouch for witnesses, as the circumstances of people do change.[114]

- Later scholars ruled that – given deteriorating social conditions, and in order to deter those who sow corruption in society – whoever incites another to wrongdoing must be held responsible for the act of wrongdoing to which this incitement led, even though the original principle states that, "The actual doer of the wrong should be held responsible, not the party who caused the wrong to be committed."[115]

- In a verdict that served to qualify the unconditional rulings of some scholars, Imam Ibn Taymiyyah and his pupil, Ibn al-Qayyim held that it was permissible for a menstruating woman to perform *ṭawāf al-ifāḍah* (the circumambulation of the Kaʿbah performed during the major pilgrimage following one's arrival from Mt. Arafah) if it would be impossible for her to stay on in Makkah until she became ritually pure again.[116] Some contemporary scholars have followed their lead in view of people's changing circumstances.

- Some muftis in our day and age have ruled that it is permissible to lock mosques between one prayer and the next, even though they are places of worship which in principle should be kept open, in order to prevent them from being burglarized or being turned to places of amusement.[117] There are, in addition, numerous other examples of rulings that have been modified by later scholars in response to changing times and conditions.[118]

- In a chapter entitled, "Changes in fatwas resulting from changing times, places, circumstances, intentions, and norms," Ibn al-Qayyim al-Jawziyyah stated:

> This is a very important topic, ignorance of which has caused untold errors in relation to Islamic law. Such errors have resulted in hardship, discomfort and onerous obligations which we know for a certainty do not have their origin in the illustrious, benevolent Shariʿah. On the contrary, the Shariʿah is founded upon wisdom and what will benefit human beings both in this life and the next. The Shariʿah is pure justice, pure benefit, and pure wisdom. Consequently, any ruling that yields injustice rather than justice, cruelty rather than mercy, harm rather than benefit, or folly rather than

wisdom does not come from the Shariʿah even though it may have been extrapolated therefrom through distorted interpretations.[119]

Perhaps this insightful statement by Imam Ibn al-Qayyim will serve to inspire jurists to give proper consideration to the environment and circumstances associated with each particular case, since many a fatwa that is useful in one age is of no use in another, and many a fatwa that is appropriate for one environment is inappropriate for another, for one person and not another, or for a given person in one situation, but not in another.

Given the importance of this truth, in what follows I will summarize three principles that should be observed when issuing fatwas in changing times, paces and circumstances:

- The basic principles of the Shariʿah are immutable; they do not change over time or in response to changing circumstances. Hence, the fact that legal rulings based on the Shariʿah differ from one case to another does not mean that the Shariʿah itself is contradictory or changeable. However, each ruling based on the Shariʿah is linked to a particular cause rooted in a given time, place and situation. Therefore, variations in people's locations and conditions will inevitably be reflected in varied fatwas, or legal rulings.[120]

- Fatwas should not change in response to mere whims, caprices, and human points of view regarding what is desirable or undesirable. Rather, there must be a valid reason for the jurist to reconsider existing fatwas. A fatwa may legitimately be modified based on altered perceptions of what serves a legitimate, recognized interest, and in light of established principles that favor a change in a previous ruling.

- The act of amending existing fatwas is the sole prerogative of qualified scholars; it is a difficult task that should not be undertaken by those with inadequate knowledge or understanding. Moreover, the greater the communal dimension in the process of researching a legal ruling, the greater the chances of the resulting verdict being valid and beneficial.[121]

9: *Investigate the commonly accepted customs of relevance to the application of a more lenient ruling.*

The word "customs" as used here has been defined by juristic scholars as "the understandings that have become ingrained in people's minds, and what has been deemed acceptable by sound minds and dispositions."[122] Jurists consider norms and customs in applying the precepts of the Shariʿah to countless situations and questions. Examples include the age when a girl should be considered capable of menstruating; puberty; acts that are incompatible with the performance of ritual prayer; the types of ritual impurity that may be overlooked; what constitutes a valid verbal affirmation in the conclusion of a contract, as well as numerous situations relating to sales, religious endowments, oaths, confessions, wills and bequests, and other matters.[123]

This is in keeping with the principle that states, "Custom is a court of law," which is based on the tradition handed down on the authority of ʿAbd Allāh ibn Masʿūd, who said, "Whatever the Muslim community deems good, is good in the sight of God."[124] Therefore, if customs and norms are given weight in the Shariʿah despite the many changes they undergo, scholars are duty-bound to take such change into account to the greatest possible extent, especially as it relates to fatwas issued in connection with new situations and unprecedented events. Of relevance here is Imam al-Qarrāfī's statement:

> Indeed, rigid adherence to rulings based on specific social customs and norms even when such customs and norms have changed conflicts with the consensus of Muslim scholars; it also reflects ignorance of the religion. Rather, every part of the Shariʿah is subject to customs. Legal rulings must change in response to changes in the customs to which they relate, conforming themselves to the requirements of these varying customs.[125]

Elsewhere he states:

> If a mufti is approached by someone seeking a fatwa, and if the mufti does not know whether the fatwa-seeker is from the same town as he is from or from the place where the fatwa is to be issued, the mufti must first ask the seeker where he [or she] is from, and whether the people of his/her town make customary usage of the relevant linguistic terms. If the people of his/her town do make customary use of the term, he should find out whether the two towns' customary usages are the same or different. Scholars agree unanimously that such an inquiry on the part of the mufti is obligatory because, if the customs in the two towns differ, the rulings regarding them will be different as well.[126]

Al-Qarrāfī affirmed this same principle elsewhere, saying:

> It is in keeping with this rule that fatwas should always be approached. When a custom evolves over time, this must be taken into consideration, and when a custom ceases to exist, this must likewise be reflected in the relevant fatwas. Do not remain rigidly observant, throughout your lifetime, of what is written in books. Rigid adherence to traditions handed down from earlier generations is bound to cause religious controversy, and reflects ignorance of the intentions of Muslim scholars and our righteous forebears in Islam.[127]

As has been mentioned, Imam Ibn al-Qayyim wrote at length about the ways in which fatwas should change from one generation to another, from place to place, from situation to situation, and in keeping with varying intentions and customs. After citing numerous examples of this phenomenon and sources of textual support for it,[128] he states that failing to take prevailing customs into account when issuing fatwas is a trap into which the uninformed mufti might easily fall, thereby misleading others. Such a mufti, states Ibn al-Qayyim, "lies to God and His Messenger and changes his religion, prohibiting what God has not prohibited, and requiring what God has not required. In God alone is our help."[129]

Given, on one hand, the importance of this principle and, on the other, the danger it might pose to people responsible for issuing legal rulings, jurists and legists have laid down four conditions that must be fulfilled in order for a given custom to be eligible for consideration when formulating a fatwa. By observing these conditions, scholars help to protect the Shariᶜah from confused, inconsistent interpretation and application. The conditions, in brief, are as follows: (1) The custom in question must be one that is observed on a widespread basis. (2) The custom on the basis of which certain behaviors are to be evaluated must have existed prior to said behaviors. (3) There must be no explicit statements [by Muslim jurists] which conflict with the custom. (4) The custom must not be opposed by an explicit legal text which would be violated by observance of said custom.[130]

As will be clear from the foregoing, every scholar or mufti studying a case that requires a legal ruling must make allowances for the customs and norms of both individuals and societies. The need for this precaution is all the greater now that people who request fatwas come from all over the world, and with varied cultural and social backgrounds. Given modern means of communication, it is easy to contact a mufti who resides in a location and community far removed from one's own. Therefore, he or she must be careful not to issue a fatwa before becoming familiar with the customs and mores of those seeking the ruling, and which precepts of the Shariᶜah apply to them. Moreover, the jurist should beware of issuing overly generalized legal rulings which may not be appropriate for the people for whom they are intended given their specific circumstances and customs. This precaution is particularly important when fatwas are being broadcast on call-in programs on television or radio.[131]

Consequently, someone preparing to issue a legal ruling should view himself not only as a mufti but, in addition, as a teacher, a reformer, a physician and a guide, since only in this way will his verdict reach its intended audience in an effective manner. Hence, all muftis and scholars should apply the aforementioned principles to the best of their ability.

There are many other rules and protocols which scholars have mentioned in connection with the work of a mufti. In the interests of simplicity and brevity, however, I have refrained from mentioning some of them due to their lack of relevance to the age in which we live.

In concluding this chapter, allow me to quote from Imam al-Khaṭīb al-Baghdādī, who summed up the principles that should guide the mufti as follows:

> The scholar, interpreter or mufti should have the following qualities: he should be skilled at inferring rulings from the relevant texts; he should be observant, prudent, patient, unhurried, and calm. Moreover, he should have insight into that which is beneficial and be willing to engage in consultation with others. He should be committed to his own religious belief and practice and be full of compassion toward his fellow religionists. He should guard his integrity, being conscientious about eating only what is Islamically permitted and wholesome, since this is vital to his success. He should shun whatever is of dubious value and legality, and refrain from invalid or unfounded textual interpretations. He should be firmly grounded in the truth, knowledgeable, and up-to-date on resources for legal rulings and methods of interpretation. He should not be neglectful or heedless, nor should he fatigue himself by staying up too late into the night; he should not be known for a lack of discipline, understanding or balance. When asked a question, he should not presume to have knowledge he lacks, or to be cognizant of things that are hidden from him.[132]

Lastly, a scholar should guard himself about the words, "I don't know" if he is unable to answer a question. Not knowing does not detract from a person's standing in any way. After all, it is impossible for anyone to possess all knowledge; there must be certain things one does not know. He who harbors the ambition to know everything is an ignoramus, and whoever undertakes a task that requires knowledge which he lacks is a liar.[133]

According to Ibn ʿAbbās, "When a scholar ceases to say, 'I don't know', he renders himself vulnerable."[134] In a similar vein, Ibn ʿUmar declared, "Knowledge consists of three things: a book that 'speaks' of its contents, established practice being actively observed in society, and the words, 'I don't know'."[135] There is abundant textual support for this notion, and statements by God-fearing scholars testify to the validity of this principle and the importance of applying it when one lacks ability or knowledge.[136]

2
Understanding *Maqāṣid al-Sharīʿah* Through Cultural Development

OVERVIEW OF THIS CHAPTER

The chapter discusses the importance of civilizational awareness, introduces the concept of a jurisprudence of human development, focuses on the need to work toward a well-guided cultural jurisprudence, and highlights the need to develop the world in a manner that strengthens and benefits humankind.
It aims to:

1. Explore the need for cultural and civilizational awareness as part of one's place in a globalised world.
2. Explore the jurisprudence of social development, which provides the theoretical basis and impetus for promoting prosperity on earth and bringing about cultural revival.
3. Explain how to maintain one's religious and spiritual identity and protect these against the effects of a secular humanist perception within the parameters of global citizenship.
4. Discuss how to maintain a balance between the material life and the spiritual hereafter.
5. Explore civilizational awareness defined as an understanding on the part of both individuals and institutions of their major responsibility toward society, their responsibility to build an integrated human personality, and to promote the process of moral and material progress and renewal through ideological, behavioral, and material reform.
6. Emphasize the importance of reading the Shariʿah to rediscover its magnanimity, the progressive nature of its ordinances, and its ability to solve societies' problems and advance human interests.
7. To critique Muslims caught up in juristic nitpicking over issues of peripheral importance, trapped in a reality imposed on them by their own weakness and decadence.

GIVEN overwhelming advances in communications technology, the Islamic community has experienced a significant rapprochement with other nations and cultures of the world. This phenomenon has enabled the civilizations of other nations, given their influential media and their ideological, economic, and political hegemony, to control the course of change in Islamic societies through the process of globalization. As a result, younger generations of Muslims have been dazzled by secular culture and values, and their religious foundations and values have been undermined. Hence, academic and societal organizations need to work towards preserving Muslims' religious beliefs and values through a sincere, dedicated, and informed return to the cultural message of Islam. Such a process has the potential of stimulating Muslims to rebuild and renew their civilization.

The juristic study of human civilization and development (*fiqh al-ʿumrān*) has long been neglected, not receiving the attention it merits in the areas of teaching, writing, and practical application. The most important means of improving Muslims' juristic understanding of culture and civilization and restoring their confidence in their religion as the remedy for social ills is to return to the goals of the Islamic legal system, reread the precepts of Islam in light of these goals, and highlight those aspects which deal with understanding civilization so that life can be ordered on this basis.

In this chapter I will be discussing the following three themes: (1) the importance of civilizational awareness, (2) an introduction to the jurisprudence of human development, and (3) the need to work toward a well-guided cultural jurisprudence.

(1) The Importance of Civilizational Awareness

God Almighty has honored human beings and given them a privileged status over all other creatures by granting them discerning minds and spirits. Consequently, human beings are the focal point of the divine messages. God declares, "Now indeed We have conferred dignity on the children of Adam, and borne them over land and sea, and provided for them sustenance out of the good things of life, and favored them far above most of Our creation" (*Sūrah al-Isrā'* 17:70). In light of this honored position, human beings have been assigned the dual tasks of worshiping God alone, and populating and developing the earth. Any failure on our part to carry out these two tasks could well turn our lives into an existence filled with distress and anxiety, disorder and misery.

Throughout the course of their history, societies have evolved and advanced through human beings' efforts and maturity, their understanding of their purpose in life, and their application of the laws God has planted in the universe. In some cases, nations and societies have weakened, fallen and faded into oblivion. They were brought to this sad end by their failure to understand the purpose of their existence, or their deviation from that purpose. And herein lies the secret of the rise and the fall of civilizations.

In order to elucidate the importance of cultural or civilizational awareness, we would do well to apply it to an examination of contemporary circumstances, including terrorist attacks, ideological extremism, and the sense of cultural inferiority that manifests itself in many aspects of life. This approach is vital if we are to diagnose the malady rather than focusing solely on symptoms.

When we are faced with a crisis, the last thing that comes to our minds is to blame ourselves; we tend to disregard the role played by our own actions in the problems we have. However, we read in the Qur'an that, "Verily, God does not change people's condition unless they change their inner selves" (*Sūrah al-Raʿd* 13:11). Similarly, we read, "And do you, now that a calamity has befallen you..., ask yourselves, 'How has this come about?' Say [O Prophet]: 'It has come about from your own selves.'" (*Sūrah Āl ʿImrān* 3:165).

The crisis we face is rooted in our failure to understand our religion and what true religiosity means, as well as individual Muslims' failure to discern the rights and obligations entailed by membership in a society. There is a veil over our eyes that has robbed us of the ability to view civilization from a sound perspective and caused us to stray onto paths of weakness, wishful thinking, and materialism. The only hope for the future of the Muslim community lies in a comprehensive awareness of the needs of both societies and their individual members. Before proceeding further, therefore, let us examine the term "civilizational awareness" more closely, thereby preparing the way for its practical application.

Awareness (*waʿy*) is a commonly used term in a variety of fields, particularly in relation to intellectual and cultural matters. The Arabic word *waʿy* (awareness) is derived from the trilateral root *w-ʿ-y*, meaning to bring together, to retain in memory, to keep and hold in a container, to hear and perceive. This last meaning is referred to by God when He speaks of Noah's ark as "a lasting reminder to you all, and that every wide-open ear (*udhunun wāʿiyah*) might consciously take it in (*taʿīyahā*)" (*Sūrah al-Ḥāqqah* 69:12), or of those who "amass [wealth] and thereupon withhold (*awʿā*) [it from their fellow human beings]" (*Sūrah al-Maʿārij* 70:18).

Over time, the word *waʿy* came to be used to indicate understanding and comprehension. The ancient psychologists defined *waʿy* as "an entity's realization of what is within itself and its environs."[1] With the advancement of knowledge and the increasing intricacy of terminologies and concepts, the word *waʿy* started taking on new, more specialized denotations in a variety of psychological, sociological, and ideological fields.

The Arabic word *waʿy* might be defined as, "a clear realization, both logical and intuitive, of what something requires for realization on the practical level." Any human project one might conceive of should be preceded by objective thinking that guarantees the soundness of the relevant action and its concordance with the rules of life. Abstract awareness devoid of action is, in my belief, mere sophistry and illusion.

As for the word *ḥaḍārah*, or civilization, its connotations vary from one culture or environment to another. The Arabic word *ḥaḍārah* is derived from the word *al-ḥāḍirah* (urban life), as opposed to *al-bādiyah* (rural life). The English word "civilization" has its roots in the Latin word *civites*, from which we derive "civic", relating to city life. Hence, the Arabic and English words have a common semantic link. However, Ibn Khaldūn, one of the first Muslim scholars to use the term *ḥaḍārah*, defines it as "the peak of a culture's development and the end of its lifetime, which heralds its decline and degeneration."[2] As defined by Ibn Khaldūn, the word *ḥaḍārah* refers to the zenith of civilization, the concluding phase of a life of material opulence that signals its imminent degeneration. However, this definition differs from that employed by contemporary scholars.

According to Will Durant, civilization is a social order that promotes increasing cultural production and which consists of four elements: economic resources, political organization, moral traditions, and the pursuit of the arts and sciences. Civilization begins where chaos and anxiety end.[3] Therefore, in Durant's view, civilization has to do simply with the existence of productivity, regardless of its extent, whereas Taylor defines civilization as a stage of cultural development in which the arts, the sciences, and political life occupy an advanced position.

As for Ralph Linton, he states that "a society is an organized group of individuals. A culture is an organized group of individually learned responses characteristic of a particular society."[4] There are other definitions that vary depending on the epistemological, historical, and ideological backgrounds of one's perspective on civilization. However, some French thinkers, among others, have expanded the concept of civilization to include all dimensions of advancement, while others, such as those belonging to the German school of thought, restrict the meaning of civilization to aspects of material advancement, while still others equate civilization with culture.

For his part, Muslim thinker Malik Bennabi has defined civilization dynamically as the "fulfillment of all ethical and material conditions that will enable a particular society to give each of its members, at every phase of his/her development, from childhood to old age, all the assistance needed at that phase."[5]

According to Malik Bennabi and many other thinkers, civilization (*al-ḥaḍārah*) is far more than mere material prosperity. Hence, some scholars draw a distinction between the Arabic terms *ḥaḍārah* and *madaniyyah*, whereby the former refers to life in a major metropolis (*al-ḥāḍirah*), and the latter to life in a town (*al-madīnah*). Realizing that the development of human life consists of two fundamental dimensions, internal and external, some scholars prefer to use the term *al-madīnah* to represent an advancement in the inner, moral substance of urban life, and the term *al-ḥāḍirah* to represent the formal aspects of such advancement, including physical means of living, tools of production, and methods of organizing the environment. However, there is no consensus on this.

The Islamic perspective on the universe places strong emphasis on the distinction between these two aspects of human advancement. God condemns nations that have made great strides in the construction of metropolises, utilization of resources, and production of tools and equipment while insolently rejecting God's commands. The corruption of the inward aspect of these people's existence has even led to their annihilation. It is in reference to this that God declares:

> Have they, then, never journeyed about the earth and beheld what happened in the end to those [deniers of the truth] who lived before their times? Greater were they in power than they are, and they left a stronger impact on the earth, and built it up even better than these are doing, and to them [too] came their apostles with all evidence of the truth, and so [when they rejected the truth and thereupon perished], it was not God who wronged them, but it was they who had wronged themselves. (*Sūrah al-Rūm* 30:9)

Speaking to the tribe of Thamūd in the midst of their material advancement, God says:

> And remember how He made you heirs to [the tribe of] ʿAd and settled you firmly on earth, so that you are [able to] build for yourselves castles on its plains and hew out mountains [to serve you] as dwellings. Remember, then, God's blessings on earth, and do not act wickedly by spreading corruption. (*Sūrah al-Aʿrāf* 7:74)

However, these people rejected faith in God. They turned away from the message they had received from Ṣāliḥ, their brother and God's messenger, with the result that "an earthquake overtook them, and then they lay lifeless, in their very homes, on the ground" (*Sūrah al-Aʿrāf* 7:78).

By contrast, the city of Madinah which witnessed the birth of the first Islamic society was no more advanced materially than some so-called Third World villages of today. However, this town came to represent the peak of civilization in moral, behavioral, and relational terms. In the society of Madinah, life's major goals were clear and unambiguous. They were so well-entrenched in people's minds, in fact, that its Muslims, including even children, vied for the honor of suffering martyrdom in a manner that was unprecedented in human history, and there were Muslims who toiled by day so that they could donate some of their wages as charity in the evening.

Members of this society were so pure and so keen to be cleansed of any sin that some men and women would come to the Prophet and confess sins they had committed. They insisted on receiving earthly punishment, even if it meant being stoned to death, in order to win God's pleasure. The government of Madinah at that time was so transparent and close to its people that the caliph's remuneration was no more than would suffice to feed and clothe him. The society was devoid of the manifestations of an overbearing state, with courts, prisons, and police being of marginal importance if they existed at all. In fact, no words could do justice to the level of moral advancement exhibited by Madinan society at that time.[6]

In sum, what I am terming civilizational awareness may be defined as an understanding on the part of both individuals and institutions of their major responsibility toward society, to wit, their responsibility to build an integrated human personality, and to promote the process of moral and material progress and renewal through ideological, behavioral, and material reform.

(2) An Introduction to the Jurisprudence of Human Development

The evolution of the study of human development, known in modern parlance as sociology, has led to a quantum leap in the way in which history is recorded. Credit for this leap goes to Abū Zayd ʿAbd al-Raḥmān Ibn Muḥammad ibn Khaldūn (d. 808 AH/1406 CE), who set forth his insights in this field in the well-known *Prolegomena* (Arabic, *al-Muqaddimah*), written initially as the introduction to his work entitled, *Kitāb al-ʿIbar wa Dīwān al-Mubtada' wa al-Khabar fī Akhbār al-ʿArab wa al-ʿAjam wa al-Barbar wa Man ʿĀsharahum min Dhawī al-Sulṭān al-Akbar* (The Book of Lessons and Records of the Reports of the Arabs, Persians, Berbers, and the Rulers Who Were Their Contemporaries).

Since the *Prolegomena* was written, no Muslim scholar has added anything of note to the field of sociology by way of research, commentary or annotation. Students of Ibn Khaldūn such as al-Maqrīzī (d. 836 AH/1442 CE) and Ibn Al-Azraq (d. 897 AH/1491 CE) recognized the historic importance of their teacher's ideas. However, they provided no significant expansion on his original contribution.

The field of sociology has now gained wide currency, and Ibn Khaldūn's role as the father of this discipline is recognized worldwide. Successive books have been written in the field, particularly in the West, and Western sociological theories have yielded a humanistic understanding of the nature of societies and their impacts on the history of nations and peoples. One of the founders of modern sociology and one of the most prominent researchers in the field is Emile Durkheim. Durkheim was preceded by Auguste Comte, who had first referred to the discipline by the term "social physics", and later coined the term "sociology" for which he became known worldwide.

Renowned British historian Arnold Toynbee describes the philosophy of history formulated and presented by Ibn Khaldūn in his *Prolegomena* as "the greatest work of its kind ever created by any mind in any time or place."[7] Ibn Khaldūn defined this new field of study as,

> a discipline that has to do with human development and society, and which treats questions concerning the successive events and circumstances experienced by people. This is, indeed, the case with every science, be it situational or rational.[8]

Ibn Khaldūn was the first to establish the logical foundations of every demonstrative science. In the beginning of his *Prolegomena*, he describes the demonstrative sciences as being founded upon four pillars: topic, manifestations, questions, and premises, and he sets out to explain "the states and stages of human development and advancement, events in human societies, the causes and reasons for phenomena and existent entities, and how people became inhabitants of their respective countries."[9] In explanation of the purpose of his field of inquiry, he states:

> It is a science that transforms the aim of the historian from that of mere narration of events and the search for unique or intriguing occurrences to that of understanding human society – world development – the nature of this development, and the states it manifests, such as savagery, sociability, tribalism, dominance by some people over others, and what such dominance gives rise to by way of sovereign rule and nation states with their varying ranks. It also examines human striving to earn a livelihood, acquire knowledge, and engage in creation and manufacturing, and the conditions yielded by such human development.[10]

This method of analyzing societies and studying the causes of individual and collective transformation is one of the most effective means of promoting needed change and reform and resolving social crises. Ibn Khaldūn's seclusion at Ibn Salamah Fortress in Algeria following the distressing events he had witnessed in Andalusia and North Africa may have been what led him to rethink the nature of social development and its impact on humankind.

My reason for introducing Ibn Khaldūn's concept of sociology is to draw attention to the cause-and-effect relationships Ibn Khaldūn observed, and to ask how these relationships can be transformed into practical mechanisms for overcoming the present degeneration in society and coping with the uncertainties of the future. To this end, the discipline of sociology needs to be linked to the science of jurisprudence so as to increase awareness of God's commands as they pertain to what is obligatory *(wājib)*, recommended (*mandūb*), undesirable (*makrūh*), and forbidden (*muḥarram*).

Therefore, the primary purpose of this discussion is to re-establish the relationship between jurisprudence as the motive force behind action, and a societal understanding that points the way to the correct and appropriate action. In order to reestablish this link, we need to understand the nature of change and, based on individual Muslims' actual circumstances, recognize where reform and social development are needed.

What I am terming "the jurisprudence of social development", which provides the theoretical basis and impetus for promoting prosperity on earth and bringing about a cultural revival in the world's societies, has been absent for much too long. Not only has there been a failure to introduce and explain this type of jurisprudence. There has, alas, been an out and out rejection of it, a failure to recognize it as part of our Shariʿah based on the mistaken notion that it represents a worldly distraction that detracts from our pursuit of the eternal Hereafter.

Thus, there is a disturbing gap between earlier periods of Muslim history which witnessed the emergence of various fields of learning within flourishing civilizations with developing infrastructures, and a modern history marked by a denigration of the material world in theory and, in practice, a pattern of feeding off the crumbs left by other nations that have picked up the torch of artistic, cultural, and technological development in our stead.

In order to bring Muslims' attention back to the central role played by the jurisprudence of human development in clarifying the actions required of us as morally accountable Muslims, I will turn in what follows to a discussion of five central points which highlight the salient features of this branch of jurisprudence and its importance to Islamic law. These five points are:

1. That God has created human beings for two principle purposes: to worship and serve their Maker, and to build up and prosper the Earth.

2. That one of the most foundational aims of Islamic law, as evidenced by both specific ordinances and the overall thrust of Islamic legal texts, is to populate and cultivate the earth in a manner that strengthens and benefits humankind.

3. That certain requirements of Islamic law are addressed not to individual Muslims, but to the Muslim community as a whole, for the purpose of benefiting the whole community without overburdening any one of its members.

4. That the Muslim community has been assigned the task of witnessing to the truth before the rest of the world by demonstrating goodness in both words and deeds, and by pursuing a path of moderation in all things.

5. That, as evidenced by both the Qur'an and the example set by the Prophet and his Companions, pursuing the Islamic path of moderation entails a balance between concern for earthly, material

well-being, and concern for spiritual realities and life in the Hereafter.

1: *God has created human beings for two principle purposes: to worship and serve their Maker, and to build up and prosper the Earth.*

The Qur'anic discourse focuses more on the concept and practice of worship than it does on material, earthly development. The reason for this is that at the time when the Qur'anic message was revealed, true worship had been tainted with polytheistic, superstitious beliefs and practices that had, in turn, been detrimental to people's physical well-being. And just as improper, misguided worship is destructive in its physical effects, sound, properly guided worship serves a corrective, healing role in people's worldly affairs. Equally, inhabiting the earth and erecting structures thereon is consistent with people's natural penchant for acquisition, competition, and proliferation. Since we need both moderation in our pursuits and a sense of duty in our activity, we need a law to guide us and a binding revelation to protect us from deviation and excess. This does not mean, however, that the Qur'an opposes or neglects our desire to seek a livelihood. On the contrary, there are many verses that encourage us to labor for the earth's development and prosperity. We read, for example, "And lo! Thy Sustainer said unto the angels, 'Behold, I am about to establish upon earth one who shall inherit it (*khalīfah*)'" (*Sūrah al-Baqarah* 2:30). Commenting on this verse, al-Bayḍāwī wrote:

> A *khalīfah* is someone who succeeds and represents someone else. The *tā' marbūṭah* added to the end of the word *khalīfah* has been placed there for emphasis. The word *khalīfah* in this verse refers to Adam, upon him be peace, who was God's vicegerent or representative on earth. The same is also true of other prophets, who were sent by God in succession with a mandate to develop the earth, lead its people, and carry out His commands among them.[11]

In affirmation of this understanding, Ibn Ashur states:

> The vicegerent (*khalīfah*) was Adam, whose vicegerency consisted in carrying out God's will to see the earth developed through divine inspiration or revelation, and by teaching his progeny what God wills for this earthly world.[12]

We read elsewhere in the Qur'an that the prophet Ṣāliḥ declared to the people of Thamūd, "He [God] brought you into being out of the earth, and made you thrive thereon" (*istaʿmarakum fīhā*) (*Sūrah Hūd* 11:61). Al-Ṭabarī understands the verbal phrase, *istaʿmara-kum*, translated above as "made you thrive" to mean, "He made you settlers therein."[13] As for al-Bayḍāwī, he interprets the phrase to mean, "He caused you to live and remain therein," or, "He gave you ability to develop and prosper it, and commanded you to do so."[14]

When we say that people were created from the earth, it is because Adam was created from the earth; hence, his origin is also the origin of his progeny. The link between humankind's creation and the earth also serves to highlight their relationship to the earth via cultivation and farming. God asks:

> Do you think that you will be left secure [forever] in the midst of what you have here and now – amidst these gardens and springs and fields, and these palm trees with slender spathes – and that you will always be able to hew dwellings out of the mountains with the same great skill? (*Sūrah al-Shuʿarā'* 26:146-148)

Moreover, because they carved dwellings out of the mountains and built fortresses on the land, God says in another verse:

> And remember how He made you heirs to [the tribe of] ʿĀd and settled you firmly on earth, so that you are [able to] build for yourselves castles on its plains and hew out mountains [to serve you] as dwellings. Remember, then, God's blessings on earth, and do not act wickedly by spreading corruption. (*Sūrah al-Aʿrāf* 7:74)

According to many Qur'anic exegetes, the verbal phrase *istaʿmarakum fīhā*, rendered above as "settled you firmly on earth", refers to building and causing to be prosperous. Hence the verse means, essentially, that God caused them to become the earth's builders through the erection of structures, cultivation, and farming.[15] These and other verses clearly indicate that the development of the earth is part of the essence of human creation, and that it is incumbent upon human beings to carry out this obligation. Imam al-Jaṣṣāṣ deems it an obligation based on the Qur'anic phrase *istaʿmarakum fīhā* since it means that God commanded people to build up the earth according to their needs. This in turn indicates the obligation to develop the earth through planting, cultivation, and the erection of structures.[16]

2: *One of the most foundational aims of Islamic law, as evidenced by both specific ordinances and the overall thrust of Islamic legal texts, is to populate and cultivate the earth in a manner that strengthens and benefits humankind.*

This principle has been enunciated by numerous scholars of Islamic jurisprudence, including Imam Ibn Ashur, who stated:

> One of the loftiest objectives of the Shariʿah is to ensure that members of the Muslim community benefit from public wealth in a manner that safeguards both communal and individual interests. This may be achieved through fair treatment of those who have toiled to earn their keep, and showing kindness toward those whose efforts have not yielded enough to meet their needs. This is one of the noblest of all the aims of Islamic law.[17]

In a similar vein Shaykh Allal al-Fasi states:

> The general objective of the Shariʿah is fulfilled by developing the earth while living in peaceful coexistence thereon. The earth's well-being is dependent on the uprightness of those who have been assigned the task of being its stewards. To wit, it depends on their acting with justice and integrity, thinking and acting soundly, making prudent use of the land, extracting its resources, and managing them judiciously for the benefit of all.[18]

Developing the land through construction, manufacturing, agriculture, and the extraction of minerals and other resources is a desirable goal for all humankind, and for Muslims in particular. Such pursuits are required by human beings' role as vicegerents of Planet Earth. In this connection Imam al-Ghazālī said, "Achieving benefit and preventing harm are among the purposes of human existence, and humans' well-being is achieved by their fulfilling their purposes."[19]

When ʿUmar ibn al-Khaṭṭāb stipulated that a tax be collected on land acquired through wars of conquest but refused to have it distributed as booty among the Muslim soldiers, it was because he wanted the land to go on flourishing under the care of its original inhabitants, who had the expertise needed to cultivate it properly. He therefore said concerning the people, "Let them inhabit and care for the land, since they know more about it, and are more capable of managing it."[20]

In so doing, ʿUmar was emulating the example set by the Prophet when he conquered Khaybar and took possession of its land and wealth. Not having sufficient workers to manage the land for him, he restored the land to its original inhabitants, allowing them to cultivate it in return for giving him half of their harvest. This arrangement continued throughout the life of the Prophet, and throughout the caliphate of Abū Bakr.

As will be seen from the foregoing, material development is not a peripheral matter. On the contrary, it is closely bound to the objectives of the Shariʿah. Hence, the activities of construction, agriculture, manufacturing and all other aspects of development are included among the objectives of the pristine Shariʿah which Muslims are expected to fulfill.

3: *Certain requirements of Islamic law are addressed not to individual Muslims, but to the Muslim community as a whole, for the purpose of benefiting the whole society without overburdening any one of its members.*

Ibn ʿAbd al-Salām defined it thus: "The purpose behind collective obligations (*furūḍ al-kifāyah*) is to achieve benefit and prevent harm without charging particular individuals with the relevant responsibilities."[21]

Development of the earth is one of most essential pursuits for the safeguarding of people's well-being, while collective obligations are likewise essential for the betterment of people's lives. After listing some of these obligations, Ibn ʿAbd al-Salām states, "other ordinances have also been legislated for the common good, and without which public order will be disturbed."[22] Needless to say, a lack of law and order is one of the greatest banes to afflict any nation or community.

According to Imam al-Qarrāfi, "One of the most important collective obligations is to monitor conditions in the Muslim community and preserve the religious community's interests."[23] As such, construction of buildings and putting things in order in the society are communal obligations that only cease to be binding when they have been performed to a sufficient extent. Otherwise, the community is guilty of having neglected its duty. If one observes the situations of today's Muslims, one will see the extent of their negligence in carrying out the obligation to develop the earth and preserve their civilization, especially in the areas of manufacturing, microtechnologies, information technology, and medical as well as scientific discoveries. Certainly no one would deny these fields' importance for Muslims, and numerous Muslim scholars deem it obligatory to meet people's collective needs in these and other areas of human endeavor. One such scholar was Imam al-Zarkashī, who said:

> Crafts, industries, and other means of livelihood such as buying and selling, farming, and other necessary functions, including even cupping and refuse disposal, are all essential tasks. The saying of the Prophet that, "Differences within my believing community are a blessing to people," is applicable in this regard, while God in his mercy has given people the aptitudes for such jobs. If people refrained from performing them, they would be held liable. Moreover, al-Rāfiʿī and al-Nawawī report no dissenting opinions among scholars on this matter.[24]

4: *The Muslim community has been assigned the task of witnessing to the truth before the rest of the world by demonstrating goodness in both words and deeds, and by pursuing a path of moderation in all things.*

God Almighty declares, "And thus have We willed you to be a community of the middle way, so that with your lives you might bear witness to the truth before all mankind, and that the Apostle might bear witness to it before you" (*Sūrah al-Baqarah* 2:143) and, "You are indeed the best community that has ever been brought forth for [the good of] mankind: you enjoin the doing of what is right and forbid the doing of what is wrong, and you believe in God" (*Sūrah Āl ʿImrān* 3:110). The attributes by virtue of which the Muslim believing community is qualified to be a witness of truth to other nations, the best community ever brought forth for humanity's good, are listed in the verses just quoted: it is a community whose members maintain a balance between extremism and laxity, and carry out their obligation to enjoin what is right and forbid what is wrong in the broadest, most inclusive sense.[25]

Therefore, the current miserable situation of the community so beautifully described in the aforementioned verses is unacceptable. No one can shoulder the responsibility of witnessing to the truth without being aware of the task at hand, and able to carry this task out. Hence, in order to witness properly to the truth before the rest of the world, the entire Muslim community is under obligation to strive for the good, to perfect its performance, to give the best it has, to spread virtue, and to eliminate the causes of harm and corruption. These are the tasks with which the first Muslims were honored, and which will fall to the final generations of Muslims as well.

5: *As evidenced by both the Qur'an and the example set by the Prophet and his Companions, pursuing the Islamic path of moderation entails a balance between concern for earthly, material well-being, and concern for spiritual realities and life in the Hereafter.*

While, on the one hand, we are encouraged to demonstrate concern for constructive civic action, we are warned, on the other hand, against being content with nothing but our earthly existence and following in the footsteps of bygone nations who were ungrateful for God's blessings and thereby merited God's wrath and chastisement. Examples of such nations are the communities of the prophets Ṣāliḥ and Hūd, and the Egyptians over whom Pharaoh ruled. Indeed, there are countless texts denigrating the material world, and many scholars have written major works devoted to the virtues of asceticism and a sole focus on the Hereafter.[26]

This brings us to an important question: Do the Prophet's words and deeds, which explain the Qur'an and clarify its rulings and objectives, condemn material development? The question can be answered with the following points:

One: Material development is not a purely material phenomenon. Rather, it is an outcome of the power of knowledge, values and a profound awareness of the laws of nature and human progress. Most texts of the divine revelation came to develop human beings spiritually and to create the necessary tools to reform their beliefs and banish all forms of superstition and paganism from their thinking and behavior. It came to free people from the residual effects of the period of ignorance that had preceded the coming of Islam and the materialistically-oriented ethics associated with that period. This can be observed in the powerful emphasis placed by the Prophet's message during the early Makkan period on the afterlife and people's relationship with God. The focus during this phase was on the creation of an inwardly pure society that would be able to bear the costs and responsibilities of the approaching renaissance, handle its preoccupations, and temper its effects on people's mentalities and conduct.

Two: The Prophet and his Companions did not live in isolation from the few meager manifestations of civilization that surrounded them. Rather, despite their involvement in calling others to faith in God and building the Islamic state, they were likewise engaged in practicing their various crafts and professions. ʿUthmān, Ibn ʿUmar, Ibn ʿAbbās, al-Zubayr, Ṭalḥah, and ʿAbd al-Raḥmān ibn ʿAwf all had a robust interest in business transactions and work. At the same time, however, they exhibited no inclination towards extravagant displays of wealth, vying for prestige with showy edifices, or forcing others to support individual projects such as palaces, estrades, and tombs as had been done by the pharaohs of Egypt, the chosroes of Persia, and the caesars of Rome.

In a refutation of the dubious notion that one should abstain from all forms of material progress under the pretext of devoting oneself to the service of God, Imam Ibn al-Jawzī said:

> When I observe Sufis and hermits, I find that most of their actions are in conflict with the Shariʿah and reflect ignorance of God's law and unfounded opinion. They support their practices by citing verses of the Qur'an whose meanings they do not understand, and Prophetic traditions that may only apply to a particular circumstance and most of which are unreliable. For example, when they hear the Qur'anic verses: "the life of this world is nothing but the enjoyment of self-delusion" (*Sūrah Āl ʿImrān* 3:185) and, "Know that the life of this world is nothing but a play and a passing delight" (*Sūrah al-Ḥadīd* 57:20), and the Prophet's saying that, "The material world means no more to God than a dead ewe to its owners," they go to the extreme in rejecting material life without investigating the real meanings of such texts. Until one knows the true nature of something, he must neither praise nor condemn it. This simple earth is the place that has been made human beings' home. It is the earth that provides us with our daily sustenance, and it is where our dead are buried. How can we revile an entity that provides us with such benefits? The water, plants, and animals on earth are all for human beings' benefit and survival, while people's survival is what makes it possible for them to recognize their Lord and be subservient to Him. Whatever serves as a means of sustenance for a devout servant of God should be praised and not condemned. Rather, we should reserve our condemnation for the actions of the ignorant and wayward. If someone makes an honest living and distributes zakah from it, he must never be criticized. We are all aware of how much wealth Ibn al-Zubayr, Ibn ʿAwf, and other Companions left after their death. The zakah distributed by ʿAli ibn Abī Ṭālib came to forty thousand [dirhams or dinars], while Ibn Masʿūd left ninety thousand [dirhams or dinars] when he died. Al-Layth ibn Saʿd used to invest twenty thousand [dirhams or dinars] every year, Sufyān used to engage in monetary transactions, and Ibn Mahdī would invest two thousand dinars every year.[27]

Three: Other texts from the Islamic tradition point to the meaning of human development, not in the outward, material sense, but in the sense of inculcating an appreciation of duty, the value of taking initiative, and a zeal for collective unity in which the individual thinks less about his/her own personal interests and aspirations than he/she does about the interests and aspirations of the community as a whole. In this connection, the Prophet is reported to have said, "If any of you, though the Day of Judgment be imminent, is holding a palm seedling in his hand, let him plant it."[28]

In the view of Imam al-Munāwī, this Prophetic tradition,

> ...encourages people to plant trees and dig wells so that Planet Earth will remain prosperous until the time when its Creator has destined it to exist no longer. If someone planted for your benefit, you should also plant to benefit others after you even if you have to do so shortly before you are gone. Such an attitude is not inconsistent with being devoted to God's service. [29]

Hence, true social and material development begins with people's awareness of their responsibilities and obligations toward one another and the planet on which they live. Without this moral awareness, development leads only to corruption, oppression, and the usurpation of people's rights in the name of "civilization." This was the point Ibn Khaldūn was making when he said, "Civilization is the bane of [true] development."[30] This happens when material development brings a society to a level of such affluence and luxury that it descends into moral decadence, societal disintegration, and the squandering of the nation's wealth on a single privileged class which brings about the downfall of the state.[31]

The jurisprudence of human development is part of a new approach to jurisprudence which Muslim societies need as they progress in areas such as banking, medicine, politics, and other areas of human endeavor. There is a dire need for a jurisprudence that will create an impetus for civil development based on Islamic concepts and principles. Such a jurisprudence will show that the Muslim community is uniquely endowed with a civilizational program that can protect the world from the adverse effects of the currently prevailing civilization with its unbridled, insidious globalization. It is hoped that this introduction to the principles of the jurisprudence of human development will encourage scholars and researchers to engage in further theorization, and to compile relevant juristic rulings that will provide a foundation for well-guided action that enhances this world while preparing for the world to come.

(3) The Need to Work Toward a Well-Guided Civilizational Jurisprudence

By this point I hope to have demonstrated the importance of civilizational awareness and the role it can play in bringing about change in backward societies, as well as the legitimacy of an Islamic jurisprudence of human development. With this groundwork laid, the next step is to bring out these aspects of Islamic thought and to form an Islamic mindset that reflects itself in all aspects of life.

No matter how well planned a project is, it can never be successful if those assigned to carry it out lack a solid understanding of their task, and commence their work without the proper know-how. Consequently, we need to re-form people's minds, deepen their thought processes, and enable them to grasp the ways in which the Islamic message encompasses all spheres of life, from worship to material development, and for all times, places, and individuals. Beginning with awareness requires that we address Muslims' intellects by encouraging them to reread the Shari'ah and rediscover its magnanimity, the progressive nature of its ordinances, and its ability to solve societies' problems and advance the interests of their individual members.

No nation develops a civilization without there first being an idea so firmly entrenched in its members' minds that they accept it as a certainty. It is this certainty that then leads to shared endeavor and civilizational development. Malik Bennabi said, "Every civilization emerges as a result of some essential idea that has impressed itself on the society concerned, and which serves as the impetus that thrusts said society into the course of history."[32] This sentiment was affirmed by Toynbee, who stressed the significance of the role played by ideas, and religious ideas in particular, in establishing civilizations.[33] It is with this in mind that I am focusing here on the importance of reviving the fundamental ideas of Islam among Muslims, and then working to entrench these ideas more firmly and deeply in their minds. As God Almighty has stated, "Thus have We willed you to be a community of the middle way, so that with your lives you might bear witness to the truth before all mankind, and that the Apostle might bear witness to it before you" (*Sūrah al-Baqarah* 2:143); and, "You are indeed the best community that has ever been brought forth for [the good of] mankind: you enjoin the doing of what is right and forbid the doing of what is wrong, and you believe in God" (*Sūrah Āl ʿImrān* 3:110).

This was the role played by the Prophet in sparking a great civilizing movement that began in Madinah and spread throughout the world. The same clarity of thought was demonstrated by Ribʿī ibn ʿĀmir who, when he was asked about the reform movement being spearheaded by the Muslims, said, "God Almighty has sent us to free people from the worship of human beings in order to worship the Lord and Sustainer of human beings, from the oppression of [misguided] religions into the expansive accommodation of Islam, from the constriction of the material world into the spaciousness of this life and the life to come, and from the injustice of [misguided] religions to the justice of Islam."[34]

Since awareness is the fuel for societal development, this development has slowed in the Muslim world over the past few centuries. Hence, our purpose in laying the foundations of a jurisprudence of human development is to rekindle Muslims' awareness and, in so doing, give them the impetus they need to pursue social and cultural reform and change. There are several reasons for the need to engage in consciousness-raising as it relates to the jurisprudence of human development.

The first reason has to do with the secular humanist-oriented globalization movement that has been taking the world by storm, including Muslim societies. This movement, which has been made possible through the influence of the mass media, has infiltrated the societies of the world on the levels of culture, economy, and politics alike. Globalization has begun invading virtually every society on earth, melting down opposing cultures under the influence of the notion that the secular humanist, profit-oriented, model alone is worthy of emulation. Consequently we are witnessing the emergence of generations of Muslims who have been stripped of their religious law and identity, so dazzled are they by the golden calf of modern secular civilization. These Muslims need to be awakened and encouraged to search, within the storehouses of their majestic religion, for sources of stability and self-esteem, and for the moral compass they have lost. Rather than having a sense of defeatism, they should recognize that their great religion is rich with concepts and values they can be proud of, and is inherently superior to that of any other nation.

The second reason to promote Muslims' awareness of the jurisprudence of human development is the weakness and decadence that pervade life in Islamic countries. The mood in these countries is one of near-despair of a renewal of any sort, and people doubt whether the Muslim community possesses the tools needed to achieve the desired revival.

The third reason to spread awareness of the jurisprudence of human development is that all previous reform efforts have failed to focus on this aspect of the change process. Islam consists of a message that offers guidance, compassion, and possibilities of advancement to humanity and the rest of the universe, whether through political action, study of the Islamic written tradition, spiritual purification, or armed struggle. Past efforts at reform have tended to focus on only one of these avenues at the expense of the others. What the Muslim community needs at the present time is for individual Muslims to recover their confidence in their religion and to develop an aptitude for real advancement based on an understanding of Islamic law as a single, integrated, flexible system that addresses all realms of life without exception

The three major starting points for creating awareness of the jurisprudence of human development might be summed up as follows:

First: Deepen people's awareness of the aims of Islamic law, linking legal rulings to these aims, and help Muslims to understand the role played by these aims in creating an integrated picture of the religion as the path to happiness in this life and the next. This process can be carried out in the following ways:

a) Encouraging heartfelt worship of God, clear thinking and sincere, dedicated effort through reflection on the verses of the Qur'an, highlighting the divine majesty in a way that will speak to people's hearts and draw them closer to their Maker at all times rather than concentrating on the academic aspects of the divine oneness (*al-tawḥīd*) or preaching fire and brimstone, both of which tend cause boredom or lethargy.

b) Educating people on the objectives of Islamic law when issuing legal rulings by mentioning the reasons for them and the wise purposes behind them. This includes applying the principle of facilitation (*al-taysīr*) in situations that involve hardship and urgent need. In addition, prohibitions should be introduced gradually, and people should be provided with permissible alternatives when a course of action has been forbidden. In these ways the mufti should fulfill his responsibility to issue rulings that are appropriate to people's ever-changing needs and circumstances.

c) Explaining religious rulings in light of the five basic essentials which Islam aims to preserve: religion, life, reason, progeny, and wealth. These five essentials should be engrained in Muslims' minds and translated into concrete approaches to social change.

Second: Give the sciences, arts and humanities the attention they deserve, and integrate them with the various fields of Islamic legal studies. They should be presented in a balanced manner, with the appropriate degree of emphasis. In this way, Muslims will be equipped with the tools required for constructive, Islamically sound human development. It should be borne in mind here that among our predecessors who lived during the Islamic awakening, hardly could one find an expert in Islamic law who was not also well-versed in other fields of learning, including medicine, engineering, technology, astronomy, mathematics, and others.

Examples of such individuals abound, but suffice it to mention the likes of Imam Ibn Rushd (Averroes) (d. 595 AH/1198 CE), al-Qurṭubī (d. 672 AH/1273 CE), al-Qarrāfī (d. 684 AH/1285 CE), al-Rāzī (d. 606 AH/1209 CE), and al-Zamakhsharī (d. 538 AH/1143 CE).

A certain British research institution organized a historical scientific exhibition which showcased scientific contributions of Muslims which changed the face of the world.[35] Writing in the British newspaper, *The Independent*, writer Paul Vallely highlighted twenty discoveries and other contributions made by Muslims, without which the contemporary world would not be as developed, civilized, prosperous, or comfortable as it is now.[36] These are only a few of numerous examples of the contributions Muslims have made to human civilization, while many of their records and manuscripts still remain to be unearthed. In a number of the world's capitals I have seen voluminous Arabic manuscripts on medicine, astronomy, engineering and agriculture. However, no one has gone to the trouble of investigating the facts they contain. One reason for this may be the modern educational system, which has cut people completely off from a huge store of inherited knowledge.

Islam's contributions to science, art, and culture, are a timeless and precious heritage, which should not lie forgotten. The achievements of Muslim civilization as well as Muslim scholars have played an important part in sowing the seeds of Europe's intellectual tradition which gave rise to the Renaissance, and whose impact is still felt today.

Third: Increase people's understanding of what it means to be a "witness" in the sense spoken of in God's declaration: "And thus have We willed you to be a community of the middle way, so that with your lives you might bear witness to the truth before all mankind, and that the Apostle might bear witness to it before you" (*Sūrah al-Baqarah* 2:143). One of the implications of being a witness is that the witness must be well acquainted with that to which he or she is bearing witness, and able to present others with persuasive evidence and arguments. The witness should be able to convey his/her message clearly to those who stand to benefit from it, and present the message in a manner that is fair and honest. At present, members of the Muslim community lack awareness of their role as witnesses to the world. Hence, those qualified to carry out this role need to be awakened to their responsibility in this respect.[37]

In sum, the jurisprudence of human development has an important role to play in reviving Islamic discourse and developing written and visual tools of ideological change. Since the ninth century AH/fifteenth century CE, Muslims have been caught up in juristic nit-picking over issues of peripheral importance, trapped in a reality imposed on them by their own weakness and decadence. However, the ongoing emergence of unprecedented situations and new Islamic legal rulings requires that we engage in research and exploration while working to free people's minds from myth and superstition. Such a process can help to restore affirmation of God's oneness and the texts of divine revelation to the vital, central place they deserve, while offering Muslims a hopeful, promising future.

3

Goals Awareness and the Crisis of Religious Extremism

OVERVIEW OF THIS CHAPTER

The chapter includes a discussion of the sensitive issue of jihad, how much the term and what it signifies has been abused by extremists and attempts to correct much misunderstanding relating to it.

It aims to:

1. Critique extremism i.e. fanatics who comb works on jurisprudence in search of statements by renowned scholars which they can use to justify their actions, or legal rulings on specific situations which they claim as a pretext for their acts of hostility and aggression.
2. Emphasize that jihad is a means to achieve justice and peace. Therefore, there is no authorization for jihad until Muslims have exhausted all options of peaceful engagement through well-intentioned, respectful dialogue. As the Prophet said, "The best jihad is a word of truth uttered in the face of a tyrant."
3. Highlight juristic parochialism, and the ways in which such parochialism destabilizes countries and endangers people's security.
4. Critique an atomistic view of Islamic legal texts that takes no account of *Maqāṣid al-Sharīʿah* overall objectives, or drawing faulty inferences from juristic textual evidence without factoring in the consequences and contingencies associated with a ruling's application.
5. Explore the crisis of ideological extremism and unawareness of *Maqāṣid al-Sharīʿah* including discussion of what constitutes legitimate resistance, and the objectives behind peacefully enjoining righteousness and prohibiting evil.

God's blessings to humankind are countless. He declares, "Should you try to count God's blessings, you could never compute them. [And yet,] man is indeed most persistent in wrongdoing, stubbornly ingrate" (*Sūrah Ibrāhīm* 14:34). Apart from faith, the greatest favors God can bestow on His servants are well-being and security. Security is the basis upon which all other aspects of human life and activity depend. Consequently, God reminds us of this blessing, so that we might be grateful for it and dedicate ourselves to Him in service and worship. He says, "Why – have We not established for them a sanctuary secure, to which, as a provision from Us, shall be gathered the fruits of all good things? But most of them are unaware [of this truth]" (*Sūrah al-Qaṣaṣ* 28:57). In affirmation of the importance of security the Prophet said, "When one wakes up in the morning secure in his dwelling, physically healthy, and with access to his daily bread, it is as though he had the whole world at his fingertips."[1]

Preservation of security in a society is one of the most fundamental objectives of the Shariʿah. As such, it is one of the most important obligations of a Muslim ruler. The position of ruler makes one a successor of the Prophet who is responsible for protecting the religion and administering worldly affairs in keeping therewith. Were it not for rulers, people would live as barbarians, in a state of neglect and anarchy.[2] In a discussion of societal security as a desideratum of Islamic law, al-Tahir ibn Ashur states:

> A thorough study of the texts of the Shariʿah dealing with the aims of Islamic legislation, both its universal principles and its specific details, will show that the overall goal of such legislation is to preserve order and well-being in the Muslim community, while the community's ongoing well-being is inseparable from the uprightness of the person who governs it.[3]

Therefore, acts that destabilize society, violate its security, and terrorize either Muslims or non-Muslims with whom Muslims have a non-aggression pact are crimes against humanity that clearly oppose the overall goal of the Shariʿah.

The bombings and other acts of sabotage that have been witnessed by a number of Muslim and non-Muslim countries confirm the powerful link between ideological extremism and juristic stagnation on one hand, and threats to the safety of innocent noncombatants on the other. Fanatics comb works on jurisprudence in search of statements by renowned scholars which they can use to justify their actions, or legal rulings on specific situations which they claim as a pretext for their acts of hostility and aggression.

At this juncture I would like to discuss three loci of juristic parochialism, and the ways in which such parochialism destabilizes countries and endangers people's security: (1) An atomistic view of Islamic legal texts that takes no account of the Shariʿah's overall objectives, or drawing faulty inferences from juristic textual evidence without factoring in the consequences and contingencies associated with such an inference and its practical application; (2) a failure to address important questions relating to the meaning and necessity of jihad; and (3) defective approaches to the issuance of legal rulings which lead, in turn, to defective application of such rulings.

1: *An atomistic view of Islamic legal texts that takes no account of the Shariʿah's overall objectives, or drawing faulty inferences from juristic textual evidence without factoring in the consequences and contingencies associated with a ruling's application.*

Jurists unanimously disapprove of issuing a hasty legal ruling before thoroughly investigating all principles and elements that might influence the interpretation of the evidence upon which the ruling is being based. Relevant principles include, for example, abrogation (*naskh*), specification (*takhṣīṣ*), and qualification (*taqyīd*). No textual proof should be relied on as a basis for a legal ruling without considering: (a) all other relevant texts, (b) all possible interpretations of said text, and (c) the overall aims of the Shariʿah.[4]

Those who have adopted violence as the only means of effecting change and who seek to force the entire Muslim community to do the same may be no different from those who, long ago, opposed the adherents of the Sunnah on many points of Islamic creed due their lack of insight and understanding and their inability to interpret things competently. Commenting on this type of situation, Ibn Taymiyyah noted, "This tends to happen when disputes arise over minor matters that are not yet completely understood from all angles."[5] In confirmation of this, Imam al-Shāṭibī stated:

> We often find ignorant people supporting their views with invalid evidence, or with valid evidence devoid of any reference to other relevant texts, whether in support of or opposed to their views. This

is the path followed by many who claim to have knowledge.[6]

Such people's failure to base their views on the consensus of the Muslim scholarly community and the example of the Prophet has led to nothing but strife, disorder, and division among members of the Muslim community.

2: *A failure to address important questions relating to the meaning and necessity of jihad.*
Some hold that aggression against Muslims by the polytheists is sufficient reason for jihad to become an obligation. However, this perspective reflects a failure to take all relevant factors into consideration. As a matter of fact, jihad is only required when the Muslims have a reasonable chance of winning a victory over the aggressor. Many Muslim jurists have ruled that fighting is prohibited in the following cases: (1) When the enemy is likely to defeat the Muslims, and/or (2) when the enemy is using Muslims as human shields.[7] Ibn Juzay said:

> If the Muslims know that they are going to be killed, it is better for them to withdraw; and, if, in addition to this, they know that they will not be able to inflict any harm on the enemy, they must retreat. According to Abū al-Maʿālī, there is no difference of opinion on this matter.[8]

Similarly, al-Shawkānī said:

> If, based on powerful circumstantial evidence, the Muslims conclude that the polytheists will be victorious over them, they should refrain from fighting them alone, recruit more fighters into the Muslim army... This position is supported by God's statement, "let not your own hands throw you into destruction" (*Sūrah al-Baqarah* 2:195). Even though this verse was revealed in a specific situation, it also has wider applicability...[9]

The task of assessing whether jihad would be in the public interest is not the responsibility of individual Muslims but, rather, of well-informed Muslim leaders and policy- and decision-makers. Those in a position to make this assessment should ascertain whether the decision meets the conditions for achieving Islamically recognized benefits; moreover, they should do so without allowing their personal feelings or inclinations to influence their conclusions. The conditions that need to be met are as follows: (1) The benefit to be achieved must not conflict with any explicit text of Islamic law, or with the overall aims of the Shariʿah. (2) The benefit in question must be real and not imaginary. (3) The benefit sought must be either certain or, at the very least, quite likely to be achieved; (4) The benefit in question must be one that will affect the general population, not one that helps certain individuals or groups while harming others.[10]

All the aforementioned conditions must be recognized as part of the process of legislating for jihad. To plunge the entire Muslim community into a war of disproportionate numbers and weapons, a war for which it is not prepared psychologically, spiritually, or militarily, reflects a clear failure to understand reality and apply religious rulings thereto. And anyone who would take such a step is unqualified to issue fatwas or to deduce legal rulings from the text of the Shariʿah. Ibn al-Qayyim said:

> No mufti or ruler can issue sound fatwas or govern justly without having two kinds of understanding. The first kind is an understanding of reality, including the ability to ascertain the facts of an occurrence through circumstantial proofs, indications, and signs. The second is an understanding of what should be done in response to the occurrence. This requires knowledge of God's rulings either through His book [the Qur'an] or through the words and actions of His Messenger as they apply to such an occurrence.[11]

When these two kinds of understanding are present, all facets of the issue become clear, and one can issue the correct ruling.

3: *Defective approaches to the issuance of legal rulings which lead, in turn, to defective application of such rulings.*

On the practical level, such defective approaches have opened the door to intellectual anarchy while preventing peaceful coexistence among differing currents of thought. The following are a few manifestations of such systematic defects in juristic understanding and application:

- Ignorance, overreliance on unaided human reason, and intellectual pride, which are a major cause of immoderation, excess, and unjustified religious innovation. God Almighty declares, "[And We said:], 'O David! Behold, We have made thee a [prophet and, thus, Our] vicegerent on earth. Judge, then, between men with justice, and do not follow vain desire, lest it lead thee astray from the path of God. Verily, for those who go astray from the path of God there is suffering severe in store for having forgotten the Day of Reckoning!'" (*Sūrah Ṣād* 38:26). In this connection Imam al-Shāṭibī said:

  > Misguided religious innovation comes about because of ignorance, overconfidence in human reason, or the pursuit of selfish desires in seeking the truth. This is what I have concluded based on an exhaustive study of the Qur'an and the Sunnah.[12]

  Ignorance is a common characteristic of people who live simply to fulfill their selfish desires. Of such people the Prophet said:

  > In later times there will appear some young people in my Muslim community whose dreams are foolish and misguided. They will quote me and recite the Qur'an, but the words will go no deeper than their throats, and they will abandon the religion with the speed of an arrow leaving a bow.[13]

- Things go awry when the views of human beings are given preference over the texts of the Shariʿah. Though no one would support such a practice in theory, reality testifies to the fact that the texts of the Islamic law are supplanted by people's opinions. Imam Ibn Qayyim al-Jawziyyah warned against this phenomenon, saying:

  > When a particular person's statements are considered so superior

that no consideration is given to what is said by anyone else, or even what is said by the law of Islam, unless it agrees with this person's affirmations, then this is unanimously ruled to be forbidden in the religion of God.[14]

- Things similarly go amiss when people refuse to learn from well-informed scholars, preferring instead to learn from incompetent, ill-educated folks or people who obey their own caprice. An example of such perversity can be seen in Jahm ibn Ṣafwān (d. 129 AH/746 CE), who was born in Kufah but settled and taught in Tirmidh. He was a very eloquent person but, like other sect leaders and speculative theologians, he never sat with or learned from well- grounded scholars. As a result, he went astray and led others astray with him.[15]

These are examples of how faulty approaches to knowledge can give birth to various contradictory inclinations, from the far right to the far left. The Arab media and internet forums manifest everything from harsh, overly austere rulings and ideas to excessive laxity. Ironically, one finds that secular writers who glory in denigrating religious extremists have fallen prey to the same extremism and narrow-mindedness they so condemn in others.

The need to maintain security in society during times of tension or crisis may compel those in authority to take additional precautions, tighten their surveillance of what they see as sources of danger, and adopt strict deterrent measures. Such steps might bear fruit if they were taken in response to a purely concrete, physical threat. However, on this battlefield of ideological convictions and influences, the only weapons are sound thinking, irrefutable proofs, and moderate, fair-minded religious concepts marked by neither extremism nor laxity. Only with weapons such as these can truth become manifest and falsehood defeated. As God declares, "Nay, but We hurl the truth against falsehood, and it crushes the latter, and lo! It withers away" (*Sūrah al-Anbiyā'* 21:18).

The Crisis of Ideological Extremism and Unawareness of the Higher Aims and Objectivesof the Shariᶜah

The ideological crisis ravaging some Muslim societies has given birth to extremist views on religious, political, and social issues alike. The causes of this extremism are numerous and complex, but the most salient causes are a lack of correct understanding of Islamic legal texts, and ignorance of the objectives of the Shariᶜah with respect to jihad and the process of commanding what is right and forbidding what is wrong.

In what follows I will discuss two issues that illustrate the importance of "goals awareness" for addressing contemporary crises. These two issues revolve around:

(1) legitimate resistance, and
(2) the objectives behind enjoining righteousness and prohibiting evil.

1: *Legitimate resistance.*
Further to the discussion of the Shariᶜah's position on "contemporary" jihad efforts, it bears noting that many jihad endeavors of today lack legitimacy or fail to yield the benefits they are intended to bring to the people and lands they strive to liberate. In fact, they are destructive causing suffering. Here again, it should be emphasized that the purpose of resistance needs to be carefully and correctly reviewed and reclarified whenever political situations change.

All religions and ideologies view resistance to an aggressor or occupier as a noble, heroic action, whatever the ideology or nationality of the occupier and whatever the goal or orientation of those engaged in the resistance. All peoples of the world take pride in their martyrs and venerate the sacrifices they have made, erecting statues in their memory and commemorating their deaths on an annual basis. All this is a manifestation of the human longing for freedom, justice, and resistance to tyranny.

Jihād is the Islamic juristic term for resistance to aggression. In fact Chapter VII of the United Nations Charter, entitled, "Action with Respect to Threats to the Peace, Breaches of the Peace, and Acts of Aggression" would be an apt description, "to maintain or restore" "peace and security" (article 39). The meaning of the term jihad and its juristic uses are based on the trilateral root *j-h-d*, which conveys the sense of exertion and effort in propagating the faith's message, and inviting people to embrace it. Thus, jihad was institutionalized as a means of preserving the religion, protecting those who convey its message, defending Muslim territories, and confronting aggressors and those seeking to appropriate Muslim lands and possessions.[16]

The Muslim leader is the standard bearer of jihad to repel aggression. As such, he bears responsibility for protecting this critical endeavor from elements of personal interest and worldly ambition lest his jihad become a vainglorious demonstration of power or a way of seeking superiority for superiority's sake.

As military leaders and their soldiers engage in resisting the enemy, they must strive to fulfill the legitimate aims of jihad, namely to preserve the religion, not destroy it, and to save lives rather than shedding innocent blood without a thought for the consequences. Muslim leaders should know that they will be held accountable, both in this world and in the next, for every death they have caused, and they should remember that every drop of blood unjustly shed is more precious to God than the Kaʿbah itself. Admittedly, some phases of Islamic history have been tainted with shameful violations of these sublime provisions. However, the Prophet and his rightly-guided successors offer us excellent models of how to engage in resistance without allowing its noble purposes to be desecrated or forgotten.

Instead of an end in itself, jihad is a means to achieve justice and peace. Therefore, there is no authorization for jihad until Muslims have exhausted all options of peaceful engagement through well-intentioned, respectful dialogue. The Prophet said, "Struggle against (*jāhidū*) the idolators with your wealth, your strength, and your tongues."[17] In other words, the concept of jihad encompasses so much more than military action alone, which God has ordained as a last resort.

If all avenues fail, then self-defence is to be carried out keeping its ultimate purpose in mind: to free civilians from oppression and to bring stability to the society. A Muslim state naturally enables its citizenry to experience Islam and the freedom to embrace it, if they so desire. However, if this is not acceptable, then, in lieu of the zakat (obligatory religious tax) which Muslim citizens give, non-Muslim citizens pay *jizyah*, a tax levied on able-bodied males, entitling them to state protection and exempting them from military service. The new Muslims state must also open its borders to allow trade and diplomacy, thereby carrying the message of Islam beyond its borders in a peaceful, non-coercive manner.

When we study the philosophy of jihad in light of all relevant texts from the Qur'an and the Sunnah, bearing in mind all related principles and objectives of Islamic law, the concept and practice of peaceful jihad can become vital means of building an ideal society where security and stability prevail. Once this has been accomplished, armed conflict would only be called for in exceptional circumstances, and under the strictest of conditions. And even then, it should not open the door to anarchy, destruction, and the violation of rights and sacred taboos.

Understood and carried out as it was intended to be, jihad is an integral part of the reform project advocated by Islam in its battle against mindless caprice, oppression, and futile customs and ways of life. Hence, when individual Muslims lack this understanding, they will also lack the moral strength they need to fulfill their responsibility to bear witness to truth on all levels.

A number of Muslim countries are suffering both covert and overt aggression, specifically the Middle East ravaged by internal division and civil war as well as external threat. Energy politics has always had a part to play in a volatile region often fought over for its oil reserves. The current situation has understandably revived the call to fight in self-defence in order to put a stop to this aggression and end oppression. However, although I do not condemn fighting for one's freedom to usher in true democracy and development there nevertheless remain important conditions that must be met and diplomatic and peaceful steps that must be taken before such action can be regarded as an effective reform project and not merely a convulsive attempt at provocation or a reckless, misguided reaction.

Liberation of one's land is one of the greatest deeds one can perform. It means the actualization of justice, the removal of oppression, the building of a society, and the provision of security for people. However, if a war of liberation is fought without the awareness that jihad is a reform project, those who struggle will fail to win their freedom and independence. The Arab revolutions that took place in the middle of the twentieth century fell into this very error, as a result of which people began pining for a return to the days of colonial rule, even if it would mean being subjected once more to a different form of injustice and oppression.

Fighters whose only goal is to rout the enemy may end up becoming their own enemies unless they refine their souls and cleanse themselves of worldly ambition and selfish interests. That is why the Afghan jihad, in which many precious lives were lost and great sacrifices were made as the oppressive Soviet army was defeated in the country's mountainous regions, failed the first real test it encountered because the Muslim fighters' souls had not been liberated from self-serving ambition. As a result, all their achievements were for naught, and Afghan society was thrust into a dark night of fragmentation and destruction.

I see no evidence of a genuine review of the contemporary jihad experience. Instead, I see the same mistakes being repeated time and time again, as legitimate jihad endeavors are turned into instruments of terror and murder. Oppressed, poor and helpless people are manipulated with empty rhetoric, only for their deceivers' ruses to be exposed in the end to all and sundry.

2: *The purposes behind enjoining righteousness and prohibiting evil and some contemporary applications.*

One of the important topics to which extremism has drawn attention is that of "enjoining righteousness and prohibiting evil" (*al-amr bi al-maʿrūf wa al-nahī ʿan al-munkar*), limitations and regulations relating to the application of this concept, ways of dealing with those who commit acts of disobedience to the Shariʿah, and the role played by this concept in reforming and changing society for the better. The principle of "enjoining righteousness and prohibiting evil" has a role to play in promoting security in society and upright conduct, which is clearly of benefit on both the individual and communal levels.

Sadly, however, this religious duty has been exploited by some as a means of achieving their own base ends by sowing discord in Muslim society. In the early centuries of Islam, the Kharijites and the Mu'tazilites deceptively raised the banner of "enjoining righteousness and prohibiting evil" as a way of sowing discord among Muslims, spreading anarchy, and inciting to murder and rebellion against their rulers. History books abound in examples of how the concept of "enjoining righteousness and prohibiting evil" has been used to sabotage the community and its interests. One such example was recorded by Ibn Jarīr al-Ṭabarī, who describes the role played by Ibn Saba' in the murder of the third caliph, ʿUthmān ibn ʿAffān. He relates:

> Abdullah ibn Saba' ... became a Muslim during the time of ʿUthmān, after which he moved from one Muslim land to another causing mischief and seeking to misguide the people. He started with Hijaz; then he went to Basrah, and from there to Kufah, and later the Levant. In the Levant he was unable to carry out his plans, and was expelled. He then went to Egypt, where he gathered about him a band of troublemakers. He drew up a plan of action which he summarized as follows: "Stir up a rebellion by defaming your rulers and claiming to promote the enjoinment of righteousness and the prohibition of evil in order to win people over to your side. Then invite them to join you in your mission." After sending these men out as his emissaries, Ibn Saba' wrote letters to corrupt people in various cities, and they responded. In secret they promoted their perverse cause, while in public they deceptively claimed to be carrying out their obligation to enjoin righteousness and prohibit evil. The trouble-makers in various regions began exchanging letters in which they fabricated charges against their rulers until their evil rumors infected Madinah itself. However, they kept their designs well-concealed, with those in one region claiming to have nothing to do with what was being done elsewhere.[18]

When "enjoining righteousness and prohibiting evil" fails to meet the necessary conditions, it may do more harm than good. The following, then, is a summary of the guiding principles relating to this Islamic obligation.

First: Enjoining righteousness and prohibiting evil should be treated as a communal obligation (*farḍ kifāyah*).[19] In certain circumstances, however, it may become an individual obligation (*farḍ ʿayn*). Ibn Taymiyyah stated:

> ...enjoining what is right and prohibiting what is wrong is not an individual duty; rather, as stipulated by the Qur'an, it is a communal obligation...Therefore, when those upon whom this duty rests fail to carry it out, each of them will be held responsible in a manner commensurate with his ability to fulfill this obligation. This is in line with the Prophet's saying, "Whoever among you sees an evil should correct it with his hand. If he is unable to do so, he should correct it with his tongue; if this, too, is impossible for him, he should correct it in his heart, which is the weakest expression of faith."[20]

Second: Matters of interpretation are not subject to criticism. Ibn Taymiyyah states:

> When, in the process of interpreting Islamic legal texts, someone adopts a certain scholar's view, no blame shall attach to this decision. Nor does any blame attach to someone who adopts one of two competing views if he is convinced that the view he has adopted has the most evidence in its favor. Otherwise, he should depend on other scholars' determination of the soundest view.[21]

As Judge Abū Yaʿlā mentions in his book, *al-Aḥkām al-Sulṭāniyyah*,[22] no one should be criticized for the position he has adopted unless said position could lead to something which has been agreed to be forbidden.

Third: Change should be limited to what the situation demands. Imam al-Ghazālī once said:

> Know that warning is due only when wrongdoing has yet to occur,

> punishment is due when wrongdoing has already occurred, and resistance is due in response to wrongdoing occurring at the present time. The only duty required of individual citizens is to resist ongoing wrongdoing. Anything beyond this, be it punishment for a past wrongdoing or a warning against wrongdoing not yet committed, they are the prerogative of legal authorities alone, and not of individuals.[23]

As for Imam al-Shawkānī, he states that the party seeking to enjoin righteousness and prohibit evil "should start with a gentle admonition. If this has no effect, he should speak more harshly, and if this, too, is ineffective, he should change the situation through action, ... if no other means brings the intended result."[24]

The aforementioned stages are governed by specific standards, as will become evident in what follows:

Fourth: One should abhor evil in one's heart under all circumstances.

> Ibn Masʿūd once heard a man say, "Whoever does not enjoin what is right or forbid what is wrong is ruined." In response Ibn Masʿūd said, "Nay, whoever does not recognize what is right and wrong in his heart is ruined." In so saying, Ibn Masʿūd was drawing attention to the fact that recognition of right and wrong in one's heart is an obligation from which no one is exempted. Hence, whoever fails to make this recognition suffers spiritual ruin. As for the obligation to oppose evil through speech and action, it varies according to one's abilities.[25]

Fifth: The extent of the obligation to effect change through words and action depends on one's ability and circumstances, and the weightiness of the human interests involved. Concerning the three means of carrying out the obligation to enjoin what is good and forbid what is evil, al-Jaṣṣāṣ wrote:

> The Prophet informed us that the prohibition of evil should take one or more of three forms, depending on one's abilities and circumstances. What he said indicates that if one cannot correct an evil

through action, he should do so through words, and if he is incapable of correcting it with words, then all he is required to do is to condemn it in his heart.[26]

As for Ibn al-Qayyim, he categorized the prohibition of evil into four types:

(1) Removing the evil or replacing it with its opposite. (2) Mitigating the evil, if not totally removing it. (These first two possibilities are consistent with the Shariʿah.) (3) Replacing the evil with an equal evil, which calls for careful interpretation. (4) Replacing the evil with a greater one, which is clearly forbidden.[27]

Sixth: One may be unable to promote virtue and prevent vice due to a fear of persecution or some other harm. Ibn Rajab says:

If anyone fears that criticizing a ruler may bring harm to his family and neighbors, he should not proceed, since doing so would be a cause of harm to others. This is the stand taken by Fuḍayl ibn ʿIyāḍ and other scholars. Therefore, if a person fears that he might be killed, flogged, jailed, chained, banished, or have his property seized, he is exempted from the obligation to enjoin rulers to do right and forbid them to do wrong. Leading scholars have made express statements to this effect, among them Imam Mālik ibn Anas, Aḥmad Ibn Ḥanbal, Isḥāq ibn Rāhwayh, and others. Imam Aḥmad said, "One should not challenge the person in the position of authority, since his sword is poised for the attack."[28]

It is, of course, considered virtuous and desirable for someone who is strong enough to bear the consequences to act and speak out against evil. As the Prophet said, "The best jihad is a word of truth uttered in the face of a tyrant."[29] However, even this is subject to the following conditions: (1) that the condemnation be likely to effect a positive result, (2) that it not bring harm to other people, and (3) that it not cause a greater harm.

Seventh: There are two competing views on enjoining the good and prohibiting evil when it is known that it will be of no use.

According to the first view, the effort to do so can legitimately be abandoned if it would be of no use. This was the position held by Ibn ʿUmar, Ibn Masʿūd, and many other Companions, as well as by scholars such as al-Awzāʿī, al-Ghazālī, al-ʿIzz, and others who based their view on the saying of the Prophet, "Continue to command what is right and forbid what is wrong until you see people becoming niggardly, controlled by selfish desires, and overconfident of their own opinions. At that point, keep to yourselves and cease your attempts to guide the general public."[30] They also supported their view by citing Prophetic sayings that encourage the God-fearing to isolate themselves in the end times when promotion of virtue and prevention of vice will do no good. According to the second view, enjoining virtue and forbidding vice remains obligatory at all times. This is the stance taken by al-Nawawī and al-Jaṣṣāṣ, who supported their position based on what is known as the incident of the Sabbath-breakers.[31]

Eighth: The following is a discussion of the matter of revolting against a tyrannical leader as it relates to the duty to enjoin what is good and prohibit what is evil. Scholars have differed over whether it is permissible to rise up against a sinful or tyrannical Muslim ruler. In this connection al-Shahristānī wrote:

> Over the course of its history, the greatest source of conflict within the Muslim community has lain in the matter of who should assume the position of leadership. Indeed, never have Muslims drawn their swords over a religious question as readily as they have drawn them over the question of who should be their leader.[32]

There is disagreement among scholars over whether it is permissible to revolt against a sinful or tyrannical Muslim ruler. Most Sunni scholars hold that it is forbidden, and according to al-Nawawī, there is unanimity on this matter.[33] As for the Muʿtazilites, the Kharijites, and the Zaydīs, they hold that it is permissible; in fact, some consider it obligatory to revolt against such a ruler.

Those who forbid revolts against repressive Muslim rulers rely on the following arguments:

1. Islamic legal texts that command obedience to the ruler and forbid one to violate an oath of allegiance. An example of this is the following hadith:

> The Prophet said, "The best among your leaders are those whom you love and bless and who love and bless you, while the worst among them are those whom you hate and curse, and who also hate and curse you." To this the Companions replied, "O Messenger of God, shall we revolt against the latter?" "No," he said, "as long as they perform the ritual prayer among you. If you see your leader disobeying God, you should detest his sins, but you should not disobey him in any respect."[34]

2. Sayings of the Prophet which prohibit infighting and warn against civil strife. One such statement reads, "After I am gone, do not show yourselves to be polytheists by striking one another with the sword."[35]

3. Statements by the Messenger indicating that certain leaders who would come after him would be corrupt, yet without commanding his people to rebel against them: "The destruction of my community will come at the hands of youths from the tribe of Quraysh."[36] Elsewhere he described certain members of the Muslim community as "those who call out at the gates of hell" (inviting others to enter).[37] Yet despite these descriptions, the Prophet did not command his followers to revolt against such people.

4. The higher objectives of the Shariʿah necessitate the prohibition of armed revolts, bearing in mind that those who, over the course of Islam history, have revolted against their leaders have rarely achieved the aims for the sake of which they revolted.

In his work entitled, *Al-Ṭabaqāt al-Kubrā*, Ibn Saʿd relates a series of events that illustrate the position taken by al-Ḥasan al-Baṣrī (d. 728 AH/1230 CE) on the issue of armed revolt.[38] On the authority of Ḥammād ibn Zayd, Ibn Saʿd reported Yūnus's statement, "al-Ḥasan was a leading scholar in opposition to civil strife and bloodshed." Hence, there are numerous lessons to be learned from al-Ḥasan al-Baṣrī's experience with the civil strife that took place during his time. Ibn Saʿd also quoted Ibn ʿAwn as saying that al-

Ḥasan refused to go out with people in the days of Ibn al-Ashʿath,[39] and people told him, "Let this man go with us." Ibn ʿAwn said, "I saw him (al-Ḥasan) between two bridges wearing a black turban. When he saw that no one was watching him, he jumped into the river as a means of escaping from the people; he nearly drowned that day." He also quoted Salmān ibn ʿAlī al-Ribʿī as stating:

> During the civil unrest in which Ibn al-Ashʿath fought against al-Ḥajjāj, ʿUqbah ibn ʿAbd al-Ghāfir, Abū al-Jawzā', and ʿAbd Allāh Ibn Ghālib set out in the company of some of their peers to meet al-Ḥasan al-Baṣrī. When they came in to see him, they asked him, "Abū Saʿīd, what is your view concerning this tyrant who has shed innocent blood, seized people's property, abandoned prayer, and done such-and-such?" They then mentioned the crimes committed by al-Ḥajjāj ibn Yūsuf. To this al-Ḥasan replied, "My view is that you should not fight him, for if he is a punishment from God, you can never ward off God's chastisement with your swords; and if he is a trial, you should bear it patiently, for God is the Best of all judges."

Al-Ḥasan said, "They left, saying, 'How can we obey this non-Arab fellow?', they themselves being Arabs. They thus marched forth with Ibn al-Ashʿath, and they were all killed."

Ibn Saʿd also reported on the authority of ʿAmrū ibn Yazīd, who said, "I heard al-Ḥasan al-Baṣrī say, 'If, when people were being afflicted by their leaders, they had borne it patiently, relief would have come to them in no time. However, they hastened towards their swords, so they were left to their own devices. By God, such people never bring any good!'"

Al-Ḥasan al-Baṣrī's stance was that one should avoid all forms of civil strife. This may be seen in the report of Sālim Ibn Abī al-Dhayyāl, who said, "Once, in the presence of some people from the Levant, I heard a man ask al-Ḥasan, 'Abū Saʿīd, what is your position regarding such tribulation as that being caused by Ibn al-Mihlab and Ibn al-Ashʿath?' Al-Ḥasan replied, 'You should side with neither party.' One of those from the Levant then asked, 'So, Abū Saʿīd, do you mean they should not side with the Commander of the Faithful, either?' With an angry wave of his hand, he repeated the man's question: 'Abū Saʿīd, do you mean they should not side with the Commander of the Faithful, either?' Then he answered the question, saying, 'No, not even with the Commander of the Faithful!'"[40]

As for those who believe in the permissibility of revolting against repressive and sinful Muslim rulers, they cite the following in support of their position:

1. General evidences indicating the obligation to promote virtue and prevent vice.
2. The Qur'anic command to fight against a group that is acting wrongfully until it repents of its disobedience to God, as in the passage that reads, "Hence, if two groups of believers fall to fighting, make peace between them. But then, if one of the two groups goes on acting wrongfully towards the other, fight against the one that acts wrongfully until it reverts to God's commandment" (*Sūrah al-Ḥujurāt* 9:9).
3. God's statement that, "My covenant does not embrace the evildoers" (*Sūrah al-Baqarah* 2:124). Since political leadership within Islam is viewed as a covenant with God then, oppressive rulers – who are evildoers – do not deserve to remain in power.
4. Islamic legal texts according to which a tyrannical ruler must be ousted, and which warn against untrustworthy leaders. One such text is the Prophet's statement, "Obedience (to political leaders) is unconditionally binding upon Muslim subjects provided they are not commanded to disobey God. However, should they be commanded to commit an act of disobedience to God, their obligation to obey their leader is voided. "[41]

The best-attested opinion – though God knows best – is that which prohibits revolt against a leader even if he is an unrighteous tyrant. This is due to the harmful consequences, such as chaos and disorder, to which such action may lead. This in no way indicates that one should be content with the situation; rather, it means simply that one should choose the lesser of the two evils, doing one's best to offer gentle admonition while exercising patience and perseverance. As Ibn Taymiyyah sagely noted, "Hardly has a group rebelled against those in authority but that its rebellion has led to greater corruption and harm than that which the rebellious group had set out to eliminate."[42]

In his work *al-Tahdhīb*, Ibn Ḥajar al-ᶜAsqalānī reflects on this topic in the context of his biography of Ḥasan ibn Ṣāliḥ ibn Ḥayy al-Hamadānī (d. 169 AH/785 CE). He states:

> Concerning their allegation against him that "he believes in the sword", they meant that he believes that armed revolts should be made against tyrannical rulers. This was the view that had been adopted by the predecessors, but it has since been abandoned when they realized that armed revolts against those in authority had led to even greater evils than those against which they had rebelled. The aftermath of the Battle of al-Ḥarrah[43] and the uprising led by Ibn al-Ashᶜath hold lessons for those willing to receive them. Moreover, despite this claim concerning al-Ḥasan ibn Ṣāliḥ, he never revolted against anyone.[44]

Imam al-Nawawī said, "Scholars have stated that the reason for prohibiting forceful removal of a tyrant or unrighteous ruler is the civil unrest, bloodshed, and corruption to which such an action may lead. For the evil of ousting a ruler is virtually always greater than that of leaving him in his post."[45]

These are, in brief, what I view as the most essential rulings and guidelines relating to the practice of "enjoining righteousness and prohibiting evil." I have contented myself for the most part with verbatim quotations from the relevant scholars, which require little or no commentary or explanation. For further detail on this important subject, readers are encouraged to consult the classic works on this subject by both early and contemporary scholars.[46]

4

Goals Awareness and Its Impact on the Muslim Mindset

OVERVIEW OF THIS CHAPTER

This chapter discusses the Muslim mindset and explores reasons for its decline. In the process of shaping a sound Muslim mentality it treats two major themes: (i) an aims-based methodology and the role it can play in revitalizing Muslim thought, (ii) Islamic rationalism, its impact on contemporary philosophy, and on the most salient features of post-modern philosophy.

It aims to:

1. Explore the need for a methodology employing tools suited to Muslim societies rather than trying to understand things through a postmodernist and secular humanist philosophy.
2. Emphasize that investigation should include an analysis of Muslim discourse and an assessment of how well it harmonizes with the changes being undergone by contemporary society. Specifically, there must be an assessment of how Islamic values and the texts of Islamic law are applied to concrete situations, and the capacity of modern Islamic discourse to serve as a vehicle of positive change in people's lives.
3. Focus on the need to refer to *maqāṣid* in regulating and guiding the formulation of Islamic legal rulings.
4. Point to guidelines for weighing the beneficial and harmful effects of competing actions.

OVER the past three decades, a number of thinkers have focused criticism on the Muslim mindset. Through this critique, scholars have attempted to identify and understand the dysfunction that has afflicted large sections of the Muslim community, and its failure to play its intended role as a witness to truth in keeping with God's declaration, "And thus have We willed you to be a community of the middle way, so that with your lives you might bear witness to the truth before all mankind, and that the Apostle might bear witness to it before you" (*Sūrah al-Baqarah* 2:143). The decline in the Muslim mentality that once played such a major role in the advancement and growth of Arab society has been attributed to the interplay between divine revelation and human interpretation; between Islamic law and human custom; and between rationality and subjective experience. Similarly, traditional tools for understanding the Qur'an and the Sunnah have been influenced by mystical interpretations and philosophical proofs. This, in addition to fruitless debates resulting from the claims of speculative theology, rigid biases in favor of specific juristic arguments and schools of thought, political tyranny, vested interests and power struggles, has undermined the Muslim community's ability to make real progress.

These problems, among others, have discouraged juristic interpretations that are at once textually sound, creative and forward-looking, and hence the disappearance of true reformers from the intellectual and scientific arenas. We have good reason, then, to reexamine the factors that have undermined the Muslim community on both the individual and communal planes. The efforts made by people such as al-Jabiri, Arkun, Shahrur, Hasan Hanafi, Jamal al-Banna and other contemporary thinkers may be seen as serious attempts to establish a reformist approach to critiquing the prevailing Muslim mindset and to liberate it from centuries-old weaknesses and shackles. However, the epistemological tools and research methodologies employed by such scholars derive from a secular intellectual environment where conclusions are not based on decisive texts from the Qur'an and the Sunnah or on juristic principles drawn from these two sources.

The secular environment to which I refer has promoted scientific and academic approaches imported from non-Muslim cultures whose critical tools emerged from Enlightenment philosophers who were questioning Christian religious authority and seeking to restore reason to its proper place. Yet, despite observable congruences between the state of Christianity during Europe's Middle Ages and what befell the Muslims after the fifth century AH/eleventh century CE, there are major differences between the nature and causes of the situations faced by the Muslim and Christian communities respectively.

It should also be remembered that these critics' analyses of the Muslim mindset are based on an incomplete examination of the

Muslim religious heritage inspired by divine revelation. Consequently, they have failed to appreciate the profundity of the principles, premises and foundations on which Muslims' methodology rests. In his work entitled *Naqd al-ʿAql al-ʿArabī*, al-Jabiri has made a significant contribution to our understanding of Muslim thought. Other thinkers' contributions, however, are less thorough and farsighted. In fact, some of them have adopted an approach so foreign to Islamic methodology that they have arrived at unrealistic philosophical conclusions whose relevance is restricted to a narrow circle of intellectuals influenced by the rationalist current, and which fail to reflect the entire spectrum of Islamic jurisprudence and recognized Islamic methods of interpretation.

In the remainder of this chapter, I will be treating two major themes: (1) aims-based methodology and the role it can play in revitalizing Muslim thought and reasoning, and (2) Islamic rationalism and its impact on contemporary philosophy, and the most salient features of post-modern philosophy.

(1) Aims-Based Methodology and The Role It Can Play In Revitalizing Muslim Thought and Reasoning

In light of the foregoing, I believe that a critique of the currently prevailing Muslim mindset calls for an in-depth investigation of the ways in which rulings are derived from textual proofs. Such an investigation should include an analysis of Islamic discourse and an assessment of how well it harmonizes with the changes being undergone by contemporary society. Specifically, there must be an assessment of how Islamic values and the texts of Islamic law are applied to concrete situations, and the capacity of modern Islamic discourse to serve as a vehicle of positive change in people's lives.

It appears to me that the attempts that have been made thus far to reform Muslim thought and method exhibit no awareness of the importance of *maqāṣid al-sharīʿah*, or the aims of Islamic law, for identifying what needs to be corrected and formulating the needed solutions. My decision to investigate an Islamic aims-based methodology as a means of reviving and reforming Muslim thought was prompted by a number of factors that can be summed up as follows:

a) *Maqāṣid al-sharīʿah* are the link that unites all branches of Islamic legislation, that is, on the levels of ritual, custom, social life, judicial concerns, and all others.
b) Viewing *maqāṣid al-sharīʿah* as a universal, all-embracing set of principles serves to regulate one's understanding of things and clarify the true purposes of human existence, including the way one should live and relate to other people, to one's circumstances in life, and to the laws of the universe.
c) People everywhere have an inborn tendency to search for a Higher Power in the universe, to surrender themselves to this Power, and to obey this Power's commands and prohibitions without seeking some material benefit for themselves. This is the sphere in which the law of divine-human, heavenly-earthly response, operates.
d) An examination of the works written on *maqāṣid al-sharīʿah* reveals that their authors served as religious and social reformers by reestablishing a connection with the universal principles of Islamic law and by fulfilling their own role in juristic research and in issuing rulings on newly emerging situations.
e) The fragmentation, weakness, and ignorance that presently afflict the Muslim community, distracting individual Muslims from the essentials and robbing them of the ability to be creative and productive, necessitate that we move quickly to recover the universal, fundamental principles and aims of Islamic law.
f) In order to correct the flaws in Muslims' ways of thinking, stress must be laid on *maqāṣid al-sharīʿah*, which can protect us from going to extremes in any direction by supplying us with rational principles that expose illusion, vacuous speculation, groundless views, and opinions with insufficient evidence in their favor.

a) As noted above, *maqāṣid al-sharīʿah* are the link that unites Islamic legislation on the levels of ritual, custom, social life, and judicial concerns. Virtually every Islamic legal ruling is based in some way on the principle of preserving the five essentials: religion, life, progeny, reason, and wealth. All legal rulings and interpretations of Islamic law are to be governed not by the personal inclinations of the jurist or interpreter, but by this central principle.

As Imam al-Shāṭibī states:

> It is the Lawgiver's purpose that a morally accountable Muslim's intention when acting should be consistent with the Lawgiver's intention when legislating. The proof for this may be clearly observed in the establishment of Islamic law... What is, therefore, required from a morally accountable Muslim is to ensure that his actions are in concordance with the intent of the Lawgiver."[1]

Moreover, these aims of Islamic law are of a general nature; as such, they apply not only to Muslims, but to people of every faith or culture. It is inconceivable that an individual or society would object to preserving these very entities in both their personal and their public affairs, since they are necessities that no one would contest. In a passage quoted earlier, Imam al-Shāṭibī writes:

> ...in affirming the intent of the Lawgiver as embodied in these principles,[2] scholars do not rely on a particular text or interpretation. Rather, based on the clear sense of countless passages, general principles, texts with universal applicability and those applicable only to specific situations, and details pertaining to cases in every area and type of jurisprudence, they have discovered that the law taken as a whole... gravitates toward support for these principles.[3]

Since *maqāṣid al-sharīʿah* are of such paramount importance in regulating and guiding the formulation of Islamic legal rulings, it is only logical that we should refer to them when seeking to identify and address problem areas in Muslims' lives, just as it is a religious duty to use them as the basis for our religious rulings and legislation. If we fail in this obligation, specific legal rulings might well conflict with the universal principles of Islam. The following practical examples will illustrate this point.

Those who view the criminal penalties prescribed in the Qur'an as undue restrictions on fundamental freedoms and overly harsh treatment of those who commit errors have failed to perceive society as a unified entity. Such people need to realize that a society's order and stability require the existence of deterrent punishments that will safeguard people's rights and freedoms. It should also be remembered that the Qur'anic verses that prescribe criminal penalties constitute no more than one-tenth of all Islamic legal rulings, and that the vast majority of Islamic ordinances concern themselves with people's improvement and inner reform.

Those who allow usury, for example, under the pretext that it is a contemporary economic necessity have not considered the ethical and social impacts of this practice. The Shariʿah prohibits usury as part of its protection of the five essentials: religion, life, reason, wealth, and progeny; hence, it is a prohibition which is necessary in order to safeguard the interests of individuals and entire societies without favoring some members of society to the detriment of others.

b) Viewing *maqāṣid al-sharīʿah* as a universal, all-embracing set of principles regulates our understanding of things and clarifies the true purposes of human existence, including the way we should live and relate to other people, to our circumstances in life, and to the laws of the universe. Keeping *maqāṣid al-sharīʿah* as one's focus helps to safeguard the mind against excess and illusion and helps one to set the proper priorities. In recognition of the role played by *maqāṣid al-sharīʿah* in shaping people's mentalities, Imam al-Tahir Ibn Ashur has listed four conditions that must be fulfilled in order for something to be included among *maqāṣid al-sharīʿah*. These conditions are as follows:

Clarity: The goal must be so clear and unambiguous that it would never be the subject of disagreement among interpreters or jurists. The law of retribution (*al-qiṣāṣ*), for example, is universally agreed upon among Muslim scholars for the preservation of life.

Certainty: The intended aim must be known to be attainable.

Moderation: The aim in question must not exceed the limits of moderation. It must not lead to hardship of the sort that Islamic law is intended to alleviate, or alienate people from the law of Islam. At the same time, it must not encourage people to be overly lax in their adherence to the law's precepts, thereby undermining the law's incentive or deterrent force and its authority over people.

Consistency: The aim in question must not be subject to change in response to differing situations, thoughts, times and places.[4]

These conditions, which determine whether a given aim is recognized by Islam, open the way to objective thinking, rational deduction, and the comprehensive understanding we need in order to play the social and cultural role that we, as Muslims, are intended to play.

c) People everywhere have an inborn tendency to search for a Higher Power in the universe, to surrender to this Power, and to obey this Power's commands and prohibitions without seeking some material benefit for themselves. This is the law of divine-human, heavenly-earthly response.[5]

Imam Ibn Ashur regards people's inborn, God-given disposition as the foundation upon which *maqāṣid al-sharīʿah* are based. If people's actions spring from this inborn, God-given nature, the aims of their actions will be in harmony with the aims of the Lawgiver. He states:

> If we closely observe Islamic legislation, we will find that its overall purpose tends towards preserving people's inborn, God-given disposition and preventing anything that would violate or corrupt it. Whatever involves a serious violation of people's inborn, God-given human nature is forbidden, whatever helps to preserve and protect it is regarded as obligatory, and whatever has no effect on it is permissible. When there is a clash between the demands of one's inborn human nature and it is not practically possible to reconcile among them, preference should be given to the demand that is most conducive to one's well-being. This is why murder is regarded as the most heinous of all crimes.[6]

Hence, we can say that inborn human nature, which is the pivotal focus of this religion, is what guides people's thinking, conduct, and morals. "And so, set thy face steadfastly towards the [one ever-true] faith, turning away from all that is false, in accordance with the natural disposition which God has instilled into man: [for,] not to allow any change to corrupt what God has thus created, this is the [purpose of the one] ever-true faith; but most people know it not" (*Sūrah al-Rūm* 30:30).

The aims of Islamic law are harmonious with "the natural disposition God has instilled" in human beings. This concordance encompasses not only physical dispositions and benefits, but ways of thinking and behaving as well. This very important aspect of inborn human nature, which has to do with regulating people's thinking and conduct, has not been properly studied despite its impact on people's lives – be it a positive impact resulting from obeying one's inborn nature, or a negative impact due to a denial of one's natural inclinations. It is hoped that an understanding of the centrality of *maqāṣid al-sharīʿah* will lead people to lend closer attention to this important aspect of themselves – their way of thinking, that is – and make efforts to give it the proper appraisal and keep it sound and healthy.

d) An examination of the works written on *maqāṣid al-sharīʿah* reveals that their authors served as religious and social reformers by reestablishing a connection with the universal principles of Islamic law and fulfilling their own role in juristic research and in issuing rulings on newly emerging situations.

The works of these reformist scholars show clearly that a proper understanding of the aims of Islamic law is what gives Muslims the incentive to correct themselves and make positive changes in themselves and society. In his pioneering work, *Al-Muwāfaqāt*, al-Shāṭibī proposed that every difference of opinion in juristic matters should be resolved in light of the fundamental objectives of the Shariʿah. He also restructured the manner in which Islamic jurisprudence is approached and freed the practice of *istidlāl* (the search for textual evidence on the basis of which one may arrive at a ruling on this or that question or situation) from the impacts of philosophical conjecture and speculative theology. Like al-Shāṭibī, al-Tahir Ibn Ashur and Allal al-Fasi made *maqāṣid al-sharīʿah* the centerpiece of their reformist methodologies as they related to both statutory legislation and the role of jurisprudence in addressing newly emerging issues and situations.

The practice of formulating legal rulings in light of the aims of Islamic law can serve as a corrective to the currently prevailing, skewed approach to Islamic jurisprudence. Therefore, this practice has an important role to play in restructuring Muslims' thought processes and helping Muslim thinkers to recover a constructive role in reform and positive change.

e) The fragmentation, weakness, and ignorance that presently afflict the Muslim community, distracting individual Muslims from the essentials and robbing them of the ability to be creative and productive, necessitate that we move quickly to recover the universal, fundamental principles and aims of Islamic law. Weak societies tend to go running after luxuries, which they consume and promote in excess. However, a renewed focus on the aims of Islamic law can restore our ability to prioritize correctly and to discern what is truly necessary and what is truly harmful. The inability to make such distinctions can cause serious difficulties in the lives of both communities and their individual members.

During times of intellectual decline, efforts are wasted on peripheral issues and useless nitpicking, which only deepens people's ignorance and widens the chasm between them and essential knowledge. What we have, as a result, is an elite class that claims a monopoly on knowledge, understanding, and the right to interpret sacred texts. This is the approach of many philosophers, both ancient and modern, who complicate the sciences of the day and claim to have sole access to knowledge and understanding while erecting barriers that others are incapable of crossing.

Hopefully, however, access to *maqāṣid al-sharīʿah* will enable broader sectors of society to grasp the fundamental, universal principles of Islam and to see how far certain pseudo-philosophers have strayed from a true engagement with society's questions and concerns. I believe that discussing *maqāṣid al-sharīʿah* can contribute to building the unity of thought which forms the foundation of a unified society. Such a discussion might also defuse sectarian conflicts and debates by restoring common ground in the form of shared concepts by means of which Muslims can address issues of mutual concern, and which provide starting points for constructive action and reform in countless areas of life.

f) In order to correct the flaws in Muslims' ways of thinking, stress must be laid on *maqāṣid al-sharīʿah*, which can protect us from going to extremes in any direction by supplying us with rational principles that expose illusion, vacuous speculation, groundless views, and opinions with insufficient evidence in their favor.

Al-ʿIzz ibn ʿAbd al-Salām classified all actions as either beneficial or harmful. He stated:

> Actions are of two kinds: the first kind includes actions that are beneficial, and these are of four types: (1) actions that bring pure benefit and no harm, whether said harm comes before, with, or after the action; such actions are always either obligatory, supererogatory, or merely permissible; (2) actions whose benefits outweigh their harmful effects; (3) actions that bring equal benefit and harm; and (4) actions whose benefits are equal to those of another action or actions; if it is possible to combine them, we should do so. Otherwise, we must choose between them. When we can distinguish which actions are the most beneficial, we should give preference to the best and the most acceptable, and not be concerned about the forfeiture of actions that have little textual evidence in their favor. As for the second kind, that is, harmful actions, it also consists of several types: The first type includes actions that are harmful in all respects and that are unconnected to any benefit that might occur before, during, or after the actions are performed. Actions of this type are always classified as either forbidden or undesirable. The second type includes actions whose harmful effects outweigh their benefits and which, for this reason, fall under the same legal classifications. The third type includes actions whose harmful effects are equal to their benefit or benefits; if it is possible to prevent the actions' harmful effects while actualizing their benefit or benefits, we should do so. Otherwise, the situation calls for an in-depth study. The fourth type consists of harmful acts whose harmful effects are equaled by those of still another action; if it is possible to avoid the harmful effects of both actions, we should do so. Otherwise, we should choose one of the two. When we are able to assess comparable harmful actions, we should be most concerned to avoid the most repugnant and dangerous of them.[7]

Scholars have established guidelines for weighing the beneficial and harmful effects of competing actions. Jurists should refer to these guidelines when formulating legal rulings, while non-jurists should memorize and refer to them as a guide to decision-making.

The following are illustrative examples of principles that serve to promote objective thinking conducive to making ethical, constructive contributions to societal development.

- Avoiding harm should be given preference over achieving benefit.
- The less beneficial of two helpful acts should be forfeited in favor of the more beneficial of them.
- An act of communal benefit should be given preference over one that offers an individual benefit.
- A source of harm may be eliminated by enduring a lesser source of harm.
- One source of harm may not be eliminated via another, equally severe source of harm.
- Something that brings harm on an individual level should be endured for the sake of warding off a source of harm on the communal level.
- Necessities render forbidden acts permissible.
- Necessities are to be assessed on a case by case basis.
- If an individual is faced with a choice between two competing benefits, preference should be given to the one that meets a more vital need over one that meets a less vital need; and preference should be given to one that meets a less vital need over one that merely enhances life.
- When one is faced with a choice between two equally beneficial acts, the act that preserves religion should be given preference over the one that preserves life; the act that preserves life should be given preference over the one that preserves reason; the one that preserves reason should be given preference over the one that preserves progeny; and the one that preserves progeny should be preferred over the one that preserves wealth.
- If there is a choice between two equally beneficial acts pertaining to the same matter, the one that benefits the community should be

given preference over the one that benefits a specific individual.

- An act whose benefit is enjoyed by others is to be preferred over one whose benefit is restricted to the person who performs it.
- An obligatory act is to be given preference over a supererogatory act.
- No weight should be attached to a supposition that has been shown to be erroneous.
- An ill-chosen means is more forgivable than an ill-conceived end.

(2) Islamic Rationalism and Its Impact on Contemporary Philosophy, and The Most Salient Features of Post-Modern Philosophy

The effects of the Enlightenment and the rationalist revolution against the Church and religion remained restricted to Europe for more than a century, at which time European colonialism began imposing its thoughts at gunpoint on its conquered subjects. Later, academic missions to the West had the effect of promoting the notion that secularist, liberal thought would liberate the world's peoples from the catastrophic weakness, poverty, and despotism from which they were suffering at the turn of the twentieth century. This cultural and philosophical movement still flourishes in Europe, though in a form different from that which prevailed during the revolution embodied in the Enlightenment, scientific advancement, materialism, and the sanctification of reason.

Unlike in the past, however, the impacts of current changes reach the rest of the world with lightning speed. In fact, knowledge now becomes internationalized within moment of its emergence. As modern intellectual developments harmonize particularly well with the direction being taken by Hollywood productions and the policies of the so-called new world order, their impact goes far beyond the educated elite to affect all members of society to one degree or another, the most powerful pull being exerted, not surprisingly, in the area of entertainment, physical pleasure, and material benefit, since these are concerns shared equally by all social classes.

The intellectual ascent of materialism and naturalism has now reached its apex, from which point it is bound to decline. The questions we now face are: Where will this decline lead? And what is the intellectual alternative to the materialistic civilization that has come to dominate the affairs of the entire world? Given the swiftness with which materialist philosophy took shape and flourished all over the globe, constituting an alternative to the ancient world religions practiced by people in Europe, the Americas, and some African and Asian countries, and the equal swiftness with which this philosophy has lost its luster, no one has answers to such questions.

Indeed, according to some contemporary philosophers, a descent to the depths is the inevitable fate of rationalistic, secular humanist, materialistic ideology. This prediction has been made not as an announcement of glad tidings or based on the belief that the approaching alternative is superior to what preceded it but, rather, based simply on a vision of the destruction into which contemporary thought is leading us. The deliberate marginalization of ancient philosophies has ushered us into a world of intellectual fluidity; or, in the words of one Muslim thinker, it has converted our materialism from a solid to a liquid.[8]

Powerful elements are now chipping away at every reality, every established base, every absolute law or comprehensive thought. This state is what is known in the secular world as post-modernism, post-structuralism, post-liberalism, post-rationalism, and any number of other anarchic, nihilistic post-isms. Post-modern theorization originated with Friedrich Nietzsche, who summed up his nihilistic view in his famous expression: "God is dead." What Nietzsche meant by this statement has been explained by German philosopher Martin Heidegger, who, in a discussion of Nihilism, wrote:

> Nihilism is the process of the devaluation of the highest values hitherto. The decline of these values is the collapse of all prior truth concerning beings as such and as a whole. The process of the devaluation of the highest values hitherto is therefore not one historical occurrence among many others but is rather the fundamental event of Western history, which has been sustained and guided by metaphysics. Insofar as metaphysics received a particular theological

> stamp through Christianity, the devaluation of the highest values hitherto must also be expressed theologically through the statement "God is dead." Here "God" means the suprasensuous realm in general, which as the "true" and eternal world "beyond" proclaims itself in opposition to this "earthly" world the only viable goal...In place of the authority of God and Church looms the authority of conscience, or the domination of reason, or the God of historical progress, or the social instinct.[9]

Hence, Nihilism entails human beings' complete liberation from every form of control imposed through moral values and constants. In the quote above, and elsewhere, Nietzsche invites others to embrace Nihilism on a permanent basis; in this invitation he is joined by other contemporary philosophers such as Martin Heidegger, Paul Sartre, and Jacques Lacan. All of them invite people to a kind of intellectual and moral anarchy and the repudiation of metanarratives in favor of the micronarratives that people formulate for themselves and in which they place their faith, far removed from any standard by which to measure their validity.

The critique of rationalism has been fueled, and its demise hastened, by the spread of the philosophy of deconstructionism, which deals the death blow to all constant meanings and facts. Jacques Derrida, Michel Foucault, and other modern Western thinkers have contributed to deconstructionist theorization as a poststructuralist phase of human history that empties postmodernist philosophies of all meaning. The following is a summary of the principle features of postmodernism.[10]

1. Religious and metaphysical considerations clearly have no place in postmodernist philosophy. This is because the materialistic modernism that originated in the Enlightenment had already marginalized the roles of religion and metaphysics. Hence, postmodernist philosophy is poised to destroy the role of reason and the centrality of humanity and nature. Postmodernism assumes that the universe consists of nothing but matter in constant motion without origin or purpose, and that the mere use of words such as truth, certainty, essence, and idealistic motives involves a regression into an unfounded metaphysical view of the universe. There is no central,

all-inclusive order, but only small, self-contained orders, each of which revolves around itself.

2. In postmodernist thought there is no such thing as an incontrovertible fact. Rather, there are facts formulated by humans themselves, who choose their own convictions regardless of how bizarre or aberrant they happen to be. However, such convictions are, in essence, nothing but a pragmatic surrender and adaptation to the status quo. The way to this Nihilism was opened by deconstructionist philosophy.

Jacques Derrida proposed the concept of Aporia, a Greek word which means "a bottomless pit." The meaning of a text is scattered and diffuse, since language possesses an uncontrollable power. Meaning is greater than a word's signification, since every reader reads his or her own meaning into a given word, as a result of which there are as many meanings as there are readers. This leads to a state of fluidity in which facts vanish and individual meanings multiply. That is why texts of the Old and the New Testaments, as well as all theories, values and principles recorded in texts, are so gelatinous that every one gives them whatever meanings suit his or her own inclinations, and they fall into the traps of poststructuralism.

3. The moral system in postmodernist philosophy is not subject to absolute value-based considerations or set standards that are respected and observed based on a culturally and religiously founded consensus. Rather, post-modernist ethics are based on agreements of limited, temporary legitimacy – in the areas of security, economics, the media, etc. – dictated by the interests of the individuals or institutions in control of society. Honesty, fairness and integrity may not be construed in their traditional senses, but they are needed based on pragmatic, temporary considerations within a milieu governed by sheer opportunism. Having dethroned reason and replaced it with materialist criteria, this philosophy proceeded to sanctify pleasure and bodily desires, and sexual desire in particular. It gave free rein to hitherto suppressed lusts without any deterrent authority, viewing sexual passion as liberation from the yokes of slavery to anything but the self.

In this philosophy the media, fashion and entertainment industries have found their desiderata. This can be seen in modern attire, from the scandalously skimpy styles now prevalent worldwide to so-called unisex fashion as a means of obliterating gender distinctions without creating true equality between men and women. The porn industry grows ever bigger and means to access it ever wider and easier including for youth. Its effects are not hard to guess. Such phenomena augur the collapse of the traditional family unit and a descent into a senseless rebellion that understands nothing but sexual pleasure in its most perverted expressions.

4. The politics of postmodernism – and here I use the word "politics", not "philosophy" – have worked hand-in-hand with a new world order ushered in by a forceful global capitalism. After suffering major losses following attempts at military hegemony and sparked resistance on the part of colonized countries, this has turned to a kind of "soft colonization" through attempts to weaken and undermine these countries' national identities and internal systems. The aim has been to persuade former colonies to open their borders to multinational corporations and imported consumer goods by transforming their political elites into investment partners and their populations into tools of consumption. This undermines the democratic spirit and true democratic principles. Religious, cultural and national identities have no place in the current world market, while entire societies are being trapped by a powerful media hailing the virtues of mindless consumerism and long-term debt.

Hollywood has also done its part toward turning people into entertainment addicts dependent on and subordinate to a materialist world order. Hollywood films and television programs have hypnotized people worldwide into mimicking wealthy secular societies, making them captive to dreams of material prosperity and worldly pleasure. Film channels, most of which are dominated by Hollywood productions that reflect postmodernism's reckless disregard for traditional ethical values, are registering an alarming increase on satellite stations of developing countries.

These, then, are some of the features of post-modernist philosophy, which has had a profound impact on Arab and Islamic culture and thought. Some of this impact is attributable to publications whose authors, whether knowingly or out of mere cultural subservience, parrot the most current secular philosophical trends.

Attempts have been made to deconstruct and reinterpret the texts of the Qur'an in keeping with readers' whims and caprices. As for the Sunnah, it has been done away with on the pretext that it is based on the words and actions of human beings who are no different from us, or that the conditions that prevailed during the days of the Prophet and his Companions differed sufficiently from those of our own day that we now need new tools for arriving at adequate understandings and inferences.

Some neo-liberal Arabs seduced by secular-humanist culture, have gone so far as to repudiate their own national identities, reject political reforms that have been proposed based on shared Middle Eastern aspirations, and disparage incontestable, religiously-based ethical values and behavioral standards as well as other rational propositions.

It now remains for us to clarify the relevance of these developments for the process of shaping a sound Muslim mentality at a time when the fundamental role of reason has been called into question. Despite the obvious weaknesses in the materialist philosophy that has been so central to the modern Western renaissance, the Islamic perspective has yet to establish its role in formulating a contemporary approach to comprehensive cultural renewal and reform. However, it should be remembered that a process of *istidlāl* based on the fundamentals of Islamic jurisprudence and the aims of Islamic law has produced pioneering sciences in the past, and can certainly do so again if developed and applied properly to the situations humanity faces today.

5

The Goals Awareness Crisis and Its Impact on Social Action

OVERVIEW OF THIS CHAPTER

This chapter discusses a number of social phenomena that demonstrate the extent to which the objectives of Islamic law have been marginalized.
It aims to:

1. Show how this marginalization of what is central to Islamic law has led in turn to excessive strictness in some situations and excessive lenience in others; it has also brought about evils that far outweigh the benefits intended.
2. Discuss phenomena that can awaken the consciousness needed to engage in analogical reasoning and proper application of the concepts inherent in the objectives of the Shariʿah.
3. To discuss how religious awakening can serve to counter religious excess, the need to spread love and harmony, the purposefulness of beauty, and the Muslim woman's role in society.

In this chapter I will be discussing a number of social phenomena that demonstrate the extent to which the aims of Islamic law have been marginalized. This marginalization of what is central to Islamic law has led in turn to excessive strictness in some situations and excessive lenience in others; it has also brought about evils that far outweigh the benefits intended. Though such phenomena are rife in our societies, I will restrict my discussion to those that can awaken the consciousness needed to engage in analogical reasoning and proper application of the noble concepts inherent in the goals of the Shariʿah.

The following themes will be discussed: (1) recreation and leisure and their place in Islam, (2) how religious awakening can serve to counter religious excess, (3) the purposefulness of a sense of national affiliation, (4) the need to spread love and harmony among Muslims, (5) the purposefulness of beauty, (6) the Muslim woman's purpose and role in society, and (7) a methodology of conscious transformation.

(1) Recreation and Leisure and Their Place in Islam

There are a number of juristic issues and questions that surface repeatedly in connection with religious events such as the fasting month of Ramadan, ʿId al-Adha (the Feast of Sacrifice), newly arising situations relating to the pilgrimage to Makkah, and events celebrated annually in the Muslim world such as the Prophet's birthday, the Night of Ascension, the middle of Shaʿban, and others. Arguments frequently occur regarding whether such events and their related activities are permissible or impermissible, legitimate or mere human innovations. Such arguments tend to grow all the more heated and complex when they are taken up for discussion on satellite television programs, which tend simply to raise further questions rather than highlighting the underlying causes behind the juristic disagreements and the conflicts over how to rule on this or that issue or situation.

It is not my intention here to resolve the juristic disputes over such issues. It would be unrealistic to expect disagreements to disappear simply because a given opinion can be shown to be well-attested in light of textual evidence and statements of well-regarded scholars, or based on the inquirer's confidence in the jurist who has issued a given legal ruling. However, the intensity of such conflicts can be mitigated if we focus on rectifying intellectual approaches and ways of thinking, nurturing faith in and reverence for the Unseen, and adopting appropriate ways of relating to those who disagree with us. Focusing on the notions that underly our disagreements can help to correct the cumulative errors that have resulted from sectarian bigotry, blind imitation, and the fear of new interpretations and understandings of religious texts.

Once, when deciding how best to spend a summer vacation, I went in search of new programs and useful ideas on a website that specializes in Friday sermons. However, even the sermons on the homepage, where one finds the best materials on the website, were unrealistic and contrary to reason, human nature, and the objectives of the Shariʿah. Most of these sermons revolved around the prohibition of activities people engage in during vacations, yet without proposing permissible alternatives. In addition, the principle of *sadd al-dharā'iʿ*, that is, prohibiting whatever has the potential of leading to a forbidden act, was misused in a number of places. For example, some types of tourism and legitimate forms of recreation were declared unlawful due to an unfounded fear that they might lead to something explicitly forbidden in the Shariʿah.

The sermons I read seemed to suspect every seeker of enjoyment and leisure of treading a path that would lead to depravity and licentiousness! Filled with warnings against summer activities that would purportedly lead to sin, the sermons were devoid of the constructive tone that would have been more in keeping with the spirit of the Shariʿah. As for alternative activities in which parents might involve their children, the sermons emphasized Qur'an memorization centers, beneficial reading, and family visits to the two Sacred Mosques, while some drew attention to scholarly courses being offered in many parts of the Kingdom of Saudi Arabia or in some Gulf capitals.

In the face of this recurrent discourse on leisure, I have a number of ideas that I believe are relevant to the discussion. As I see it, leisure is no longer a marginal issue in people's lives. Vacation expenses have become priorities in families' budgets. In the business world, it has been suggested that tourism-based economies will soon occupy first place in world expenditure, with tourist nations becoming the world's wealthiest in place of industrial nations, which are currently the wealthiest, and agricultural nations, which previously held first place in terms of national income. Even culture comes to reflect not what benefits people and promotes their scientific and intellectual advancement, but, rather, what they want and enjoy.

Muslims are not far removed from these changes on the world scene. On the contrary, their impact on the Muslim community is at once powerful and profound. Countless members of Muslim societies take out loans to cover just a few days of vacation! These same individuals may buy modern-day satellite dishes and the most sophisticated cell phones without being able to cover their families' medical and educational expenses. It may be impossible to halt the advance of the culture of leisure; however, we can redirect its course and mitigate its destructive effects on our values if we make concerted efforts to create awareness and search for acceptable substitutes.

In regard to the Shariʿah's stand on developments taking place in the world of leisure, one notes that Muslim jurists shy away from addressing the frenzied craving, particularly among youths and young children, for contemporary modes of entertainment. Some Muslim preachers and scholars hold that enrolling in Qur'an memorization courses, reading books and participating in scholarly programs are the only viable antidotes to an addiction to fun, excitement and leisure. However, such solutions are suitable for only a tiny segment of society; hence, this approach undermines such scholars' claim to objectivity, as well as the claim that Islam's teachings are applicable to all times and places.

One of the goals of making sound laws that are relevant to people's lives is to provide permissible, inviting substitutes for prohibited actions. We need urgently to reexamine some actions which have been declared forbidden in the past for fear that they might lead to other actions that are explicitly prohibited by Islamic law. Examples include sports activities in their various forms for men and women; purposeful art, recreational hobbies, educational games, travel, tourism, and others. If we critically examine all of these, we will discover that they fall within the category of what is permissible. Instead of declaring them to be fundamentally prohibited and measuring someone's honor or piety based on whether or not he or she engages in them, we can work to purge the activities themselves of harmful elements.

This austere and excessively cautious point of view should not be imposed on everyone without exception or legislated as a mandatory educational approach. The Sunnah of the Prophet actually encourages forms of recreation and leisure which, were people to indulge in them in our day, would be deemed shameful and unlawful! It was reported that Abū al-Dardā' said, "I grant myself relaxation by engaging in certain kinds of lawful enjoyment, since this gives me strength to uphold the truth."[1]

In the Qur'anic account of the prophet Joseph and his brothers, God informs us that his brothers said to their father, "Let him go out with us tomorrow, that he may enjoy himself and play, and verily, we shall guard him well" (*Sūrah Yūsuf* 12:12). Commenting on this passage, al-Qāḍī Abū Bakr ibn al-ʿArabī states:

> Be aware, may God grant you success, that there is nothing reprehensible in the play referred to here. After all, it is related in the tradition that men played with their horses, their families and their arrows. The play that Joseph's brothers engaged in would have involved either foot-racing or archery. This may be concluded from the verse that reads, "O our father! Behold, we went off racing with one another ..." (*Sūrah Yūsuf* 12:17) And there is certainly nothing blameworthy in this.[2]

ʿĀ'ishah is related to have said:

> I saw the Messenger of God standing by the door to my room while the Abyssinians were playing with their spears in the mosque. He concealed me with his garment so that I could watch them play. He continued standing there for so long, in fact, that I was the one to take my leave. Imagine a young girl being that interested in such fun.[3]

According to the version of this hadith found in the *Musnad*, the Prophet then added, "So that the Jews may know that there is a wide scope for action in our religion, because I have been sent with a rightly guided, magnanimous religion."[4]

In *Fatḥ al-Bārī*, Ibn Ḥajar wrote that, "Al-Nasā'ī recorded via ʿĀmir ibn Saʿd, on the authority of Quraẓah ibn Kaʿb and Abū Masʿūd, both of whom were among the Prophet's Helpers, that we (Muslims) have been granted a concession to enjoy ourselves at weddings."[5]

The Sunnah attests to various forms of permissible recreation and diversion, including foot racing, horse racing, wrestling, archery, banter and play. Of relevance here is an account which affirms the need for balance among the various facets of life. We are told that Salmān [al-Fārisī] once said to Abū al-Dardā', "Certainly your soul has a claim on you; your Lord has a claim on you; your guest has a claim on you, and your family has a claim on you. So give to everyone his due, and to everything its due." The Prophet then said approvingly, "Salmān has spoken the truth."[6]

The Prophet permitted certain Abyssinians to practice their sport in his mosque; he allowed two young girls to sing for ʿĀ'ishah; he allowed play with dolls; and he allowed leisure, joking, racing and other kinds of recreation, all of which shows that just as our religion enjoins seriousness, exertion and struggle, it also permits various forms of recreation, enjoyment and relaxation.

(2) How Religious Awakening Can Serve to Counter Religious Excess

Ideological extremism constitutes a threat to society, particularly when it is translated into concrete action. Hence, we need to identify and analyze the causes behind such extremism in our Islamic societies. Given the importance of this analysis and the role it can play in leading us to a suitable solution, it should be undertaken not by individuals, whatever their expertise, but by various institutions through collective and organized efforts.

Nevertheless, perhaps due to my firsthand experience with extremism and the fact that I have traced its development in local communities, I consider myself obliged to do a bit of theorizing on the matter of extremism. In brief, I believe that patterns of thinking that militate against objectivity, however insignificant they are and however weak their initial impacts may seem, should never be overlooked, since such patterns of thought may, over time, grow less and less moderate and objective to the point where they turn into full-blown ideological extremism. Blind adherence to a particular individual, juristic school, or sect causes an individual to see the truth solely through the lens of that individual, school or sect. As a consequence, he comes to think with other people's logic rather than his own, and he rejects whatever view or approach opposes that of the person, school or sect he follows without question. The result of such blind allegiance is widening societal divisions that have the potential to develop into violent disputes and even internecine wars.

As a result of the exaggerations common to extremist thought, an individual may criticize his opponents to the extent of defaming and alienating them, while at the same time lauding those he agrees with to the point of idolizing them and seeing them as infallible! Such a phenomenon contributes to the formation of mentalities that see things through a purely emotional prism, or which look at issues, situations and even matters of religion from one perspective only, insisting that this perspective is the one and absolute truth. However, knowing only half of a reality is worse than being completely ignorant of it. This is because someone that knows half of something usually presumes that he knows everything, while he only possesses the knowledge of a part thereof.

The major factor that gives rise to unidimensional mentalities, whether among extremists or others, is the absence of an intellectual or cultural environment that would enable one properly to analyze problems and cope with crises. Such people's thinking is trapped within a narrow box that contains the entirety of their intellectual wealth and life experiences. This is why scholars stipulate that whoever wants to engage in ijtihad must have the scholarly and intellectual qualifications that will enable him or her to do a thorough, fact-based study of the question at hand.

Those with a unidimensional mentality find it hard to dialogue calmly with others and listen to criticism without bitterness or rancor. This is because someone with this mentality sees himself as a perfect individual who has a monopoly on truth and correctness; it follows logically, therefore, that whoever disagrees with him must be religiously or intellectually deficient. Indeed, one hallmark of extremists is their tendency to oversimplify major issues and problems rather than subjecting them to thorough study and logical analysis. Such oversimplification prevents a society from benefiting from other cultures and the knowledge they might contribute toward finding solutions to its problems, thereby making its problems even worse.

Even if extremism has not yet been observed openly or sparked acts of violence and destruction, it should not be ignored, since most infernos begin from the tiniest of sparks. It is incumbent upon societal institutions to remold people's thinking, deepen and broaden their awareness via objective thinking, stress the importance of dialogue, teach a proper etiquette of disagreement, and formulate an educational curriculum that develops an objective, open-minded mode of thinking and instruction.

Many of the world's societies have their own share of intellectual extremism. However, its impact varies from one society to another depending on the level of awareness of its citizenry and government officials. It is only in atmospheres governed by a unidimensional mentality that the scourge of extremism thrives and proliferates.

Given its perilous impacts on individuals and the state, decision makers in Muslim societies are now placing priority on addressing the phenomenon of extremism. The security measures being taken to curtail the spread of this ideology and contain the threat it poses are quite important. However, development and reform efforts should not be put on hold until extremism has been eradicated. Rather, priority should be given during this phase to spreading a jurisprudence of revival and civilization that prompts everyone to build up their society, look to the future, and vie with others to achieve progress and advancement.

Many nations have passed through intellectual crises and witnessed violent confrontations in relation to social and political visions and orientations. Rather than allowing these crises and disputes to stop them from charting the path of advancement and revival, they quickly joined hands to repel whatever might endanger their civilization or curtail their advancement. Examples of such nations in our time are India and China. To my knowledge, no other countries have experienced a greater degree of religious and racial diversity, intellectual and sectarian conflict, or economic hardship than have these two, and this with the added burden of burgeoning populations. Nevertheless, in the year 2003, India's economy grew by 8 percent which is a commendable rate by international economic indexes.[7]

As for China, its tremendous economic achievement over the last several decades has enabled it to overcome all the exceptional circumstances it has faced. Its gross domestic product (GDP) in 2013 was more than US$ 9 trillion, second largest in the world after the United States, which had a GDP of close to US$ 17 trillion.[8] The number of poor people in China declined from 451 million in 1999 to 84.1 million in 2011. The difference of 366.1 million people who have been lifted out of poverty during this relatively short period is greater than the current population of the United States.[9]

As we seek to address extremism and the crisis it has generated in modern times, our educated elites should concern themselves with promoting a jurisprudence of revival while exploring a variety of developmental options rather than entrenching themselves in ivory towers from which they can theorize and market temporary solutions.

(3) The Purposefulness of A Sense of National Affiliation

The "industry" of reform projects has flourished in most Muslim countries as a result of the various internal crises through which their societies are passing. The growth of this industry has been encouraged by globalization and its political clout, which have flooded the markets of Muslim countries with imported goods while undermining all things local. Given this situation, there is a weak demand for local goods even though they are available in abundance, since the allure of imported goods has duped many of those in decision-making positions to accept and promote them.

Similarly, the unconditional acceptance of imported solutions distorts national identity and endangers the nation's future. A keen observer of the experiences of nations and civilizations will realize the enormity of the hazard that such imported solutions pose to a Muslim society's culture and thinking. One of the few Muslim thinkers to realize this danger, Malik Bennabi, states:

> No one should suggest solutions and present plans without regard for the circumstances of his community and his native land. Rather, his thoughts, his sentiments, his words and his actions should be in consonance with the demands of whatever phase his nation is passing through. Importing solutions from East or West only renders local efforts fruitless and exacerbates whatever ailment is already afflicting society. Hence, every act of blind imitation is a suicidal act of ignorance.[10]

In this atmosphere of crisis, it is vital that we revive and ingrain a sense of patriotism in citizens' minds. This is the first protective shield – both preventive and curative – for both individuals and the nation. The following, in brief, are three fundamentals that will help to deepen a society's national consciousness.

First: Clearly implant in people's minds and hearts the greatest purpose of their existence, which is to worship God, so that this awareness can influence the way they live their lives. It is God who "has created death as well as life, so that He might put you to a test [and thus show] which of you is best in conduct, and [make you realize that] He alone is Almighty, Truly Forgiving" (*Sūrah al-Mulk* 67:2). God declares, "I have not created the invisible beings and men to any end but that they may [know and] worship Me" (*Sūrah al-Dhāriyāt* 51:56). God has thus made all life's activities to be means of winning His pleasure. Attaining success in this great trial of life on earth will root true civilization in people's minds, hearts and actions, spurring them to give unceasingly and to strive to be witnesses to truth and goodness among other nations and societies: "And thus have We willed you to be a community of the middle way, so that with your lives you might bear witness to the truth before all mankind, and that the Apostle might bear witness to it before you" (*Sūrah al-Baqarah* 2:143).

People in many parts of the world live in distress and crisis. Though the building blocks of civilization are present, the goals of people's frantic activity are vague and confused, and fail to reflect the sound inclinations with which human beings were born. However, when people have a clear sense of purpose and understand the goals set out in the Shariʿah for the life of society and its individual members, they realize their true place, that is, their duties and the role they were intended to play in life. I sincerely doubt that people with an awareness of their true purpose will be satisfied to live their lives on the margins, or to be depraved in their actions.

A critical examination of the state of Arab society before the coming of the Prophet will show clearly how backward and decadent it was, both materially and socially. This is why the Arabs received virtually no mention in the annals of history until after Muhammad's advent. His prophethood heralded a comprehensive civilizational resurgence and the birth of one of the most influential and advanced nations in the world. The essential reason for this marvelous transformation is the divine revelation which God sent down upon His messenger Muhammad. As God said to the Prophet, "And thus too, [O Muhammad,] have We revealed unto thee a life-giving message, [coming] at Our behest. [Ere this message came unto thee,] thou didst not know what revelation is, nor what faith [implies]: but [now] We have caused this [message] to be a light, whereby We guide whom We will of Our servants: and, verily, [on the strength thereof], thou, too, shalt guide [people] onto the straight way" (*Sūrah al-Shūrā* 42:52). As we read in the verse just quoted, this revelation was the spirit that resurrected the body of an Arab society that had been devoid of all vitality, the light that illumined their darkness and dissipated the confusion that had reigned during their days of ignorance.

The Prophet's Companion, Abū Saʿīd al-Khudrī, once illustrated the remarkable transformation that had occurred in the lives of the desert Arabs of the Prophet's time in the following story:

> A wolf once chased a sheep and caught it. The shepherd then pursued the wolf and seized the sheep from it. Squatting on its tail, the wolf asked, "Do you not fear God? Why do you deprive me of the provision God had bestowed on me?" "How amazing!" exclaimed the shepherd. "A wolf is talking to me as though he were a human being!" Then the wolf asked, "Shall I tell you something even more amazing? Muhammad is in Yathrib telling people about events that happened long before his time."[11]

This is why Ibn Khaldūn states in *The Prolegomena* that "for the most part, Arabs only obtain authority to rule based on some religious justification, whether it be [a claim to] prophethood, sainthood, or some other significant religiously based influence."[12]

Civilizational awareness can only bear fruit when joined with spiritual highmindedness and heartfelt faith. Given the presence of these elements, such awareness is the true motive force behind civilizational advancement, spurring individuals to be active, productive, and creative. It also orders relations among individuals, clarifying their roles and responsibilities with fairness and impartiality. In this connection, Malik Bennabi states:

> It has been observed that no civilization arises apart from some religious creed. Hence, when studying a given civilization, we must search for its religious origin. Perhaps it would not be unreasonable to suggest that Buddhism planted the seeds of Buddhist civilization, and that Brahmanism provided the nucleus for Brahmanic civilization. Civilization invariably emerges in the garb of a revelation sent down from Heaven which provides people with a law to follow. At the very least, its foundations guide people to an invisible deity in the most general sense. It is as though human beings are destined never to witness the emergence of a civilization unless they look beyond their own earthly lives or their own era. For when human beings discover the true meaning of their existence, they also discover the truest meanings of the things that govern and interact with their genius.[13]

Second: Strengthen and deepen people's sense of belonging to this land which God honored by choosing it as the place where He would reveal His final message to humankind, and the place toward which all Muslims are to turn daily in prayer. Given these special privileges, it should be clear that fulfilling the duty to preserve this land's security, stability, growth, and advancement brings benefits that accrue not only to its citizens, but to all other Islamic nations as well. The Muslim's religious obligation to preserve this region is no less pressing than his or her national or patriotic obligation.

This sense of belonging can only be deepened in an atmosphere of mutual trust, and only when citizens feel that they share common interests with the state's various institutions (political, economical and social). When an individual feels debased, demeaned or disregarded and is being denied his/her legitimate rights, this will be reflected in the way he/she carries out his/her responsibilities. If such a situation continues, the individual's thoughts and concerns may shift to a kind of absolute individualism that serves only his/her personal interests, even to the detriment of others, and an excessive selfishness which prevents him/her from making any sacrifice for his/her nation or cooperating with others. If this mentality is coupled with punishments from the state, then the affected individual will develop an increasing aversion to the state and keep more and more to himself/herself. After all, patriotism is something that must develop spontaneously in response to the individual's feeling that his/her needs and problems are recognized by society and that he or she will receive the social support he or she needs in times of crisis.

Third: Formulate policies and laws that govern the life of individual citizens and regulate society's affairs. Such policies and laws are a prerequisite for a society's progress and development, since they embody the society's principles in relation to citizens' rights and obligations. In civilized nations, such principles are held sacred by all, just as they were in the first generation of Muslims.

In backward societies, laws are tools that protect only the interests of the powerful and influential; hence, they are respected by no one but those who benefit from them. Because laws are tools of oppression and corruption, their enforcement becomes a manifestation of social collapse and a cause of destruction. The Prophet Muhammad warned against this phenomenon when he said, "What destroyed those before you is that if an influential person committed theft, they would free him, but if an unimportant person did so, they would punish him by cutting off his hand."[14]

Most countries in the world today are governed by laws and constitutions, and their governments have independent judicial systems. As for countries with nothing but the outward trappings of civilization, they suffer from a kind of "legal duplicity" in that alongside every written law there is an unwritten one. The latter reflects the actual law of the land, while the former is a mere façade; hence, "right" always belongs to the one who can pay more or who is the most intimidating.[15]

Legal organization and systems of reward and deterrence are indispensable for the protection of a society from rebellion and negligence on the part of some its members. However, the punishments instituted by civilized nations are not what bring a society into being; rather, they only serve to protect and preserve it. Whoever considers the Qur'anic verses dealing with criminal penalties will find that they make up no more than one-fifth of the entire Holy Book, while the remaining four-fifths focus on building up people's inner beings by developing their awareness and urging them to monitor themselves and correct their own behavior.

The atmosphere in which patriotic consciousness comes into being requires a willingness on the part of all ethnic groups and social classes, thinkers and educated elites, to concede some of their distinctive views and social privileges in favor of the collective national framework of which everyone is meant to be a part. This willingness to feel with others and sacrifice for them is one of the most significant signs of social and cultural advancement. A careful observer of the effect of Islam on the Arabian Peninsula, which hitherto had been embroiled in power struggles and wars that were sparked for the most trivial reasons, will discover that within a very short period of time, Islam was able to unite these people, despite their differences and dissimilarities, into a cultural identity that embraced a broad human spectrum.

It behooves us here to learn some lessons about self-sacrifice and dedication from the world of insects. The function of a queen bee, for example, is to lay eggs. The queen bee feeds on a substance produced by glands in the worker bees' heads. Yet, despite there being only one queen for each colony, none of the worker bees complains about the division of power! Worker bees are the backbone of the hive. They do most of the work and, despite being "barren," they feed and take care of the young, as well as cleaning and aerating the hive. The tremendous efforts expended by the worker bees render their bodies incapable of living very long, and their average lifespan is only about six weeks. As for the drones, they die immediately after mating with the queen bee. Nevertheless, they undertake this act as if they were sacrificing their lives for the sake of their species' survival. The bee's motto is always, "My life is of no value if my community's well-being is in danger."

One of the basic requirements of a patriotic mindset is that educational and media institutions carry out their responsibility to raise consciousness on both the individual and collective levels. Our educational institutions at all levels have the obligation to formulate a purposeful, integrated plan to form each individual's character and instill in him/her the needed civilizational consciousness. Schools, universities, families, teachers, public speakers, and imams alike should be prepared to participate in this noble endeavor under the banner of the sacred injunction: "And say [unto them, O Prophet]:

'Act! And God will behold your deeds, and [so will] His Apostle, and the believers...'" (*Sūrah al-Tawbah* 9:105). In modern times, the media has become one of the most crucial instruments of social progress and retrogression alike. Unless the media conveys and reinforces progressive values and principles that help its recipients to leave behind trivial concerns, sensationalism, blind imitation of others and short-sightedness, it will become a means of rapid destruction, however solid the nation's structure, and however many its builders.

(4) The Need to Spread Love and Harmony Among Muslims

Many concepts are influenced by people's relationship to their environment. One's environment serves to form and shape one's way of thinking, the types of psychological and emotional influences at work in one's life, as well as one's ability to change and live harmoniously with others.

Owing to their closeness to harbors, their exposure to commercial exchange and their openness to the sea, coastal environments tend to promote more flexible mindsets and openness to diversity than do other areas. As for desert environments with their aridity, isolation, and harsh conditions, they tend to produce an obstinate, irascible, closed-minded character. Similarly, we find that moutainous regions, urban areas, rural areas, moderate climates, severely cold environments, and severely hot ones all leave a clear mark on their inhabitants in terms of their way of thinking, behavior, and emotions. Ibn Khaldūn cites numerous examples to illustrate this principle.[16]

Whoever observes people's emotions, thinking, and behavior in our Arab society will discover that they vary according to climate and topography, although this is not always the case, since the growing interconnection among societies and the sudden emergence of modern communications technology and satellite channels have greatly impacted the manner in which this principle applies to people everywhere.

Nevertheless, there is reason to believe that an arid environment may, in fact, lead to a kind of emotional dryness and an absence of feeling in broad sectors of society in both Saudi Arabia and the Gulf States. The spheres for feelings of love and affection have narrowed greatly. There are certain people who limit their shows of affection to themselves and those closest to them, while appearing unconcerned about other members of society. The lack of feeling may be due to tribal affiliation, color, social status, or other factors. However, the Qur'an calls upon us to break out of this misguided mentality. God says, "Behold, We have created you all out of a male and a female, and made you into nations and tribes, so you might come to know one another. Verily, the noblest of you in the sight of God is the one who is most deeply conscious of Him" (*Sūrah al-Ḥujurāt* 49:13). When God broadened the diversity among people, He recalled them to unity and cooperation based on the principle of 'knowing one another', the foundation of which is God-consciousness, so that genuine collective advancement might be achieved among the different races of humankind.

One finds that even people's love for those closest to them, including spouses, children, and siblings, is often left unexpressed in either words or actions, whereas the Prophet said, "If a man loves his brother (in Islam), he should tell him so."[17] In affirmation of the importance of such expressions, the Prophet said, "No two persons love each other for the sake of God but that the more beloved of them to God, the Mighty and Sublime, shows more love to his companion."[18] He also said, "On Resurrection Day, God will say, 'Where are those who love one another for the sake of My Majesty? I shall protect them with My shade on the day when there shall be no shade but My shade.'"[19]

If it is this important to show love for brothers and companions, then how much worthier of such love must spouses and children be? Unfortunately, our present situation confirms the fact that there is an emotional indifference between spouses and a failure to show affection even for children, even though the expression of such feelings may be even more important to them than satisfying their material needs. In fact, I would venture to state that the most critical cause of some broken homes is a lack of love for wives and young girls or a failure to express adequate affection for them. This situation can cause the deprived spouse to go looking for affection in illicit sexual relationships and emotional attachments. Meanwhile, present-day temptations to infidelity are more powerful than those of yesteryear, whether they come through satellite programs, online conversations, or any of a number of other media that now invade every household in our society.

The spread of true affection devoid of lust and base motives, both in the family and in society at large, would help to ensure stronger cohesion, compassion and solidarity, which would in turn do away with the various forms of tension, indifference, hatred and malice among people. Such a process represents one of the most important aims of the Shariʿah. Otherwise, it would not have been mentioned more than 83 times in the Qur'an, and the Prophet would not have enjoined it on so many occasions. In fact, he went so far as to declare that mutual love guarantees admittance to Paradise. He stated, "By the One in Whose hand is my soul, you cannot enter Paradise unless you have faith, and you cannot have faith unless you love one another."[20]

I marvel at the intense emotion that was evinced by the Prophet when, as he preached in the mosque, his two grandsons al-Ḥasan and al-Ḥusayn entered, prompting him to come down from the pulpit, put his arms around them and plant kisses on their cheeks! More marvelous still is the way he showed affection to animals and even to inanimate objects! When he ascended Mount Uḥud he said, "Here is a mountain that loves us and that we love in return!"[21]

So I wonder: Can we overcome the stultifying influence of the climate of estrangement that surrounds us, and respond to the feelings of love and goodwill in our hearts? How badly we need to access that emotional, sentimental realm in which the doers of good and doers of evil vie for the opportunity to spread sincere awareness in society. In this race, there are as many reasons to do good as there are to do evil, and I believe that if we joined in such a race, we might open many a closed heart.

(5) The Purposefulness of Beauty

"Indeed, God is beautiful and loves beauty."[22] This prophetic dictum encapsulates a comprehensive religious goal that is relevant to many aspects of the Shariʿah. It urges Muslims to perceive the beauty with which God has imbued the cosmos, to nurture it within themselves, and, when its manifestations seem to be absent, to contemplate it in their mind's eye. Surely there is no sound-minded individual but that he/she loves beauty, finds refreshment in its manifestations, and seeks out its varied expressions whether by gazing at a lovely sight, listening to a melodious strain, perceiving the subtle harmony manifested in Nature's cycles and movements, or breathing in a sweet aroma. The greater the impact such perceptions of beauty have on the person who experiences them, the more clearly they will be reflected in his/her thoughts and behavior, and the more able he/she will be to live in harmony with reality and the laws of the cosmos.

According to Malik Bennabi, "The beauty found in a given sphere containing colors, sounds, aromas, movements, and shapes has a suggestive effect on one's thoughts and leaves its special imprint, whether in the form of refined, lovely taste, or of loathsome ugliness." Does beauty produce/have a significant impact on the generation of ideas or accepting its reality. There is no doubt that there is an impact. But is this impact intentional during the process of formulation and change or does it emerge spontaneously?

In my view, the role of beauty in change and transformation has been neglected by many in their contemporary reform efforts, and Muslims in particular, as evidenced by the move away from the arts and personal experience, and an absence of efforts to foster aesthetic awareness. Given that beauty and perfection are among the divine attributes, and that God loves to see the effects of His grace and beauty in His creation, then both Islamic law and common sense dictate that God's splendrous design should be manifest in all our affairs. One of the most pertinent proofs of this from the law of Islam is its concern for orderliness in Muslims' daily affairs. Prayer, for example, has stipulated time periods, and rules dictating how it is to be performed in congregation; fasting has prescribed days, conditions and defined goals; the amount of zakah is clearly stipulated, and there is a clearly defined minimum amount of wealth on the basis of which it is calculated, while the pilgrimage to Makkah is associated with specific verbal, physical, and inward rites. When performed in keeping with the divine injunctions, these acts of worship enthrall the heart and captivate the eye, while the mosaic of human diversity displayed in their performance makes the sight of them all the more awe-inspiring.

The Shariʿah also concerns itself with the importance of doing our work well and maintaining good hygiene and a neat appearance, all of which demonstrates the fact that outward beauty is one of the goals of Islamic law. How could it be otherwise, when Muslims are commanded to observe and contemplate the beauty of God's creation as manifested in the sky and the stars, mountains and streams, flora and fauna? When speaking of the blessings, both practical and aesthetic, embodied in a particular kind of animal, God says, "And He creates cattle: you derive warmth from them, and [various other uses]; and from them you obtain food; and you find beauty in them when you drive them home in the evenings and when you take them out to pasture in the mornings" (*Sūrah al-Naḥl* 16:5-6). Indeed, the Qur'an in its entirety, with its picturesque style, its elegant forms of expression, and the lucidity of its messages, delights the heart and the ear while drawing the mind and the soul into submission. Is this not sufficient proof that beauty is among God's purposes even in the realm of thought, study, and reflection?

The expressions of beauty that surround Muslims in their rites of worship and reside in their hearts have a powerful impact on their characters and thoughts. Beauty contributes to mildness of manner and refinement of character while mitigating harshness of temper and intransigence. At the same time, it sparks a desire to look for the good in circumstances and the virtue in other individuals rather than being on the lookout for their failings and mistakes. The lover of beauty doesn't allow himself/herself to live in a state of languor and ignominy, servility and cynicism.

The Arabian Peninsula, where the Qur'an was revealed, was a place of sparse beauty. Nevertheless, Islam so impressed images of beauty on the souls of its hearers that its teachings became an established creed through which believers could envision the unspeakable splendor and bliss of Paradise. This experience created such a sense of beauty in their minds and hearts that one of the Prophet's

Companions exclaimed that he could "smell the scent of Paradise from beyond Mount Uḥud."

My purpose in discussing beauty as a goal of Islamic law is to stress the need to reclaim the Islamic aesthetic values that can revive feelings of love and kindness both in ourselves and in others, while healing the scars left by hatred and violence that have marred life's beauty and disturbed relations among all living things. The aesthetic values rooted in Islam promise to improve people's chances of living a decent life filled with happiness and gratification. Knowing this, it grieves me to see falsehood being showcased in a specious, alluring garb, while the truth is presented in the most dreadful, repellent of forms. International news about Muslims is filled with scenes of killing, violence, wars and harsh, fanatical pronouncements, and it is with these images and words that Muslims are now associated throughout the world.

Our exemplar, the Prophet Muhammad, was endowed with exceptional beauty, his words were exceedingly wonderful, and he would never allow any rite of Islam to be presented in anything but the most appealing form. Bilāl ibn Rabāḥ was not the first to be inspired with the Islamic call to prayer; however, he was appointed as the first muezzin because he had been endowed with the most resonant, melodious voice. Similarly, the Companion Diḥyah al-Kalbī was chosen to serve as the Prophet's emissary to a number of monarchs because of his eloquence and comely appearance.

Is it not time, then, that the beauty of our religion manifested itself in our words, our actions, and the manner in which we present ourselves to others?

(6) The Muslim Woman's Purpose and Role in Society

Contemporary women's issues have provoked controversy in virtually all sectors of society. This topic, which has been widely discussed and analysed, has yielded countless articles and studies only a few of which have been translated into reality, and even these few fail to reflect the nature of the reality in which we live at present. Consequently, I would like to discuss a number of ideas adopted by an educated group who have emerged as spokespersons on behalf of the silent majority of society's women. Of particular interest are Saudi women involved in public leadership, journalistic writing, or speaking for Saudi women from an Islamic perspective. These ideas are as follows:

Firstly: There has been intensive, even obsessive, discussion of the rapid change our society is undergoing, the remarkable development of mechanisms by which it can open itself to the world, and the imminent danger faced by women in the wake of this flood of change. As a result of this discourse, most women's activities have come to revolve around accusing others of being the cause of this tsunamic wave, their purpose being to vindicate themselves and resist the symptoms of change without delving into the causes of society's ills. These developments have led to the emergence of a jurisprudence that focuses around legal issues which are products of this change, such as whether women should be required to wear a loose, flowing outer garment, whether they should be permitted to drive, vote, or travel without a *maḥram* (a male relative with a degree of consanguinity that would preclude marriage to the woman in question), and other questions, none of which has been central over the course of Islam's history, and the rulings on which are by no means written in stone.

Despite the importance of these issues, they should not be allowed to gain priority over more crucial matters to which insufficient attention is being devoted, such as women's various rights, their role in development, and their participation in the institutions of society.

As I see it, women's role during this current phase has shrunk in response to a fear for their identity, that is, a fear of losing themselves in the identity of others. This phenomenon has curtailed women's role and undermined their potentials, potentials not enjoyed by women in many other societies. What we possess by way of Islamic values, the higher aims of Islamic law, and a divinely inspired approach to life guarantee women the ability to make a difference and play an active role in social reform. This ability needs to be highlighted in this critical phase of the history of the Saudi woman. However, this can only be attained by setting up developmental programmes and constructive projects through social institutions, research centers, and technical and economic institutes that can attend to all women's problems and needs and involve all sectors of society without marginalizing or discriminating against anyone. In so doing, we can shift from a defensive position to on offensive one, engaging ourselves in progressive developmental projects that open new vistas in areas of vital importance worldwide.

Secondly: The limited opportunity to engage in critical thought and objective thinking on the part of many educated Muslim women may serve to delay numerous developmental initiatives on behalf of the society's women. This delay might also be explained as being due to the lack of effective means of communicating and implementing their ideas via existent policies and legislation, as well as the fact that men are viewed as women's guardians in virtually all aspects of life. As a consequence of this situation, many efforts have been expended in vain, with viable ideas having been neglected for lack of efforts and funding.

The absence of logical thinking, limited knowledge, the lack of sophistication on the part of Saudi Arabia's female elites, and the sparsity of academic institutions to stimulate intellectual activity have spawned numerous negative social phenomena, including a mounting craving for luxuries, cosmetics, and the latest fashions that surpasses any found in non-Muslim societies! Such factors have dampened women's interest in issues of real significance and rendered them more receptive to "old wives' tales" and rumors, as well as, possibly, magic and charlatanry. Women's capitulation to their sentimental tendencies at the expense of logic and common sense has taken its toll on their family's stability and their capacity to tackle their personal problems. They have become more vulnerable to emotional influences whatever their source. I believe this tendency has affected numerous social groups, albeit to varying degrees. However, its commonality among women in particular has made it a primarily female phenomenon in Saudi society.

Thirdly: What we hope to see from our educated elites is an awakening that springs out of the pristine Shariʿah and its general objectives, and which yields practical ideas that can be applied to projects that advance women's role in society. This can only be achieved through conscious thought, sound plans, and joint efforts that give birth to Islamic projects which address contemporary changes without squandering time and effort on responding to or attacking the imported ideas that may have gained ground among Muslim women.

The current generation of Muslim women has numerous urgent questions having to do with freedoms, rights, fairness, full equality with men, and other issues. The best answers to these inevitable questions are to be found, it seems to me, in the developmental programmes in which they involve themselves, and through which they can play their role in building up society, since in this way, the concepts of freedom, justice, equality, revival, and civilization can take concrete shape both in their minds and in their communities. It is high time that this step be taken. It is time for theorists to descend from their ivory towers and take part in the work of real construction. Even if the Day of Resurrection is imminent and a woman holds a date palm seedling in her hand, let her plant it!

(7) A Methodology of Conscious Transformation

Political domination and material oppression may be the most detestable forms of transgression against the individual's dignity and humanity. However, although physical oppression may be painful in its effects, intellectual oppression is more lethal, because it kills people's drive to seek freedom and suppresses their will to express their convictions by subjugating them to the dictates of someone who believes that he/she has absolute knowledge of everything, including even knowledge of the Unseen. Material oppression strikes with a rod of iron, while intellectual oppression strangles with a cord of silk! Once people's minds have been tamed through intimidation, marginalization and oversimplification, society then becomes a vast prison where people are deprived of thinking and expressing their views. They languish in the chains of fear of criticizing or antagonizing the idol who rules them, while everyone with the courage of his/or convictions becomes a pariah, a rebel against the cowering majority. This is what happened to the Germans under Hitler, the Italians under Mussolini, the Chinese under Mao Zedong, and the Russians under Stalin. These are all glaring examples of mass mental slavery and sacred cows, and subjugated populations will only hold their heads high again once these tyrants have been stripped of their power.

However, due to the availability and variety of international means of communication, we have now entered a stage in which it is impossible to fetter people's minds entirely with closed ideas. Consequently, Islamic societies are now faced with a confusing plethora of reform options, and find themselves drawn to thought trends that are vying with each other for control over new domains. The individual Muslim may even find himself in crisis as he/she attempts to discern which of the various imported ideas is most appropriate and applicable to his or her situation.

Muslims have the tendency to believe that because certain ideas and schemes were successful in the countries where they originated, they must represent the solution to the problems they face in their own countries. For example, at one point the various competing currents in the Islamic world jumped on the bandwagon of democracy. However, when democracy was transplanted onto Islamic soil by holding elections and broadening the participation of political parties in administering power, the result was a miserable regression to tribalism, racism, regionalism, and sectarianism. This led to the partition of single states into statelets which were ready to flare up at the slightest provocation. The best and safest way to transplant such a scheme from one place to another would have been first to test the recipient soil to see whether it would be a suitable medium for the new breed of crop. However, individuals and nations with vested interests hastened to carry out the operation without undertaking the needed preparation, which turned the whole process into a risky venture that now hovers between life and death.

At this point certain questions present themselves: Why are we Muslims so fearful of the proposal of new ideas, or objective treatments of our current crises based on social and philosophical analyses that enable us to verify new ideas' acceptability or unacceptability against the established values of our religion? Why do we always see a thinker as a rebel against the religion and a conspirator against Muslims, particularly at a time when some atheist thinkers are coming back to Islam and renouncing modern rationalism? Have negative historical images of certain thinkers made us averse to benefiting from theories of change or reform projects applied in other parts of the world based on shared human values that merit attention and application? These questions call for well-thought out responses, and a willingness to reopen issues that have lain dormant for far too long.

There is another issue I might also mention on this occasion. Muslims are witnessing frustrating circumstances whose long-term effects they cannot easily perceive. Examples include clashes among local political wings and groups, rival intellectual and ideological affiliations, the collapse of religious values in the face of overpowering materialistic inclinations, and hasty, unthinking adoption of the cultures of colonizing nations in response to the global media. Hence, in order to ward off the destructive effects of rationalist theories or extremist ideologies, the Muslim community needs to strengthen its defenses against cultural imperialism and penetration by rebuilding its intellectual foundations.

Given this reality, we need urgently to return to a religious consciousness in order to remain steadfast in our faith, and to develop civilizational awareness that will bring about a reawakening in the Muslim community. We need to adopt the motto: "faith and action" embodied in the Qur'anic prayer to God: "Thee alone do we worship; and unto Thee alone do we turn for aid" (*Sūrah al-Fātiḥah* 1:50). We should avoid being like those who provoke God's wrath by refusing to act on what they know, or those who act without adequate knowledge or understanding.

Our need for civilizational awareness under the present circumstances may be seen clearly based on the following two points:

Firstly: Whoever ponders the various phases of Islamic history will see that they are like links in a chain. Some are stronger than others; however, they are compatible due to the commonality of religion and civilization ingrained in Muslims' hearts. Once the role of faith, knowledge, and sound reasoning begins to recede, the links weaken and the chain begins to fall apart. Alternatively, one might liken this history to a relay race in which one generation hands the baton of faith and sound reasoning to the one that follows it. The race continues until a weak and inept person (or generation) holding the baton causes the entire team to lag behind. This is why spiritual and intellectual factors together have such a great impact on the strength of a nation or community.

For those who possess the essential awareness, there are today opportunities to correct these weaknesses in the Muslim community. I am certain that those with intellectual and religious awareness are the missing link that will enable everyone to begin working together in a cooperative spirit, and whose projects will draw more and more willing participants. Every reformer who has occupied a special place in the history of the Muslim community has made critical efforts to overcome the Muslim community's intellectual shortcomings and to fill in the gaps in its knowledge. Overall, however, the Muslim community has neglected its duty to fortify Muslims' minds against superstition and illusion, and to make use of its ideas in such a way as to modernize itself and, at the same time, revive and strengthen its Islamic faith.

Secondly: The contemporary challenges that face Muslims in all areas of life have raised urgent questions in their minds. They wonder what stance they should take on openness to other cultures and religions, and on the need for peaceful coexistence with them in view of their common interests. Which values should be unfailingly preserved, and which of them allow for some flexibility? What does the future hold for them in the face of aggressive multinational companies and the satellite media? How should they cope with rampant unemployment and consumerism, and resist erroneous and perverse behaviors? There are only some of the questions which our political, intellectual, and scholarly elites are afraid to address with solutions that are practical and convincing, especially to young people. Are they afraid that the solutions they propose won't sit well with certain sectors of the society? Have they fallen prey to the illusion that they can simply avoid intellectual controversies? It is indeed an illusion, since the sharpness of such controversies has not abated over time. On the contrary, it continues to intensify. In the meantime, confused youths are left wandering and wondering, awaiting the emergence of a guide who will demonstrate real concern for their future. The fear of attending to these problems has led to the emergence of preachers the likes of Salman al-Awdah, Amr Khalid, Tariq al-Suwaydan, and others. These scholars, few though they be, have distinguished themselves from numerous other scholars and thinkers who, though they witness the deadly attacks being launched against the ideas of entire generations, fail to lift a finger to change the situation. It is only natural, then, that Muslim youths seek out those who can understand their plight and offer realistic ways of helping them out of their predicaments, however simplistic and unworkable some of the proposed remedies may be.

Like it or not, within the space of less than a decade, those who are our youth today will become our leaders. With every passing day I become more convinced that what we need in the present phase of our history is to create and reinforce awareness on the individual and communal levels alike; and that any suppression of awareness or neglect of its effectiveness in preaching, education, and reform will mark the beginning of an era of intellectual extremism, violence, communal strife, and the return to a primitive society.

Conclusion

I HOPE this book has helped readers to realize the importance of applying the aims and higher objectives of Islamic law (*maqāṣid al-sharīʿah*) to all facets of their lives. I make no claim to having exhausted all the ways in which people's lives are impacted by putting *maqāṣid al-sharīʿah* into practice; however, the examples I have cited should be sufficient to demonstrate my points, and I hope my readers will communicate with me to the end that I might clarify whatever needs further clarification, and communicate things in the most suitable manner.

In order to help the general public better understand and apply *maqāṣid al-sharīʿah*, and to help jurists rule on newly emerging situations in light of this understanding, there is a need for further research and writing on this topic. *Maqāṣid al-sharīʿah* encompass all branches of the Islamic religion, and they undergird all Islamic rulings. The Muslim who understands these objectives and how they relate to the overall framework of Islamic law will safeguard against deviations, and will develop an awareness of actions that should be avoided. He/she will know which actions are to be given priority in a particular situation and which can reasonably be delayed. Equally, he/she will clearly understand the benefits of the Shariʿah for men, women and children, and the happiness and fulfillment that can come from conscious practice of the religion based on an understanding of *maqāṣid al-sharīʿah*.

May Almighty God guide me to what is correct, bring my statements and actions into conformity with the truth, and endow me with sincerity in all my actions. I seek forgiveness from Him, exalted is He, for my sins and errors. He is the All-Knowing, the Most Wise, and the One who guides to the straight path. May God's blessing and mercy be upon Muhammad, his household, and his Companions one and all.

NOTES

PREFACE

1 The abbreviation SWT represents the Arabic phrase *subḥānuhu wa taʿālā*, meaning "May He be praised and exalted," or "praiseworthy is He, and exalted."

2 (ṢAAS) – *Ṣallā Allāhu ʿalayhi wa sallam*. May the peace and blessings of God be upon him. Said whenever the name of Prophet Muhammad is mentioned.

3 Meaning literally, "those with a point of view or opinion," the term *Ahl al-Ra'y* refers to those who base their rulings on independent reasoning rather on blind imitation of earlier thinkers or tradition.

4 Meaning, "the people of the hadith", or simply, traditionists, the term *Ahl al-Ḥadīth* came to refer to scholars who relied exclusively on the written traditions handed down on the authority of the Prophet and his Companions (hadith) and the rulings that had previously been derived from such traditions.

INTRODUCTION

1 Abū Isḥāq Ibrāhīm ibn Mūsā ibn Muḥammad al-Lakhmī al-Shāṭibī, *Al-Muwāfaqāt*, Introduction by Bakr ibn Abd Allah Abu Zayd, text arrangement, introduction, commentary and sourcing of hadiths by Abu Ubaydah Mashhr ibn Hasan Al Salman (Khobar: Dār Ibn ʿAffān, 1417 AH/1997 CE), vol. 2, p. 9.

2 Ibid., vol. 2, p. 13.

3 See Muhammad al-Tahir ibn Ashur, *Maqāṣid al-Sharīʿah al-Islāmiyyah* (Tunis: Al-Sharikah al-Tūnisiyyah li al-Nashr, 1978), pp. 20-22, and Wahbah Mustafa al-Zuhayli, *Uṣūl al-Fiqh al-Islāmī* (Damascus: Dār al-Fikr, 1406 AH/1985 CE), vol. 2, p. 1018.

4 See Yusuf Hamid al-Alim, *Al-Maqāsid al-ʿĀmmah li al-Sharīʿah al-Islāmiyyah*, A Series of University Publications, 2nd edn., (Virginia: International Institute of Islamic Thought, 1414 AH/1993 CE), pp. 106-107; Zayd al-Rummani, *Maqāṣid al-Sharīʿah al-Islāmiyyah* (Dār Al-Ghayth, 1415 AH/1994 CE), pp. 20-29; Nur al-Din Mukhtar al-Khadimi, *Al-Ijitihād al-*

Maqāṣidī: Hujiyyatuhu, Ḍawābiṭuhu, Majālātuhu (Kitāb al-Ummah, no. 65, 1419 AH/1998 CE), pp. 58-59.

5 Ibn Ashur, *Maqāṣid al-Sharīʿah al-Islāmiyyah*, p. 5.

6 See Abū al-Maʿālī ʿAbd al-Malik ibn ʿAbd Allāh al-Juwaynī (*Al-Burhān fī Uṣūl al-Fiqh)*, vol. 2, pp. 810-811 and 911-923.

7 Abū Ḥāmid Muḥammad ibn Muḥammad al-Ghazālī, *Al-Mustaṣfā min ʿIlm al-Uṣūl* (Bulaq: Al-Maṭbaʿah al-Amīriyyah, 1322 AH/1904 CE), vol. 2, pp. 285-315; and *Shifā' al-ʿGhalīl fī Bayān al-Shabah wa al-Makhīl wa Masālik al-Taʿlīl*, p. 161.

8 See ʿIzz al-Dīn ʿAbd al-ʿAzīz ibn ʿAbd al-Salām, *Qawāʿid al-Aḥkām Fī Maṣāliḥ al-Anām* (Dār al-Ṭibāʿ, 1413 AH/1992 CE), and *Mukhtaṣar al-Fawā'id Fī Aḥkām al-Maqāṣid al-Maʿrūf bi al-Qawāʿid al-Ṣughrā*, introduced, edited and annotated by Salih ibn Abd al-Aziz ibn Ibrahim al-Mansur (Riyadh: Dār al-Furqān, 1417 AH/1997 CE).

9 See Abū al-ʿAbbās Aḥmad ibn Idrīs al-Qarrāfī, *Al-Furūq*, vol. 1, p. 118 and vol. 2, pp. 32ff, and *Sharḥ Tanqīḥ al-Fuṣūl*, 2nd edn., (Al-Maktabah Al-Azhariyah, 1414 AH/1993 CE), p. 391.

10 See Abū al-ʿAbbās Aḥmad ibn ʿAbd al-Ḥalīm ibn Taymiyyah al-Ḥarrānī, *Majmūʿ Fatāwā Shaykh al-Islam Aḥmad ibn Taymiyyah*, compiled and arranged by ʿAbd al-Raḥmān ibn Muḥammad ibn Qāsim al-ʿĀṣimī al-Najdī al-Ḥanbalī, assisted by his son, Muḥammad, (Riyadh: Maṭābiʿ al-Riyāḍ, 1381-1383 AH/1961-1963 CE), vol. 11, p. 354; vol. 20, p. 583, and vol. 32, p. 234.

11 See Abū ʿAbd Allāh Muḥammad ibn Abī Bakr ibn Qayyim al-Jawziyyah, *Shifā' al-ʿAlīl fī Masā'il al-Qaḍā' wa al-Qadar wa al-Ḥikmah wa al-Taʿlīl*, pp. 400ff.; *Miftāḥ Dār al-Saʿādah wa Manshūr Wilāyat al-ʿIlm wa al-Irādah*, vol. 2, p. 408 and *Iʿlām al-Muwaqqiʿīn ʿan Rabb al-ʿĀlamīn* (Beirut: Dār al-Kutub al-ʿIlmiyyah, 1408 AH/1987 CE), vol. 3, p. 9, and many others.

12 See *Bayān Ahammiyat al-Muwāfaqāt* in Ahmad al-Raysuni, *Naḍariyat al-Maqāṣid ʿInda al-Imām al-Shāṭibī*, University Publications Series, No. 1, 2nd edn., (Virginia: International Institute of Islamic Thought, 1412 AH/1991 CE), p. 93; and Hammadi al-Ubaydi, *al-Shāṭibī wa Maqāṣid al-Sharīʿah*, pp. 97-116.

13 Al-Shāṭibī, *Al-Muwāfaqāt*, vol. 3, pp. 23-24.

14 Ibid., vol. 3, p.24, footnote.

15 Recorded by al-Bukhārī, *The Book of Soul-Enrichers (kitāb al-raqā'iq)*, Chapter on Intention and Constancy in Deeds, No. 6098.

16 See Abū al-Faḍl Muḥammad ibn Makram ibn Manẓūr, *Lisān al-ʿArab* (Dār al-Fikr, 1410 AH/1989 CE), vol. 3, pp. 354-356; Al-Fayrūz Ābādī, *Al-Qāmūs*

Al-Muḥīṭ, p. 396; Abū al-Ḥusayn Aḥmad ibn Zakariyyā ibn Fāris, *Muʿjam Maqāyīs al-Lughah,* edited by Abd al-Salam Muhammad Harun, (Dār al-Jīl, 1411 AH/1990 CE), vol. 5, p. 95; Muḥammad ibn Abī Bakr al-Rāzī, *Mukhtār al-Ṣiḥāḥ*, p. 472; and Aḥmad ibn Muḥammad ibn ʿAlī al-Fayyūmī, *Al-Miṣbāḥ al-Munīr* (Beirut: Maktabat Lubnān, 1990), pp. 260-261.

17 See *Lisān Al-ʿArab*, vol. 8, p. 174; *Al-Qāmūs Al-Muḥīṭ*, p. 946; ʿAlī ibn Muḥammad al-Jurjānī, *al-Taʾrīfāt*, p. 176; Abū Zakariyyā Yaḥyā ibn Sharaf al-Nawawī, *Tahdhīb al-Asmāʾ wa al-Lughāt* (Dār al Fikr, 1416 AH/1995 CE), vol. 3, p. 153.

18 Al-Raysuni, *Naḍariyat al-Maqāṣid ʿind al-Imām al-Shāṭibī*, p. 5.

19 See al-Shāṭibī, *Al-Muwāfaqāt*, vol. 1, pp. 67-72; and Muhammad Sad al-Yubi, *Maqāṣid al-Sharīʿah al-Islāmiyyah wa ʿAlāqatuhā bi al-Adillah al-Sharʿiyyah* (Riyadh: Dār al-Hijrah li al-Nashr wa al-Tawzīʿ, 1418AH/1997CE), p. 34.

20 Ibn Ashur, *Maqāṣid al-Sharīʿah a- Islāmiyyah*, p. 51.

21 Al-Raysuni, *Naḍariyat al-Maqāṣid ʿinda al-Imām al-Shāṭibī*, p. 7.

22 Ibid.

23 Yusuf Hamid al-Alam, *Al-Maqāṣid al-ʿĀmmah li al-Sharīʿah al-Islāmiyyah*, 2nd edn., University Publication Series, (Herndon, Virginia: International Institute of Islamic Thought, 1414 AH/1993 CE), p. 83.

24 Al-Zuhayli, *Uṣūl al-Fiqh al-Islāmī*, vol. 2, p. 1017.

25 See al-Yubi, *Maqāṣid al-Sharīʿah*, p. 37; Awad al-Qarni, *Al-Mukhtaṣar al-Wajīz fī Maqāṣid al-Tashrīʿ* (Jeddah: Dār al-Andalus al-Khaḍrāʾ, 1419 AH/1998 CE), p. 19; Al-Ubaydi, *al-Shāṭibī wa Maqāṣid al-Sharīʿah*, p. 119; Al-Rummani, *Maqāṣid al-Sharīʿah al-Islāmiyyah*, p. 14; Al-Khādimī, *Al-Ijtihād al-Maqāṣidī*, pp. 52-53; and Muhammad Riyad, *Uṣūl al-Fatwā wa al-Qaḍāʾ fī al-Madhhab al-Mālikī*, p. 280.

26 Muḥammad ibn Idrīs al-Shāfiʿī, *Al-Risālah*, p. 512.

27 ʿAlāʾ al-Dīn ʿAbd al-ʿAzīz ibn Aḥmad al-Bukhārī, *Kashf al-Asrār ʿan Uṣūl Fakhr al-Islām al-Bazdawī* (Beirut: Dār al-Kitāb al-ʿArabī, 1414 AH/1993 CE), vol. 1, p. 12.

28 Al-Qarrāfī, *Sharḥ Tanqīḥ al-Fuṣūl*, p. 406.

29 See al-Shāṭibī, *Al-Muwāfaqāt*, vol. 2, pp. 9-13; Taqī al-Dīn Muḥammad ibn Aḥmad al-Fattūḥī ibn al-Najjār, *Sharḥ al-Kawkab al-Munīr*, also known as *Mukhtaṣar al-Taḥrīr,* or *al-Mukhtabar al-Mubtakir Sharḥ al-Mukhtaṣar fī Uṣūl al-Fiqh*, ed. Muhammad al-Zuhayli and Nazih Hammad, 2nd edn., (Makkah: Umm al-Qurā University, 1413 AH/1992 CE), vol. 1, p. 312; An annotation by the scholar al-Banānī on al-Jalāl Shams al-Dīn Muḥammad ibn Aḥmad al-Maḥallī's commentary on *Jamʿ al-Jawāmiʿ* by Imam Tāj al-Dīn

ʿAbd al-Wahhāb ibn al-Subkī, with a marginal statement by Shaykh al-Islam Abd al-Rahman al-Sharbini, vol. 2, p. 233; Tāj al-Dīn Abū al-Naṣr ʿAbd al-Wahhāb ibn ʿAlī al-Subkī, *Al-Ibhāj fī Sharḥ al-Minhāj*, being a commentary on al-Bayḍāwī's *Minhāj al-Wuṣūl ilā ʿIlm al-Uṣūl*, vol. 3, p. 41; Muhammad Mustafa Shalabi, *Taʿlīl al-Aḥkām ʿArḍ wa Taḥlīl li Ṭarīqat al-Taʿlīl wa Taṭawwurātihā fī ʿUṣūr al-Ijtihād wa al-Taqlīd*, pp. 94-135.

30 Al-Shāṭibī, *Al-Muwāfaqāt*, vol. 2, p. 9.

31 For a discussion of the historical development of juristic terminology, see Muṣṭafā Aḥmad al-Zarqa, *Al-Istiṣlāḥ wa al-Maṣāliḥ al-Mursalah fī al-Sharīʿah al-Islāmiyyah wa Uṣūl Fiqhihā: Dirāsah Muqāranah fi al-Madhāhib al-Fiqhiyyah al-Thamāniyah, maʿa Muqaddimah Tamhīdiyah Mūjazah ʿan al-Maṣādir al-Fiqhiyyah al-Arbaʿah wa al-Istiḥsān* (Damascus: Dār al-Qalam, 1988 CE), pp. 58-60.

32 Fakhr al-Dīn Muḥammad ibn ʿUmar al-Rāzī, *Al-Kāshif ʿan Uṣūl al-Dalā'il wa Fuṣūl al-ʿIlal*, p. 53.

33 Al-Ghazālī, *Al-Mustaṣfā min ʿIlm al-Uṣūl*, vol. 2, pp. 286-287.

34 See al-Shāṭibī, *Al-Muwāfaqāt*, vol. 2, p. 86, and Ibn ʿAbd al-Salām, *Qawāʿid al-Aḥkām*, vol. 1, pp. 22-29.

35 See, for example, Ibn Qayyim al-Jawziyyah, *Iʿlām al-Muwaqqiʿīn* (Beirut: Dār al-Kutub al-ʿIlmiyyah, 1408 AH/1987 CE), vol. 1, pp. 292-301 and vol. 2, pp. 49-119; and Abū al-ʿAbbās Aḥmad ibn ʿAbd al-Ḥalīm ibn Taymiyyah al-Ḥarrānī, *Al-Fatāwā al-Kubrā*, vol. 2, p. 29.

36 Abd al-Aziz ibn Abd al-Rahman ibn Ali al-Rabiah, *Al-Sabab ʿinda al-Uṣūliyyīn*, 3 vols, (Riyadh: Imam Muḥammad Ibn Saʿūd Islamic University, 1980 CE), vol. 2, pp. 17-18. See also al-Qarrāfī, *Sharḥ Tanqiḥ al-Fuṣūl*, p. 406; Abū al-Maḥāsin Yūsuf ibn ʿAbd al-Raḥmān ibn al-Jawzī, *Al-Īḍāḥ fī Qawānīn al-Iṣṭilāḥ (fī al-Jadal al-Uṣūlī al-Fiqhī)*, edited, with commentary and introduction by Fahd ibn Muhammad al-Sadhan, (Riyadh: Maktabat al-ʿUbaykān, 1412 AH/1991 CE), p. 38; Al-Jurjānī, *Al-Taʿrīfāt*, p. 123; Al-Raysuni, *Naḍariyat al-Maqāṣid*, pp. 9-10; and Shalabi, *Taʿlīl al-Aḥkām*, p. 136.

37 See Shalabi, *Taʿlīl al-Aḥkām*, p. 13.

38 Ibid.

39 Al-Shāṭibī, *Al-Muwāfaqāt*, vol. 1, p. 410-411.

40 Shams al-Dīn Abū ʿAbd Allāh Muḥammad ibn Maḥmūd al-Iṣfahānī, *Sharḥ al-Minhāj li al-Bayḍāwī fī ʿIlm al-Uṣūl*, edited, with an introduction and commentary by Abd al-Karim ibn Ali ibn Muhammad al-Namlah, 2 vols., (Riyadh: Maktabat al-Rushd, 1989), vol. 2, p. 682.

41 Ibid.

42 Ḥasan ibn Muḥammad al-ʿAṭṭār, *Hāshiyat al-ʿAṭṭār ʿalā Jamʿ al-Jawāmiʿ* (Beirut: Dār al-Kutub al-ʿIlmiyyah, n.d.), vol. 2, p. 322.

43 Al-Ghazālī, *Al-Mustaṣfā*, vol. 2, p. 297. See ʿAlī ibn Muḥammad ibn Sayf al-Dīn al-Āmidī, *Al-Iḥkām fī Uṣūl al-Aḥkām*, ed. Sayyid al-Jamili, 2nd edn., (Beirut: Dār al-Kitāb al-ʿArabī, 1406 AH/1985 CE), vol. 3, p. 294; Jamāl al-Dīn al-Isnawī, *Nihāyat al-Sūl fī Sharḥ Minhāj al-Wuṣūl*, 4 vols, (Beirut: ʿĀlam al-Kutub, n.d.), vol. 4, pp. 76-104; Badr al-Dīn Abū ʿAbd Allāh Muḥammad al-Zarkashī, *Al-Baḥr al-Muḥīt fī Uṣūl al-Fiqh*, ed. Abd al-Qadir Abd Allah al-ʿĀnī, revised by ʿUmar Sulaymān al-Ashqar, 6 vols, 2nd edn., (Kuwait: Ministry of Endowments and Islamic Affairs, 1413 AH/1992 CE), vol. 5, pp. 206-208; Ibn al-Najjār, *Sharḥ al-Kawkab al-Munīr*, vol. 4, pp. 153-157; Muḥammad ibn ʿAlī al-Shawkānī, *Irshād al-Fuḥūl ilā Taḥqīq al-Ḥaqq min ʿIlm al-Uṣūl* (Nizār al-Bāz, 1417 AH/1996 CE), p. 203.

44 For other terms of relevance, see al-Khadimi, *Al-Ijitihād al-Maqāṣidī*, pp. 47-52; Abd al-Wahhab ibn Ibrahim Abu Sulayman, *Manhaj al-Baḥth fī al-Fiqh al-Islāmī: Khaṣā'isuh wa Naqā'iṣuhu* (Beirut: Dār Ibn Ḥazm, 1996), pp. 90-93; Al-Zarqa, *Al-Istiṣlāḥ wa al-Maṣāliḥ al-Mursalah*, pp. 58-60; and al-Raysuni, *Naḍariyyat al-Maqāṣid*, pp. 8-15.

45 The principles spoken of here refer to the notions of essentials (*al-ḍarūriyyāt*), needs (*al-ḥājiyyāt*), and enhancements (*al-taḥsīniyyāt*). See al-Shāṭibī, *Al-Muwāfaqāt*, vol. 2, p. 79, footnote.

46 See Ibid., vol. 2, p. 82.

47 Ibid., *Al-Muwāfaqāt*, vol. 2, p. 9.

48 Ibid., vol. 2, p. 18.

49 Ibn al-Qayyim al-Jawziyyah, *Miftāḥ Dār al-Saʿādah*, p. 408.

50 Similarly, there are more than a hundred Qur'anic passages in which God is described as *Al-Karīm* (The Most Generous). See Muhammad Fuad Abd al-Baqi, *Al-Muʿjam al-Mufahras li Alfāḍ al-Qur'ān al-Karīm*, pp. 214-215.

51 Ibn al-Qayyim al-Jawziyyah, *Shifā' al-ʿAlīl*, p. 400. See also Fakhr al-Dīn Muḥammad ibn ʿUmar al-Rāzī, *Al-Maḥṣūl fī ʿIlm Uṣūl al-Fiqh* (Beirut: Dār al-Kutub al-ʿIlmiyyah, 1408 AH/1987 CE), vol. 2, p. 328.

52 There are over two hundred-fifty places in the Qur'an where God is described as *Al-Raḥmān* (The All-Merciful). See al-Rāzī, *Al-Maḥṣūl*, vol. 2, pp. 306-309.

53 See Ibn al-Qayyim al-Jawziyyah, *Shifā' al-ʿAlīl*, p. 426; and al-Rāzī, *Al-Maḥṣūl*, vol. 2, p. 329.

54 Narrated by al-Bukhārī (hadith no. 5887), and Muslim (hadith no. 2156).

55 See al-Shāṭibī, *Al-Muwāfaqāt*, vol. 2, pp. 11- 13; and Ibn Ashur, *Maqāṣid al-Sharīʿah al-Islāmiyyah* (Tunis: al-Sharikah al-Tūnisiyyah li al-Tawzīʿ, 1978), p. 20.

56 In this connection, see Yaqub Abd al-Wahhab al-Buhusayn, *Raf^c al-Ḥaraj fī al-Sharīʿah al-Islāmiyyah: Dirāsah Uṣūliyyah Ta'ṣīliyyah*, 2nd edn., (Dār al-Nashr al-Dawlī, 1416 AH/1995 CE), pp. 49-92; Salih ibn Abd Allah ibn Hamid, *Rafʿ al-Ḥaraj fī al-Sharīʿah al-Islāmiyyah: Ḍawābiṭuhu wa Taṭbīqātuhu*, Book 30, (Makkah, Umm al-Qurā University: Markaz al-Baḥth al-ʿIlmī wa Iḥyā' al-Turāth al-Islāmī, 1403 AH/1983 CE), pp. 25-94; and Adnan Muhammad Jumah, *Rafʿ al-Ḥaraj fī al-Sharīʿah al-Islāmiyyah* (Damascus: Dār al-Imām al-Jārī, 1979), pp. 25-120.

57 See Ibn Ashur, *Maqāṣid al-Sharīʿah al-Islāmiyyah*, pp. 143-205; and al-Yubi, *Maqāṣid al-Sharīʿah*, pp. 481-484.

58 Al-ʿIzz ibn ʿAbd al-Salām, *Qawāʿid al-Aḥkām*, p. 642.

59 See Muhammad al-Amin al-Shanqiti, *Aḍwā' al-Bayān fī Īḍāḥ al-Qur'ān,* vol. 3, pp. 409-457.

60 Recorded by Ibn Mālik in *Al-Muwaṭṭa'*, hadith no. 1426, and Imam Aḥmad in *Al-Musnad,* hadith no. 2867. Together with its corroborating narratives, this hadith is judged to be authentic. See Nur al-Din Ali al-Haythami, *Majmaʿ Al-Zawā'id wa Manbaʿ al-Fawā'id* (Beirut: Dār al-Kutub al-ʿIlmiyyah, 1408 AH/1987 CE), vol. 4, p. 110; and Muḥammad Nāṣir al-Dīn al-Albānī, *Irwā' al-Ghalīl fī Takhrīj Aḥādīth Manār al-Sabīl*, vol. 3, p. 408.

61 Abū al-Faraj ʿAbd al-Raḥmān ibn Aḥmad ibn Rajab, *Jāmiʿ al-ʿUlūm wa al-Ḥikam fī Sharḥ Khamsīn Ḥadīth min Jawāmiʿ al-Kalim,* ed. Shuayb al-Arnaut and Ibrahim Bahis, 2nd edn., (Oman: Mu'assasat al-Risālah, 1413 AH/1992 CE), vol. 2, p. 212.

62 Al-Yubi, *Maqāṣid al-Sharīʿah*, pp. 106-118.

63 Ibn al-Qayyim al-Jawziyyah, *Shifā' al-ʿAlīl,* p. 429; and al-Rāzī, *Al-Maḥṣūl*, vol. 2, p. 328.

64 Al-Yubi, *Maqāṣid al-Sharīʿah*, p. 120.

65 Al-Rāzī, *Al-Maḥṣūl*, vol. 2, p. 329.

66 See al-Yubi, *Maqāṣid al-Sharīʿah*, pp. 120-121.

67 Ibn ʿAbd al-Salām, *Mukhtaṣar al-Fawā'id*, p. 108.

68 Imam al-Shāṭibī divided *maqāṣid al-sharīʿah* into two categories; objectives of the Lawgiver (*maqāṣid al-Shāriʿ*), and objectives of those accountable under the Law (*maqāṣid al-mukallaf*). He further divided the first category into four classes: (1) the Lawgiver's fundamental aim of instituting the Shariʿah as a complete, perfect system for regulating human existence; (2) the Lawgiver's aim of making the Shariʿah comprehensible to those it addresses; (3) the Lawgiver's aim of defining the conditions for human accountability before the Shariʿah (being a discerning adult, being in possession of all one's mental faculties, etc.); and (4) the Lawgiver's aim of enabling human beings to comply

with the Shari'ah by helping them to overcome the pull of personal desire and to willingly subject themselves to the divine law's claim on them. See al-Shāṭibī, *Al-Muwāfaqāt*, vols. 2 and 3. In this study of ours, we will be drawing on various aspects of al-Shāṭibī's thought as it applies to the process of arriving at legal rulings appropriate to specific situations.

69 Al-Shāṭibī, *Al-Muwāfaqāt*, vol. 2, pp. 17-18.

70 Ibn al-Najjār, *Sharḥ al-Kawkab al-Munīr,* vol. 4, p. 159. see also Jalāl al-Dīn Muḥammad ibn al-Maḥallī, *Sharḥ Jamʿ al-Jawāmiʿ*, vol. 2, p. 280.

71 Ibn al-Najjār, *Sharḥ al-Kawkab al-Munīr*, vol. 4, p. 160; Al-Ghazālī, *Al-Mustaṣfā*, vol. 2, p. 287; ʿAbd al-ʿAlī ibn Muḥammad ibn Muḥammad al-Laknawī al-Anṣārī, *Fawātiḥ al-Raḥmūt* (Bulaq: al-Maṭbaʿah al-Amīriyyah, 1322 AH/1904 CE), vol. 2, p. 262; and the annotation by al-Banānī on Jalāl Shams al-Dīn Muḥammad ibn Ahmad al-Maḥallī's commentary on *Jamʿ al-Jawāmiʿ* by Imam Tāj al-Dīn ʿAbd al-Wahhāb ibn al-Subkī, with a marginal statement by Shaykh al-Islam Abd al-Rahman al-Sharbini, vol. 2, p. 280.

72 Al-Shāṭibī, *Al-Muwāfaqāt*, vol. 1, p. 31. For other arrangement of the essentials, see al-Rāzī, *Al-Maḥṣūl*, vol. 2, p. 320; and al-Zarkashī, *Al-Baḥr al-Muḥīṭ*, vol. 5, p. 209.

73 Scholars of *uṣūl al-fiqh* have differed over whether to refer to the essential translated above as "progeny" (*nasl*) as *nasab*, that is, lineage, descent, or kinship. Scholars such al-Ghazālī, al-Shāṭibī, al-Āmidī, Ibn Ḥājib, al-Fatūḥī, and al-Shawkānī used the word *nasl*, translated above as progeny, while al-Rāzī, al-Qarrāfī, Ibn al-Subkī, Ibn Qudāmah, al-Ṭūfī and others preferred the term *nasab*, or lineage. The word *nasl* may be viewed as more general or inclusive than *nasab*, in that its meaning implies the preservation of one's lineage or descent. See Ibn al-Najjār, *Sharḥ al-Kawkab al-Munīr*, vol. 4, p. 160; Al-Banānī's annotation of al-Maḥallī's commentary on *Jamʿ al-Jawāmiʿ*, vol. 2, 280; and al-Isnawī, *Nihāyat al-Sūl*, vol. 4, p. 84.

74 See Sulaymān ibn ʿAbd al-Qawī al-Ṭūfī, *Al-Bulbul fī Uṣūl al-Fiqh*, which is an abridged version of *Rawḍat al-Nāẓir* by al-Muwaffaq ibn Qudamah, 2nd edn., (Riyadh: Maktabat al-Imām al-Shāfiʿī, 1410 AH/1989-1990 CE), p. 144; And al-Banānī's annotation of al-Maḥallī's commentary on *Jamʿ al-Jawāmiʿ*, vol. 2, p. 280.

75 Al-Shāṭibī, *Al-Muwāfaqāt*, vol. 1, p. 31.

76 Muḥammad ibn Amīr al-Ḥājj, *Al-Taqrīr wa al-Taḥbīr: Sharḥ Ibn Amīr al-Ḥājj* (Bulaq: al-Maṭbaʿah al-Amīriyyah, 1416 AH/1995 CE), vol. 3, p. 144.

77 Al-Shāṭibī, *Al-Muwāfaqāt*, vol. 2, p. 18.

78 See al-Ghazālī, *Al-Mustaṣfā*, vol. 2, pp. 287-289; Al-Rāzī, *Al-Maḥṣūl*, vol. 2, pp. 320-321; Al-Anṣārī, *Fawātiḥ al-Raḥmūṭ*, vol. 2, p. 262; Al-Qarrāfī, *Sharḥ*

Tanqīḥ al-Fuṣūl, p. 391; Al-Zarkashī, *Al-Baḥr al-Muḥīṭ*, vol. 5, p. 209; Al-Isnawī, *Nihāyat al-Sūl*, vol. 4, pp. 83-84; Al-Banānī's annotation of al-Maḥallī's commentary on *Jam^c al-Jawāmi^c*, vol. 2, p. 280; Ibn al-Najjār, *Sharḥ al-Kawkab al-Munīr*, vol. 4, pp. 160-162; Al-Āmidī, *Al-Iḥkām*, vol. 3, pp. 300-301; Ibn Ashur, *Maqāṣid al-Sharī^cah al-Islāmiyyah*, p. 79; Muhammad Said Ramadan al-Buti, *Ḍawābiṭ al-Maṣlaḥah fī al-Sharī^cah al-Islāmiyyah*, 6th edn., (Mu'assasat al-Risālah, 1413 AH/1992 CE), pp. 56 and 105.

79 Al-Shāṭibī, *Al-Muwāfaqāt*, vol. 2, pp. 18-19.

80 Ibid., p. 21.

81 Al-Ghazālī, *Al-Mustaṣfā*, vol. 2, p.289; Al-Isnawī, *Nihāyat al-Sūl*, vol. 4, p. 84; Al-Āmidī, *Al-Iḥkām*, vol. 3, p. 301; Al-Rāzī, *Al-Maḥṣūl*, vol. 2, p. 321; Ibn al-Najjār, *Sharḥ al-Kawkab al-Munīr*, vol. 4, p. 164; Al-Anṣārī, *Fawātiḥ al-Raḥmūṭ*, vol. 2, p. 262; Al-Zarkashī, *Al-Baḥr al-Muḥīṭ*, vol. 5, p. 210; Al-Zarkashī, *Tashnīf al-Masāmi^c bi Jam^c al-Jawāmi^c li Tāj al-Dīn al-Subkī*, vol. 3, p. 293; Al-Qarrāfī, *Sharḥ Tanqīḥ al-Fuṣūl*, p. 391; Al-Banānī's annotation of al-Maḥallī's commentary on *Jam^c al-Jawāmi^c*, vol. 2, p. 281; Ibn Ashur, *Maqāṣid al-Sharī^cah al-Islāmiyyah*, pp. 79-80; and al-Alim, *Al-Maqāṣid al-^cĀmmah*, pp. 163-164.

82 Al-Shāṭibī, *Al-Muwāfaqāt*, vol. 2, pp. 21-22.

83 Ibid., p. 233; See also Ibn Hamid, *Raf^c al-Ḥaraj fī al-Sharī^cah*, p. 34.

84 Al-Āmidī, *Al-Iḥkām*, vol. 3, p. 301.

85 Al-Shāṭibī, *Al -Muwāfaqāt*, vol. 2, p. 22.

86 Al-Āmidī, *Al-Iḥkām*, vol. 3, p. 302, al-Ghazālī, *al-Mustaṣfā*, vol. 1, p. 290; Al-Isnawī, *Nihāyat al-Sūl*, vol. 3, p. 54; Al-Banānī's annotation of al-Maḥallī's commentary on *Jam^c al-Jawāmi^c*, vol. 2, p. 281; Al-Iṣfahānī, *Bayān al-Mukhtaṣar: Sharḥ Mukhtaṣar Ibn al-Ḥājib*, vol. 2, p. 241; Al-Qarrāfī, *Sharḥ Tanqīḥ al-Fuṣūl*, p. 391; Al-Zarkashī, *Al-Baḥr al-Muḥīṭ*, vol. 5, pp. 211-212; Al-Anṣārī, *Fawātiḥ al-Raḥmūt*, vol. 2, p. 263.

87 Al-Qarrāfī, *Sharḥ Tanqīḥ al-Fuṣūl*, p. 391.

88 Ibn Ashur, *Maqāṣid al-Sharī^cah al-Islāmiyyah*, p. 83.

89 Al-Shāṭibī, *Al-Muwāfaqāt*, vol. 2, pp. 22-23.

90 See Ibid., p. 24; Al-Zarkashī, *Tashnīf al-Masāmi^c*, vol. 3, p. 293; Ibn al-Najjār, *Sharḥ al-Kawkab al-Munīr*, vol. 4, p. 163; Al-Āmidī, *Al-Iḥkām*, vol. 3, p. 301; Al-Qarrāfī, *Sharḥ Tanqīḥ al-Fuṣūl*, p. 391; Al-Banānī's annotation of al-Maḥallī's commentary on *Jam^c al-Jawāmi^c*, vol. 2, p. 281; Al-Isnawī, *Nihāyat al-Sūl*, vol. 4, p. 85.

91 Ibn al-Najjār, *Sharḥ al-Kawkab al-Munīr*, vol. 4, p. 163.

92 This is because, if someone with a higher social standing is killed in retribution

for the death of someone of a lower social standing, the former's relatives will rise up in rebellion and, as a consequence, the purpose for which retribution was legislated in Islamic law will not be achieved.

93 This is because, if the couple are compatible in terms of education, ways of thinking, etc., this is more conducive to a lasting union, and thus the purpose of marriage is more likely to be achieved.

94 Al-Shāṭibī, *Al-Muwāfaqāt*, vol. 2, pp. 24-25.

95 Ibid., pp. 26-27.

96 Ibid., vol. 3, p. 31.

97 Ibid., vol. 2, p. 300.

98 Ibid.

99 Ibid., vol. 2, p. 301.

100 Ibid., vol. 2, p. 302.

101 Al-Shāṭibī, *Al-Muwāfaqāt*, vol. 3, p. 154-155; Al-Yubi, *Maqāṣid al-Sharīʿah*, pp. 353-363; And al-Khadimi, *Al-Ijitihād al-Maqāṣidī*, p. 56.

102 Ibn Ashur, *Maqāṣid al-Sharīʿah al-Islāmiyyah*, p. 51.

103 Ibn Ashur, *Maqāṣid al-Sharīʿah al-Islāmiyyah*, pp. 89–90; Al-Yubi, *Maqāṣid al-Sharīʿah*, p. 391; and al-Alim, *Al-Maqāṣid al-ʿĀmmah*, pp. 172-173.

104 Al-Shāṭibī, *Al-Muwāfaqāt*, vol. 1, p. 541.

105 See Ibn Ashur, *Maqāṣid al-Sharīʿah al-Islāmiyyah*, pp. 155-182; Al-Yubi, *Maqāṣid al-Sharīʿah*, p. 411; Al-Khadimi, *Al-Ijitihād al-Maqāṣidī*, p. 54; and al-Rummani, *Maqāṣid al-Sharīʿah al-Islāmiyyah*, pp. 95-110.

106 See, for example, Ibn Taymiyyah, *Al-Qawāʿid al-Nūrāniyyah al-Fiqhiyyah* (Beirut: Dār al-Kutub al-ʿIlmiyyah, 1414 AH/1993 CE), pp. 13, 56, 77, 93 and 96; Ibn al-Qayyim al-Jawziyyah, *Iʿlām al-Muwaqqiʿīn*, vol. 1, pp. 264-302 and vol. 2, pp. 3-119; and Abd Allah Ahmad Qadiri al-Ahdal, *Al-Islām wa Ḍarūriyyāt al-Ḥayāh* (Jeddah: Dār al-Mujtamaʿ, 1406 AH/1985 CE).

CHAPTER 1

1 See al-Qarrāfī, *Al-Furūq*, vol. 2, pp. 217-218.

2 Abū al-ʿAbbās Aḥmad ibn Idrīs al-Qarrāfī, *Al-Iḥkām fī Tamyīz al-Fatāwā ʿan al-Aḥkām wa Taṣarrufāt al-Qāḍī wa al-lmām*, p. 99.

3 Ibn al-Qayyim al-Jawziyyah, *Iʿlām al-Muwaqqiʿīn*, vol. 4, pp. 205-310.

4 Abū ʿAmrū ʿUthmān ibn ʿAbd al-Raḥmān ibn Ṣalāḥ, *Adab al-Muftī wa al-Mustaftī*, p. 72.

5 *Saḥīḥ al-Bukhārī*, hadith no. 100.

6 Shihāb al-Dīn Aḥmad ibn ʿAlī ibn Ḥajar al-ʿAsqalānī, *Fatḥ al-Bārī Sharḥ Ṣaḥīḥ al-Bukhārī* (Al-Maktabah al-Salafiyyah, 1407 AH/1986 CE), vol. 1, p. 236.

7 See al-Shāṭibī, *Al-Muwāfaqāt*, vol. 5, p. 253.

8 *Saḥīḥ Muslim*, hadith no. 1478, vol. 2, p. 1104.

9 *Ṣaḥīḥ al-Bukhārī*, vol. 2, p. 5 and *Ṣaḥīḥ Muslim*, vol. 1, p. 220, hadith no. 1732.

10 *Ṣaḥīḥ al-Bukhārī*, vol. 2, p. 79 and *Ṣaḥīḥ Muslim*, vol. 3, p. 1358, hadith no. 1732.

11 See Yusuf al-Qaradawi, *Al-Fatwā bayna al-Inḍibāṭ wa al-Tasayyub* (Cairo: Dār al-Ṣaḥwah: 1988), p. 111.

12 Ibn Ashur, *Maqāṣid al-Sharīʿah al-Islāmiyyah*, pp. 92-93.

13 Yusuf al-Qaradawi, *Al-Ijtihād al-Muʿāṣir bayna al-Inḍibāṭ wa al-Infirāṭ* (Cairo: Dār al-Tawzīʿ wa al-Nashr al-Islāmiyyah, 1414 AH/1994 CE), p. 90.

14 For examples of such fatwas, see Ibid., pp. 62-88, Hammud al-Tuwayjiri, *Taghlīẓ al-Malāmʿalā al-Mutasarrʿīn ilā al-Futyā wa Taghyīr al-Aḥkām*, pp. 58-88, and Jamal al-Din Muhammad ibn Muhammad al-Qasimi, *Al-Fatwā fī al-Islām*, p. 125.

15 See Abū ʿAbd Allāh Muḥammad Mufliḥ al-Qāqūnī, *Al-Ādāb al-Sharʿiyyah*, vol. 2, p. 45.

16 For a discussion of this issue, see Abū Zakariyyā Yaḥyā ibn Sharaf al-Nawawī, *Al-Majmūʿ*, vol. 1, pp. 90-91; Al-Maḥallī, *Sharḥ Jamʿ al-Jawāmiʿ*, vol. 2, p. 393; Al-Qarrāfī, *Sharḥ Tanqīḥ al-Fuṣūl*, p. 432; Abū al-ʿAbbās Aḥmad ibn ʿAbd al-Halīm ibn Taymiyyah al-Ḥarrānī, Majd al-Dīn Abū al-Barakāt ʿAbd al-Salām ibn ʿAbd Allāh ibn al-Khiḍr, and Shihāb al-Dīn Abū al-Maḥāsin ʿAbd al-Ḥalīm, *Al-Musawwadah fī Uṣūl al-Fiqh*, p. 465; Ibn al-Najjār, *Sharḥ al-Kawkab al-Munīr*, vol. 4, p. 574; and ʿAlī ibn Burhān, *Al-Wuṣūl ilā al-Uṣūl*, 2 vols, ed. by Abd al-Hamid Ali Abu Zunayd, (Riyadh: Maktabat al-Maʿārif, 1404 AH/1983 CE), vol. 2, p. 369.

17 *Majmūʿ Fatāwā Shaykh al-Islām Aḥmad ibn Taymiyyah*; compiled and arranged by Abd al-Rahman ibn Muhammad ibn Qasim al-Asimi al-Najdi al-Hanbali with assistance from his son Muhammad, (Riyadh: Maṭābiʿ al-Riyāḍ, 1381-1383 AH/1961-1963 CE), vol. 20, pp. 208-209.

18 See al-Qaradawi, *Al-Ijtihād al-Muʿāṣir*, p. 88; and al-Qaradawi, *Al-Ijtihād fī al-Sharīʿah al-Islāmiyyah: Maʿa Naḍarāt Taḥlīliyyah fī al-Ijtihād al-Muʿāṣir* (Kuwait: Dār al-Qalam, 1985), p. 175.

19 See Muḥammad ʿAlī ibn Ḥusayn al-Mālikī, *Tahdhīb al-Furūq wa al-Qawāʿid al-Saniyyah fī al-Asrār al-Fiqhiyyah*, vol. 4, p. 120. *Tahdhīb al-Furūq* is a marginal gloss on Qāsim ibn ʿAbd Allāh ibn al-Shāṭ's commentary on al-Qarrāfī's *Al-Furūq* entitled *Idrār al-Shurūq ʿalā Anwā' al-Furūq*. See also Ibn Taymiyyah, *Al-Fatāwā al-Kubrā*, vol. 4, p. 581.

20 See al-Zarkashī, *Al-Baḥr al-Muḥīṭ*, vol. 1, p. 215; Taqī al-Dīn Abū Bakr Abū Muḥammad al-Ḥiṣnī, *Kitāb al-Qawāʿid*, vol. 1, p. 478; Al-Subkī, *Al-Ibhāj*,

vol. 3, p. 177; Al-Isnawī, *Nihāyat al-Sūl*, vol. 4, p. 352; Jalāl al-Dīn ʿAbd al-Raḥmān ibn Abū Bakr al-Suyūṭī, *Al-Ashbāh wa al-Naẓā'ir* (Beirut: Dār al-Kitāb al-ʿArabī, 1407 AH/1986 CE), p. 133. This principle is confirmed by the saying of the Prophet, "The permissible is whatever God has declared permissible in His Book; the forbidden is whatever He has forbidden in His Book, and whatever He has kept silent about, He has overlooked." This saying is recorded by al-Tirmidhī in his "Book on Clothing; the chapter concerning the wearing of furs" (vol. 4, p. 220); and by Ibn Mājah in his "Book on Foods; the chapter on the eating of cheese and clarified butter" (vol. 2, p. 1117).

21 See Muhammad ibn al-Hasan al-Hajawi, *Al-Fiqh al-Sāmī fī Tārīkh al-Fiqh al-Islāmī* (Beirut: Dār al-Kutub al-ʿIlmiāyah, 1416 AH/1995 CE), vol. 1, p. 215.

22 See Abū ʿUmar Yūsuf Ibn ʿAbd Allāh Ibn ʿAbd al-Barr, *Al-Kāfī*, vol. 1, p. 355; Shams al-Dīn Muḥammad ibn Aḥmad al-Sharbīnī, *Mughnī al-Muḥtāj ilā Maʿrifat Maʿānī Alfāẓ al-Minhāj*, vol. 2, p. 377; Ibrāhīm ibn Muḥammad ibn Mufliḥ, *Al-Mubdiʿ fī Sharḥ al-Muqniʿ*, vol. 3, p. 250; and Sharaf al-Dīn Abū al-Najā Mūsā ibn Aḥmad al-Ḥijjāwī, *Al-Iqnāʿ*, vol. 1, p. 390.

23 See ʿAlā' al-Dīn Abū Bakr ibn Masʿūd al-Kāsānī, *Badā'iʿ al-Ṣāniʿ*, vol. 2, p. 137; Shaykh Muhammad ibn Salih Uthaymin, *Al-Sharh al-Mumtiʿ ʿalā Zād al-Mustaqniʿ*, compiled and arranged by Sulayman ibn Abd Allah ibn Hammud Abu al-Khayl and Khalid ibn Ali ibn Muhammad al-Mushayqih, (Riyadh: Mu'assasat Āsām li al-Nashr, 1995-1997), vol. 7, p. 385; and Muhammad al-Musnid, ed., *Fatāwā al-Ḥajj wa al-ʿUmrah wa al-Ziyārah*, p. 110.

24 See al-Kāsānī, *Badā'iʿ al-Ṣāniʿ*, vol. 2, p. 138; Abū Bakr Muḥammad ibn Aḥmad al-Sarkhasī, *Al-Mabsūṭ*, vol. 4, p. 68; Al-Sharbīnī, *Mughnī al-Muḥtāj*, vol. 3, p. 328; And Abd al-Rahman al-Nafisah, "Risālah fī Fiqh al-Ḥajj wa al-ʿUmrah [A Treatise on the Jurisprudence of the Major and Minor Pilgrimages to Makkah]," in *Majallat al-Buḥūth al-Fiqhiyyah al-Muʿāṣirah* [The Journal of Contemporary Juristic Studies], (Riyadh, no. 33, 1416 AH/1995 CE), pp. 22-25.

25 Abd al-Rahman al-Nafisah, *Fiqh al-A'immah al-Arbaʿah bayna al-Zāhidīna fīhi wa al-Mutaʿaṣṣibīna lahu*, p. 66.

26 Championed first by Dāwūd ibn ʿAlī al-Ẓāhiri (d. circa 219 AH/834 CE) in the mid-third century AH/mid-ninth century CE, and later by Ibn Ḥazm al-Andalusī (d. 456 AH/1064 CE), the Ẓahirī school of jurisprudence sought to derive legal rulings by relying solely on the literal, most apparent meaning of the Qur'an, the Sunnah, and the unanimous views of the Prophet's Companions. It rejected reliance on anything it viewed as merely speculative,

including personal opinion (*al-ra'y*), analogical deduction (*al-qiyās*), juristic preference (*al-istiḥsān*), and unrestricted interests (*al-maṣāliḥ al-mursalah*).

27 See al-Qaradawi, *Al-Ijtihād al-Muʿāṣir*, p. 88.

28 Ibn al-Qayyim al-Jawziyyah, *Iʿlām al-Muwaqqiʿīn*, vol. 4, p. 134.

29 Quoted in Abd al-Rahman al-Luwayhiq, *Al-Ghulū fī al-Dīn fī Ḥayāt al-Muslimīn al-Muʿāṣirah: Dirāsah ʿIlmiyyah ḥawla Maẓāhir al-Ghulū wa Mafāhīm al-Taṭarruf wa al-Uṣūliyah* (Beirut: Mua'ssasat al-Risālah, 1992), p. 273.

30 Ibn al-Qayyim al-Jawziyyah, *Iʿlām al-Muwaqqiʿīn*, vol. 3, p. 109.

31 Al-Qarrāfī, *Sharḥ Tanqīḥ al-Fuṣūl*, pp. 448-449 and *Al-Furūq*, vol. 2, p. 33; and al-Yubi, *Maqāṣid al-Sharīʿah*, pp. 574-584.

32 See Yusuf al-Qaradawi, *Al-Siyāsah al-Sharʿiyyah fī Ḍaw' Nuṣūṣ al-Sharīʿah wa Maqāṣidiha: Naḥwa Waḥdah Fikriyyah li al-ʿĀmilīna li al-Islām* (Cairo: Maktabat Wahbah, 1419 AH/1998 CE), p. 231.

33 See al-Qarrāfī, *Sharḥ Tanqīḥ al-Fuṣūl*, p. 449; And Ibn al-Qayyim al-Jawziyyah, *Iʿlām al-Muwaqqiʿīn*, vol. 3, p. 109.

34 See Yusuf al-Qaradawi, *Markaz al-Mar'ah fī al-Ḥayah al-Islāmiyyah*, pp. 130-150; and Badriyyah al-Azzaz, *Al-Mar'ah: Mādhā baʿd al-Suqūṭ?*, pp. 199-216.

35 See al-Qaradawi, *Al-Ijtihād al-Muʿāṣir*, p. 88.

36 See al-Shāṭibī, *Al-Muwāfaqāt*, vol. 1, pp. 184-194; and Munib Mahmud Shakir, *Al-ʿAmal bi al-Iḥtiyāṭ fī al-Fiqh al-Islāmī* (Riyadh: Dār al-Nafā'is, 1418 AH/1997 CE), p. 118.

37 See al-Suyūṭī, *Al-Ashbāh wa al-Naẓā'ir*, p. 257; and al-Qarrāfī, *Al-Furūq*, vol. 4, p. 210.

38 See Ibid., p. 258; Shakir, *Al-ʿAmal bi al-Iḥtiyāṭ*, pp. 254-257, Ibn Hamid, *Rafʿ al-Ḥaraj fī al-Sharīʿah*, pp. 337-348; and Yaqub Abd al-Wahhab al-Buhusayn, *Rafʿ al-Ḥaraj fī al-Sharīʿah al-Islāmiyyah*, pp. 115-130.

39 Ibid., pp. 115-116.

40 See al-Buti, *Ḍawābiṭ al-Maṣlaḥah*, p. 110.

41 Ibid., p. 187. See also al-Ghazālī, *Al-Mustaṣfā*, vol. 2, p. 293; Ibn al-Najjār, *Sharḥ al-Kawkab al-Munīr*, vol. 4, p. 432; Al-Qarrāfī, *Sharḥ Tanqīḥ al-Fuṣūl*, p. 446; Al-Zarkashī, *Al-Baḥr al-Muḥīṭ*, vol. 6, pp. 78-79; Abū al-Qāsim Muḥammad ibn Aḥmad ibn al-Juzayy al-Kalbī, *Taqrīb al-Wuṣūl ilā ʿIlm al-Uṣūl*, ed. Muhammad al-Mukhtar al-Shanqiti, (Maktabat Ibn Taymiyyah, 1414 AH/1993 CE), p. 412; Al-Shawkānī, *Irshād al-Fuḥūl*, p. 242; Al-Zarqa, *Al-Istiṣlāḥ wa al-Maṣāliḥ al-Mursalah*, p. 75; Al-Qaradawi, *Al-Siyāsah al-Sharʿiyyah*, pp. 245-261; and Husayn Hamid Hassan, *Naḍariyat al-Maṣlaḥah fī al-Fiqh al-Islāmī* (Maktabat al-Mutanabbī, 1918 CE), pp. 525-552.

42 Muhammad al-Ghazali, *Al-Sunnah al-Nabawiyyah bayna Ahl al-Fiqh wa Ahl al-Ḥadīth*, pp. 47 and 50.

43 *Ṣaḥīḥ al-Bukhārī*, hadith no. 4073.

44 For a refutation of the former mufti's view, see Ali Ahmad al-Salus, *Al-Iqtiṣād al-Islāmī wa al-Qaḍāyā al-Fiqhiyyah al-Muʿāṣirah* (Beirut: Mu'assasat al-Rayyān, 1996), vol. 1, pp. 330-356. The book is a rebuttal of the views of those who, like Abd al-Munim Namr, al-Fanjari and others, hold that it is permissible to receive interest.

45 Ibn Hamid, *Rafʿ al-Ḥaraj fī al-Sharīʿah*, pp. 312-313; Fahmi Huwaydi, *Tazyīf al-Waʿī*, 3rd edn., (Dār al-Shurūq, 1420 AH/1999 CE), p. 79. In his book *Al-Mujtamaʿ wa al-Sharīʿah wa al-Qānūn* (Cairo: Dār al-Hilāl, 1986, pp. 78 and 88), Muhammad Farhat expresses the view that the Islamic prohibition against usury is unrealistic and ill-suited to people's best interests.

46 See al-Qaradawi, *Al-Siyāsah al-Sharʿiyyah*, p. 253, and *Al-Ijtihād al-Muʿāṣir*, pp. 70-82.

47 See the debate between Said al-Ghamidi and Yusuf al-Qaradawi on the permissibility of women working as actresses, published in *Majallat al-Mujtamaʿ*, no. 1321.

48 See al-Haythami, *Majmaʿ al-Zawā'id*, vol. 3, p. 162; He states, "Al-Ṭabarānī recorded it in *al-Kabīr*...and narrators in his chain of transmission are reliable." See also Jalāl al-Dīn ʿAbd al-Raḥmān ibn Abū Bakr al-Suyūṭī, *Saḥīḥ al-Jāmiʿal-Saghīr wa Ziyādatuh (al-Fatḥ al-Kabīr)*, ed. Muhammad Nasir al-Din al-Albani, vol. 1, p. 383, hadith no. 1885.

49 Al-Haythami, *Majmaʿ al-Zawā'id*, vol. 1, p. 186;
narrated by al-Haythamī on the authority of Muʿādh. Al-Haythamī states, "It was recorded by al-Ṭabarānī in all *al-Muʿjam al-Kabīr*, *al-Muʿjam al-Awsaṭ*, and *al-Muʿjam al-Ṣaghīr*; its chain of transmission includes ʿAbd al-Ḥakīm ibn Manṣūr, whose hadiths are to be rejected." He cites some supporting narrations, though they are rather weak. It is also recorded in Abū Bakr Aḥmad ibn al-Ḥusayn al-Bayhaqī, *Shuʿab al-Īmān*, vol. 2, and vol. 3, p. 347. This hadith has a number of supporting narrations, some of which are traceable to the Messenger of God, and some of which are traceable to one of his Companions and which, taken together, bring the hadith up to the level of *ḥasan*, or "good." (Such a hadith is considered *ḥasan*, "good", due to the existence of other well-attested hadiths that deal with the same issue and have essentially the same message.) See Abū ʿUmar Yūsuf ibn ʿAbd Allāh ibn ʿAbd al-Barr, *Jāmiʿ Bayān al-ʿIlm wa Faḍlihi* (Al-Dammam: Dār ibn al-Jawzī, 1994), vol. 2, p. 980; Abū Bakr Aḥmad ibn ʿAlī al-Khaṭīb al-Baghdādī, *Al-Faqīh wa al-Mutafaqqih*, ed. Abu Abd al-Rahman Adil ibn Yusuf al-Gharazi, 2 vols.,

(Dammam: Dār ibn al-Jawzī, 1417 AH/1996 CE), vol. 2, p. 26; and Abū Nuʿaym Aḥmad ibn ʿAbd Allāh al-Isbahānī, *Ḥilyat al-Awliyā' wa Ṭabaqāt al-Aṣfiyā'*, vol. 4, p. 196.

50 See Wahbah Mustafa al-Zuhayli, *Al-Fiqh al-Islāmī wa Adillatuhu*, vol. 9, p. 41; Sad al-Anzi, "Al-Talfīqu fī al-Fatwā," *Majallat al-Sharīʿah wa al-Dirāsāt al-Islāmiyyah*, year 14, no. 38, 1420 AH/1999 CE, pp. 274-305. See articles published in *Majallat Majmaʿ al-Fiqh al-Islāmī*, year 1, no. 8, pp. 41-65. This issue has been discussed by Wahbah al-Zuhayli, Abd Allah Muhammad Abd Allah, Shaykh Khalil al-Mis, Shaykh Muhammad Rafi al-Uthmani, Hamd al-Kubaysi, Shaykh Mujahid al-Qasimi, and Hamdati Shabihuna Ma al-Aynayn, among others. Some of the aforementioned thinkers hold that it is permissible to adopt rulings from more than one juristic school of thought and to seek out concessions (*al-akhdh bi al-rukhaṣ*). They attribute this position to Imam al-Qarrāfī, most scholars of the Shāfiʿī juristic school, and the Ḥanafī juristic school. It is also the position favored by Ḥanafī jurist Ḥāfiẓ ibn al-Humām (d. 861 AH/14 CE). See ʿAbd al-ʿAlī Muḥammad ibn Niẓām al-Dīn al-Laknawī, *Fawātiḥ al-Raḥamūt bi Sharḥ Muslim al-Thubūt*, 2 vols., ed. Abd Allah Mahmud Umar, (Beirut: Dār al-Kutub al-ʿIlmiyyah, 2002); also Kamal al-Din Muhammad ibn Abd al-Wahid ibn al-Hammam, *Sharḥ Fatḥ al-Qadīr* (Beirut: Dār al-Fikr, 1998).

51 See al-Ghazālī, *Al-Mustaṣfā*, vol. 2, p. 390; Al-Qarrāfī, *Sharḥ Tanqīḥ al-Fuṣūl*, p. 432; Al-Qarrāfī, *Al-Iḥkām fī Tamyīz al-Fatāwā ʿan al-Aḥkām wa Taṣarrufāt al-Qāḍī wa al-Imām*, p. 230; Al-Anṣārī, *Fawātiḥ al-Raḥmūt*, vol. 2, p. 404; Al-Zarkashī, *Al-Baḥr al-Muḥīṭ*, vol. 6, p. 325; Ibn al-Najjār, *Sharḥ al-Kawkab al-Munīr*, vol. 4, pp. 571 and 577; Abū Muḥammad ʿAbd Allāh ibn Aḥmad ibn Qudāmah al-Maqdisī, *Rawḍat al-Nāḍir wa Jannat al-Munāḍir fī Uṣūl al-Fiqh ʿalā Madhhab al-Imām Aḥmad ibn Ḥanbal*, edited and annotated by Abd al-Karim ibn Ali ibn Muhammad al-Namlah, 3rd edn., (Riyadh: Maktabat al-Rushd, 1415 AH/1993 CE), vol. 3. p. 1024; and al-Shawkānī, *Irshād al-Fuḥūl*, pp. 271-272.

52 See al-Shāṭibī, *Al-Muwāfaqāt*, vol. 5, footnote; and Muhammad al-Dasuqi, *Al-Ijtihād wa al-Taqlīd fī al-Sharīʿah al-Islāmiyyah* (Doha: Dār al-Thaqāfah, 1987), p. 233.

53 See al-Zarkashī, *Al-Baḥr al-Muḥīṭ*, vol. 6, p. 326.

54 See al-Shāṭibī, *Al-Muwāfaqāt*, vol. 5, p. 99, and Ibn al-Ṣalāḥ, *Adab al-Muftī wa al-Mustaftī*, pp. 125-126.

55 See Ibn Humayd, *Rafʿ al-Ḥaraj fī al-Sharīʿah*, p. 58.

56 See Ibn al-Ṣalāḥ, *Adab al-Muftī wa al-Mustaftī*, p. 125.

57 See Ibn ʿAbd al-Barr, *Jāmiʿ Bayān al-ʿIlm wa Faḍlihi*; Ibn al-Najjār, *Sharḥ al-*

Kawkab al-Munīr, vol. 4, p. 578; Al-Anṣārī, *Fawātiḥ al-Raḥmūt*, vol. 2, p. 406; Al-ʿAṭṭār, *Hāshiyat al-ʿAṭṭār ʿalā Jamʿ al-Jawāmiʿ*, vol. 2, p. 442.

58 Al-Shāṭibī, *Al-Muwāfaqāt*, vol. 5, pp. 79-105.

59 See Ibn al-Shāṭ's commentary on al-Qarrāfī's *Al-Furūq* entitled *Idrār al-Shurūq ʿalā Anwā' al-Furūq*, vol. 2, p. 117.

60 See al-Shāṭibī, *Al-Muwāfaqāt*, vol. 5, p. 97.

61 See al-Zarkashī, *Al-Baḥr al-Muḥīṭ*, vol. 6, p. 325; and al-Shawkānī, *Irshād al-Fuḥūl*, p. 272.

62 Al-Shawkānī, *Irshād al-Fuḥūl*, p. 272.

63 Commenting on this hadith in his annotation on the *Sunan* of Abū Dāwūd, Ibn al-Qayyim writes, "Ibn Baṭṭah and others recorded it with a good chain of narrators." He adds that al-Tirmidhī judged its chain of transmission to be sound. See Sulaymān ibn al-Ashʿath al-Sijistānī Abū Dāwūd, *ʿAwn al-Maʿbūd: Sharḥ Sunan Abī Dāwūd*, with a commentary by al-Ḥāfiẓ ibn al-Qayyim al-Jawziyyah, vol. 9, p. 244.

64 Ibn al-Salāḥ, *Adab al-Muftī wa al-Mustaftī*, p. 111; Al-Nawawī, *Al-Majmūʿ*, vol. 1, p. 81; Burhān al-Dīn Ibrāhīm ibn ʿAlī ibn Farḥūn, *Tabṣirat al-Ḥukkām fī Uṣūl al-Aqḍiyah wa Manāhij al-Aḥkām*, vol. 1, p. 51, Al-Shāṭibī, *Al-Muwāfaqāt*, vol. 5, p. 91; Ibn al-Qayyim al-Jawziyyah, *Iʿlām al-Muwaqqiʿīn*, vol. 4, p. 175; and al-ʿAṭṭār, *Hāshiyat al-ʿAṭṭār ʿalā Jamʿ al-Jawāmiʿ*, vol.2, p. 442.

65 See al-Qarrāfī, *Al-Iḥkām fī Tamyīz al-Fatāwā ʿan al-Aḥkām wa Taṣarrufāt al-Qāḍī wa al-lmām*, p. 250.

66 Ibn Farḥūn, *Tabṣirat al-Ḥukkām*, vol. 1, p. 64.

67 The reference here is to the fact that, when she saw her husband's patient perseverance in the face of abject misery, Job's wife chided him for his faith, saying, "Curse God, and die!" (The Bible, Job 2:9). According to some Qur'an commentaries, Job swore that if he recovered, he would punish his wife's blasphemy with a hundred stripes, but later regretted his hasty oath, having realized that her words were simply an expression of her distress at his suffering. God then revealed to Job that he could keep his oath in a symbolic way by taking a handful of grass and striking his wife with it a single time, saying: "Now take in thy hand a small bunch of grass, and strike therewith, and thou wilt not break thine oath!" (*Sūrah Ṣād* 38:44). See Muhammad Asad's commentary on this Qur'anic verse in Muhammad Asad, *The Message of the Qur'an* (Gibraltar: Dar al-Andalus, 1984), p. 700.

68 Ibn al-Qayyim al-Jawziyyah, *Iʿlām al-Muwaqqiʿīn*, ed. Muhammad Abd al-Salam Ibrahim (Beirut: Dār al-Kutub al-ʿIlmiyyah, 1991), vol. 4, pp.170-171.

69 More specifically, *bayʿ al-ʿīnah* refers to the practice of selling merchandise to

someone on credit, then buying the same merchandise back from the person for cash, and for a lesser price. It is forbidden because it is viewed as a deceptive means of practicing usury.

70 See Ibn Taymiyyah, *Al-Fatāwā al-Kubrā*, vol. 3, pp. 430ff; and al-Shāṭibī, *Al-Muwāfaqāt*, vol. 3, pp. 108-116, and vol. 5, p. 187.

71 See al-Shāṭibī, *Al-Muwāfaqāt*, vol. 5, pp. 276-278.

72 Ibid., vol. 2, p. 286; Ibn al-Ṣalāḥ, *Adab al-Muftī wa al-Mustaftī*, pp. 111-112; and al-Nawawī, *Al-Majmūʿ*, vol. 1, p. 51.

73 See Ibn ʿAbd al-Barr, *Jāmiʿ Bayān al-ʿIlm wa Faḍlihi*, vol. 1, p. 784.

74 See al-Qasimi, *Al-Fatwā fī al-Islām*, p. 59; Al-Qaradawi, *Al-Ijtihād al-Muʿāṣir*, p. 91; Al-Qaradawi, *Al-Ijtihād fī al-Sharīʿah*, p. 178; Al-Qaradawi, *Al-Fatwā*, p. 111; Abd al-Hamid Mahyub, *Aḥkām al-Fatwā wa al-Istiftā'* (Cairo: Dār al-Kitāb al-Jāmiʿī, 1404 AH/1984 CE), pp. 112-115; And Muhammad Riyad, *Uṣūl al-Fatwā wa al-Qaḍā' fī al-Madhhab al-Mālikī*, p. 232.

75 We are told by Muslim and Ibn ʿAbd al-Barr that ʿAlqamah ibn Waqqāṣ al-Laythī al-Madanī was born during the lifetime of the Messenger of God, while Ibn Mandah includes him among the Prophet's Companions. In *Al-Taqrīb*, al-Ḥāfiẓ ibn Ḥajar al-ʿAsqalānī said, "He was trustworthy and reliable; however, those who class him among the Companions are in error." See al-Ḥāfiẓ ibn Ḥajar al-ʿAsqalānī, *Taqrīb al-Tahdhīb*, (No. 4701) and *Tahdhīb al-Tahdhīb*, vol. 7, p. 237 and p. 240. As for ʿAlqamah ibn Qays al-Nakhʿī, he was a student of Ibn Masʿūd, whom he resembled in character and conduct. Some of the Companions would ask him questions and seek fatwas from him. He died in the year 62 AH, and was referred to by Mālik as a Companion of the Prophet, though in an honorary sense. See Abū al-Faraj ʿAbd al-Raḥmān ibn ʿAlī ibn al-Jawzi, *Ṣifat al-Ṣafwah*, vol. 3, p. 27.

76 See Abū al-Faḍl ʿIyāḍ ibn Mūsā al-Qāḍī ʿIyāḍ, *Tartīb al-Madārik wa Taqrīb al-Masālik li Maʿrifat Aʿlām Madhhab Mālik*, ed. Said Aghrab, 3rd edn., (Rabat: Ministry of Religious Endowments and Islamic Affairs, 1403 AH/1983 CE), vol. 1, p. 179.

77 See al-Khaṭīb al-Baghdādī, *Al-Faqīh wa al-Mutafaqqih*, vol. 2, pp. 386-428; Ibn ʿAbd al-Barr, *Jāmiʿ Bayān al-ʿIlm wa Faḍlihi*, vol. 1, pp. 501-559; Al-Qāqūnī, *Al-Ādāb al-Sharʿiyyah*, vol. 2, pp. 44-55; Al-Tuwayjiri, *Taghlīẓ al-Malām*, pp. 6-47; and Riyad, *Uṣūl al-Fatwā*, pp. 218-219.

78 Ibn ʿAbd al-Barr, *Jāmiʿ Bayān al-ʿIlm wa Faḍlihi*, vol. 2, p. 848; al-Qaradawi, *al-Fatwā*, pp 72-73; and Salman al-Awdah, *Ḍawābiṭ al-Dirāsāt al-Fiqhiyyah*, pp. 89-92.

79 Recorded by Abū Bakr Aḥmad ibn al-Ḥusayn al-Bayhaqī in *Al-Sunan al-Kubrā*, vol. 10, p. 135.

80 See al-Khaṭīb al-Baghdādī, *Al-Faqīh wa al-Mutafaqqih*, vol. 2, p. 390; al-Shāṭibī, *Al-Muwāfaqāt,* vol. 5, pp. 323-324; Al-Qarrāfī, *Al-Iḥkām*, pp. 236-237; and Abd al-Aziz ibn Abd al-Rahman ibn Ali al-Rabiah, *Al-Muftī fī al-Sharīʿah al-Islāmiyyah*, p. 31.

81 Recorded by Imam Aḥmad ibn Muḥammad ibn Ḥanbal in *Musnad al-Imām Aḥmad ibn Ḥanbal,* vol. 1, p. 321; The hadith was judged authentic by Abū ʿAbd Allāḥ Muḥammad ibn ʿAbd Allāh al-Hākim al-Nīsābūrī in *al-Mustadrakʿ alā al-Ṣaḥīḥayn fī al-Ḥadīth*, to which *Talkhīṣ al-Mustadrak* is appended, vol. 1, p. 183, No. 61; al-Dhahabī shares al-Ḥākim's view.

82 Recorded in Abū Muḥammad ʿAbd Allāh ibn ʿAbd al-Raḥmān al-Dārimī, *Sunan al-Dārimī*, vol. 1, p. 69.

83 Recorded by al-Khaṭīb al-Baghdādī in *Al-Faqīh wa al-Mutafaqqih,* vol. 2, p. 416; and Ibn ʿAbd al-Barr in *Jāmiʿ Bayān al-ʿIlm wa Faḍlihi*, vol. 2, p. 1124.

84 See Ibn Qayyim al-Jawziyyah, *Iʿlām al-Muwaqqiʿīn*, vol. 1, p. 64.

85 See al-Qāḍī ʿIyāḍ, *Tartīb al-Madārik*, vol. 1, p. 178.

86 Ibid.

87 See al-Shāṭibī, *Al-Fatāwā*, compiled and edited by Muhammad Abu al-Ajfan, p. 83.

88 See Ibn al-Qayyim al-Jawziyyah, *Iʿlām al-Muwaqqiʿīn*, vol. 1, p. 9.

89 See al-Qaradawi, *Al-Ijtihād fī al-Sharīʿah al-Islāmiyyah*, p. 176.

90 See Abd al-Nasir Abu al-Basal, "Al-Madkhal ilā Fiqh al-Nawāzil," *Abḥāth al-Yarmūk*, year 13, no. 1, 1997, p. 130.

91 See al-Khaṭīb al-Baghdādī, *Al-Faqīh wa al-Mutafaqqih*, vol. 2, p. 390; Ibn al-Qayyim al-Jawziyyah, *Iʿlām al-Muwaqqiʿīn*, vol. 4, p. 197; and Ibn al-Ṣalāḥ, *Adab al-Muftī wa al-Mustaftī*, p. 138.

92 Ibn al-Qayyim al-Jawziyyah, *Iʿlām al-Muwaqqiʿīn*, vol. 4, p. 123.

93 Ibid. p. 200.

94 Ibid.

95 Ibid.

96 *Saḥīḥ al-Bukhārī*, hadith no. 6659.

97 Ibid., vol. 4, p. 122; al-Qasimi, *Al-Fatwā fī al-Islām*, p. 83; and al-Nawawī, *al-Majmūʿ*, vol. 1, pp. 83 and 87.

98 See al-Ghazālī, *Al-Mustaṣfā*, vol. 1, p. 141; al-Qarrāfī, *Sharḥ Tanqīḥ al-Fuṣūl*, p. 446; al-Zarkashī, *Al-Baḥr al-Muḥīṭ*, vol. 6, pp. 79 and 87; al-Āmidī, *Al-Iḥkām*, vol. 4, p. 32; al-Banānī's annotation of al-Maḥallī's commentary on *Jamʿ al-Jawāmiʿ*, vol. 2, pp. 274-283; Ibn al-Najjār, *Sharḥ al-Kawkab al-Munīr*, vol. 4, p. 432; al-Kalbī, *Taqrīb al-Wuṣūl*, p. 410; al-Shawkānī, *Irshād al-Fuḥūl*, p. 242; Abd al-Karim Zaydan, *Al-Wajīz fī Uṣūl al-Fiqh* (Dār al-Tawzīʿ, 1414 AH/1993 CE), p. 240; and al-Buhusayn, *Rafʿ al-Ḥaraj fī al-Sharīʿah al-Islāmiyyah*, p. 270.

99 Al-Āmidī, *Al-Iḥkām*, vol. 4, p. 32.

100 See al-Ghazālī, *Al-Mustaṣfā*, vol. 1, p. 296; al-Isnawī, *Nihāyat al-Sūl*, vol. 5, pp. 77-90; Ibn al-Najjār, *Sharḥ al-Kawkab al-Munīr*, vol. 4, pp 170-171; al-Banānī's annotation of al-Maḥallī's commentary on *Jamᶜ al-Jawāmiᶜ*, vol. 2, pp. 285 and 584; al-Qarrāfī, *Sharḥ Tanqīḥ al-Fuṣūl*, p. 446; Al-Shawkānī, *Irshād al-Fuḥūl*, p. 242; and al-Buti, *Ḍawābiṭ al-Maṣlaḥah*, pp. 115-272.

101 See Ibn Humayd, *Rafᶜ al-Ḥaraj fī al-Sharīᶜah*, p. 48.

102 See Adnan Muhammad Jumah, *Rafᶜ al-Ḥaraj*, p. 25.

103 *Ṣaḥīḥ al-Bukhārī*, hadith no. 38.

104 See Ibn Humid, *Rafᶜ al-Ḥaraj fī al-Sharīᶜah*, p. 42.

105 See Zayn al-Dīn ibn Ibrāhīm ibn Nujaym, *Al-Ashbāh wa al-Naẓā'ir*, p. 92.

106 See Abū Bakr Aḥmad ibn ᶜAlī al-Jaṣṣāṣ *Aḥkām al-Qur'ān* (Beirut: Dār al-Kutub al-ᶜIlmiyyah, 1415 AH/1994 CE), vol. 3, p. 310; al-Shāṭibī, *Al-Muwāfaqāt*, vol. 2, pp. 268-278; al-Suyūṭī, *Al-Ashbāh wa al-Naẓā'ir*, p. 168 and Ibn Humayd, *Rafᶜ al-Ḥaraj fī al-Sharīᶜah al-Islāmiyyah*, pp. 292-293.

107 See al-Shāṭibī, *Al-Muwāfaqāt*, vol. 5, p. 179.

108 *Ṣaḥīḥ al-Bukhārī*, hadith no. 3257, and *Ṣaḥīḥ Muslim*, hadith no. 4682.

109 *Ṣaḥīḥ al-Bukhārī*, hadith no. 126. The implication here is that had the Prophet undertaken such an action, people would have reacted by rising up against him for desecrating what they viewed as a sacred symbol of the religion of their pagan forefathers (the Kaᶜbah having become associated with polytheistic rites after having originally been dedicated to the worship of the one Deity).

110 See al-Suyūṭī, *Al-Ashbāh wa al-Naẓā'ir*, pp. 322-325; Ibn Qayyim al-Jawziyyah, *Iᶜlām al-Muwaqqiᶜīn*, vol. 3, pp. 108-110; and Hassan, *Naḍariyat al-Maṣlaḥah*, p. 193.

111 Al-Shāṭibī, *Al-Muwāfaqāt*, vol. 5, p. 178.

112 See Muḥammad Amīn ibn ᶜĀbidīn, *Majmūᶜat Rasā'il ibn ᶜĀbidīn*, 2 vols., (Beirut: ᶜĀlam al-Kutub, n.d.), vol. 2, p. 123; and al-Zarqa, *Al-Madkhal al-Fiqhī al-ᶜĀmm*, 10th edn., (Dār al-Fikr, 1387 AH/1967 CE), vol. 2, pp. 923-924.

113 See Ahmad al-Zarqa, *Sharḥ al-Qawāᶜid al-Fiqhiyyah* (Damascus: Dār al-Qalam, 1409 AH/1989 CE), p. 227; and Muhammad Sidqi Burnu, *Al-Wajīz fī al-Qawāᶜid al-Fiqhiyyah* (Beirut: Mu'assasat al-Risālah, 1416 AH/1995 CE), p. 254.

114 See ᶜUthmān ibn ᶜAlī al-Zaylaᶜī, *Tabyīn al-Ḥaqā'iq fī Sharḥ Kanz al-Raqā'iq* (Bulaq: Al-Maṭbaᶜah al-Amīriyyah, 1315 AH/1897 CE), Part 6, p. 211.

115 Mashhur ibn Hasan Al Salman, ed., *Qawāᶜid ibn Rajab*, vol. 1, p. 127 and vol. 2, p. 597.

116 See Ibn Taymiyyah, *Majmūʿ Fatāwā Shaykh al-Islām Aḥmad ibn Taymiyyah*, vol. 26, pp. 224-243; and Ibn al-Qayyim al-Jawziyyah, *Iʿlām al-Muwaqqiʿīn*, vol. 3, pp. 19-31.

117 See al-Burnu, *Al-Wajīz fī al-Qawāʿid al-Fiqhiyyah*, p. 255.

118 See Ibn al-Qayyim al-Jawziyyah, *Al-Ṭuruq al-Ḥukmiyyah fī al-Siyāsah al-Sharʿiyyah*, p. 162; Kamal al-Din Muhammad ibn Abd al-Wahid ibn al-Hammam, *Sharḥ Fatḥ al-Qadīr*, Part 1, p. 249; Ibn ʿĀbidīn, *Majmūʿat Rasā'il ibn ʿĀbidīn*, part 2, pp. 123-136; al-Zarqa, *Sharḥ al-Qawāʿid al-Fiqhiyyah*, pp. 227-229; and Abd Allah al-Ghutaymil, "Taghayyur al-Fatwā: Mafhūmuhu wa Ḍawābiṭuhu wa Taṭbīqātuhu," in *Majallat al-Buḥūth al-Fiqhiyyah al-Muʿāṣirah*, no. 35 (1418 AH/1997 CE), pp. 22-60.

119 See Ibn al-Qayyim al-Jawziyyah, *Iʿlām al-Muwaqqiʿīn*, part 3, p. 11.

120 Ibid., pp. 36-38; and Ibn al-Qayyim al-Jawziyyah, *Ighāthat al-Lahfān min Maṣā'id al-Shayṭān*, vol. 1, pp. 330-331.

121 Muhammad Bazmul, *Taghayyur al-Fatwā* (Al-Thuqbah: Dār al-Hijrah, 1415 AH/1994 CE), p. 56; Abd Allah al-Ghutaymil, "Taghayyur al-Fatwā: Mafhūmuhu wa Ḍawābiṭuhu wa Taṭbīqātuhu," , pp. 21-22; and Husayn al-Tarturi, "Fiqh al-Wāqiʿ: Dirāsah Uṣūliyyah Fiqhiyyah," in *Majallat al-Buḥūth al-Fiqhiyyah al-Muʿāṣirah*, no. 34 (1418 AH/1997 CE), pp. 71-114.

122 See Abū al-Barakāt ʿAbd Allāh ibn Aḥmad al-Nasafī, *Kashf al-Asrār: Sharḥ al-Muṣannif ʿalā al-Manār*, vol. 2, p. 718; ʿAlī ibn Muḥammad al-Jurjānī, *Al-Taʿrīfāt*, p. 193; Ibn ʿĀbidīn, *Majmūʿat Rasā'il ibn ʿĀbidīn*, vol. 2, p. 112; Al-Banānī's annotation of al-Maḥallī's commentary on *Jamʿ al-Jawāmiʿ*, vol. 2, p. 356; al-Qarrāfī, *Sharḥ Tanqīḥ al-Fuṣūl*, p. 448; Ibn Juzay al-Kalbī, *Taqrīb al-Wuṣūl*, p. 404; Ibn al-Najjār, *Sharḥ al-Kawkab al-Munīr*, vol. 4, p. 48; and Ibn Nujaym, *Al-Ashbāh wa al-Naẓā'ir*, p. 101.

123 Ibn Nujaym, *Al-Ashbāh wa al-Naẓā'ir*, pp. 102-114; al-Suyūṭī, *Al-Ashbāh wa al-Naẓā'ir*, pp. 182-183; Abd Allah ibn Abd al-Muhsin al-Turki, *Uṣūl Madhhab al-Imam Aḥmad: Dirāsah Uṣūliyyah Muqāranah*, 3rd edn., (Beirut: Mu'assasat al-Risālah, 1410 AH/1989 CE), p. 736.

124 Cited by al-Khaṭīb al-Baghdādī in *Al-Faqīh wa al-Mutafaqqih*, vol. 1, p. 422; and Ibn ʿAbd al-Barr in *Jāmiʿ Bayān al-ʿIlm wa Faḍlihi*, vol. 2, p. 855; and by al-Haythami in *Majmaʿ al-Zawā'id*, vol. 1, pp. 177-78. Commenting on this tradition, al-Haythamī states, "It was recorded by Aḥmad, al-Bazzār and al-Ṭabarānī in *Al-Kabīr*, and its narrators are reliable."

125 See al-Qarrāfī, *Al-Iḥkām fī Tamyīz al-Fatāwā*, p. 218.

126 Ibid. p. 232.

127 See al-Qarrāfī, *Al-Furūq*, vol. 1, p. 167.

128 See Ibn al-Qayyim al-Jawziyyah, *Iʿlām al-Muwaqqiʿīn*, vol. 3, pp. 11-30.

129 Ibid., vol. 4, p. 176.

130 See Ibn Nujaym, *Al-Ashbāh wa al-Naẓā'ir*, pp. 110-114; al-Suyūṭī, *al-Ashbāh wa al-Naẓā'ir,* pp. 185, 192-193; Ibn ᶜĀbidīn, *Majmūᶜat Rasā'il ibn ᶜĀbidīn*, vol. 2, pp. 113-114; al-Zarqa, *Al-Madkhal al-Fiqhī al-ᶜĀmm*, vol. 2, pp. 783-881; al-Buhusayn, *Rafᶜ al-Ḥaraj fī al-Sharīᶜah al-Islāmiyyah*, pp. 349 and 352; al-Turki, *Uṣūl Madhhab al-Imām Aḥmad*, pp. 588-589; and Bazmul, *Taghayyur al-Fatwā*, pp. 47-50.

131 Bazmul, *Taghayyur al-Fatwā*, pp. 47-50; Ibn al-Ṣalāḥ, *Adab al-Muftī wa al-Mustaftī*, p. 115; al-Nawawī, *Al-Majmūᶜ*, vol. 1, p. 82; Al-Qaradawi, *Al-Fatwā*, pp. 95-105; Riyad, *Uṣūl al-Fatwā wa al-Qaḍā' fī al-Madhhab al-Mālikī*, p. 236; and Ali Abbas al-Hikmi, *Uṣūl al-Fatwā wa Taṭbīq al-Aḥkām al-Sharᶜiyyah fī Bilād Ghayr al-Muslimīn*, pp. 57-71; and al-Rabiah, *Al-Mufti fī al-Sharīᶜah al-Islāmiyyah*, p. 30.

132 See al-Khaṭīb al-Baghdādī, *Al-Faqīh wa al-Mutafaqqih*, vol. 2, p. 333.

133 Riyad, *Uṣūl al-Fatwā wa al-Qaḍā' fī al-Madhhab al-Mālikī*, p. 231.

134 Recorded by Ibn ᶜAbd al-Barr in *Jāmiᶜ Bayān al-ᶜIlm wa Faḍlihi*, vol. 2, p. 840.

135 Ibid., vol. 1, p. 753.

136 Ibid., vol. 2, pp. 826-843; al-Khaṭīb al-Baghdādī, *Al-Faqīh wa al-Mutafaqqih*, vol. 2, pp. 360-370; *Al-Ādāb al-Sharᶜiyyah*, vol. 2, pp. 44-51; and Ibn al-Qayyim al-Jawziyyah, *Iᶜlām al-Muwaqqiᶜīn*, vol. 1, p.27.

CHAPTER 2

1 See Abd al-Karim Bakkar, *Tajdīd al-Waᶜy: Al-Riḥlah ilā al-Dhāt* (Damascus: Dār al-Qalam, 2000), p. 6, and (Cairo: Dār al-Taḥrīr, 1980), p. 157.

2 See Ibn Khaldūn, *Al-Muqaddimah*, vol. 3, p. 877.

3 See Will Durant, *The Story of Civilization*, 11 vols., (New York: MJF Books, 1993), especially vol.1.

4 See Ralph Linton, *Tree of Culture* (Shajarat al-Ḥaḍārah), translated by Ahmad Fakhri, (Cairo: Maktabat al-Anjalū-Maṣriyah, n.d.), vol. 1, p. 65.

5 See Ibn Khaldūn, *Al-Muqaddimah*, vol. 2, p. 36.

6 See Abd al-Karim Bakkar, *Tajdīd al-Waᶜy*, pp. 120-126, and *Muqaddimātun li al-Nuhūḍ bi al-ᶜAmal al-Daᶜwī* (Dār al-Muslim, 1417AH/1996 CE), p. 353.

7 See Muhammad Abid al-Jabiri, *Fikr ibn Khaldūn: Al-ᶜAṣabiyyah wa al-Dawlah: Maᶜālim Naḍariyyah Khaldūniyyah fī al-Tārīkh al-Islāmī*, 7th edn., (Beirut: Markaz Dirāsāt al-Waḥdah al-ᶜArabiyyah, 2001), p. 130.

8 Ibn Khaldūn, *Al-Muqaddimah*, vol. 1, p. 33.

9 Ibid., vol. 1, p. 70.

10 Ibid., vol. 1, p. 32.

11 Al-Bayḍāwī, Abū Saᶜīd ᶜAbd Allāh ibn ᶜUmar, *Tafsīr al-Qāḍī al-Bayḍāwī:*

Tafsīr Anwār al- Tanzīl wa Asrār al-Ta'wīl, vol. 1, p. 64.

12 Muhammad al-Tahir ibn Ashur, *Al-Taḥrīr wa al-Tanwīr: Al-Muqaddimāt wa Tafsīr Sūrah al-Fātiḥah wa Juz' ʿĀmma*, vol. 1, p. 208. Ibn al-Qayyim al-Jawziyyah presents a useful, detailed discussion of the concept of divine vicegerency on earth in his book, *Miftāḥ Dār al-Saʿādah wa Manshūr Wilāyat al-ʿIlm wa al-Irādah*, vol. 1, p. 151.

13 Abū Jaʿfar Muḥammad ibn Jarīr al-Ṭabarī, *Tafsīr al-Ṭabarī: Jāmiʿ al-Bayān ʿan Ta'wīl Āy al-Qur'ān*, vol. 15, p. 368.

14 Al-Bayḍāwī, *Tafsīr al-Qāḍī al-Bayḍāwī*, vol. 3, p. 103.

15 Ibn Ashur, *Al-Taḥrīr wa al-Tanwīr*, vol. 7, p. 163.

16 Al-Jaṣṣāṣ, *Aḥkām al-Qur'ān*, vol. 3, p. 378.

17 Ibn Ashur, *Al-Taḥrīr wa al-Tanwīr*, vol. 2, p. 449.

18 Allal al-Fasi, *Maqāṣid al-Sharīʿah al-Islāmiyyah wa Makārimuhā*, 5th edn., (Dār al-Gharb al-Islāmī, 1993), pp. 41-42.

19 Al-Ghazālī, *Al-Mustaṣfā*, vol. 1, p. 483.

20 Abd Allah al-Kaylani, *Ijtihād ʿUmar ibn al-Khaṭṭāb fī Arḍ al-Sawād wa Ṣilatuhū bi al-Siyāsah al-Iqtiṣādiyyah al-Sharʿiyyah* (Amman: Al-Dār al-Athariyyah, 2008), pp.31-32.

21 Ibn ʿAbd al-Salām, *Qawāʿid al-Aḥkām*, vol. 1, p. 69.

22 Al-Shāṭibī, *Al-Muwāfaqāt*, vol. 2, p. 180.

23 Al-Qarrāfī, *Al-Furūq*, vol. 4, p. 92.

24 Badr al-Dīn Abū ʿAbd Allāh Muḥammad al-Zarkashī, *Al-Manthūr fī al-Qawāʿid*, vol. 3, p. 35; And al-Suyūṭī, *Al-Ashbāh wa al-Naẓā'ir*, vol. 2, p. 251.

25 Abū al-Ḥasan ʿAlī ibn Muḥammad al-Māwardī, *Al-Nukatu wa al-ʿUyūn: Tafsīr al-Māwardī*, vol. 1, p. 252; Abū Muḥammad al-Ḥusayn ibn Masʿūd al-Baghawī, *Maʿālim al-Tanzīl fī al-Tafsīr wa al-Ta'wīl*, vol. 2, p. 89; and Ibn Ashur, *Al-Taḥrīr wa al-Tanwīr*, vol. 3, p. 186.

26 Examples include Aḥmad ibn Muḥammad ibn Ḥanbal, *Kitāb al-Zuhd*; Hunād ibn al-Sirrī, *Al-Zuhd*; Wakīʿ ibn al-Jarrāḥ, *Al-Zuhd*; Abū ʿAbd al-Raḥmān ʿAbd Allāh ibn al-Mubārak, *Al-Zuhd wa al-Raqā'iq*, ed. Habib al-Rahman al-Azami, (Makkah: Dār al-Bāz, n.d.); Ibn Abū ʿĀṣim, *Al-Zuhd*, and many others.

27 Abū al-Faraj ʿAbd al-Raḥmān ibn ʿAlī ibn al-Jawzī, *Ṣayd al-Khāṭir*, vol. 1, p. 27.

28 Recorded in Aḥmad ibn Muḥammad ibn Ḥanbal, *Musnad al-Imām Aḥmad ibn Hanbal*, hadith no 13240.

29 ʿAbd al-Ra'ūf Muḥammad ibn ʿAlī al-Munāwī, *Fayḍ al-Qadīr: Sharḥ al-Jāmiʿ al-Ṣaghīr min Aḥādīth al-Bashīr al-Nadhīr*, vol. 3, p. 30.

30 Ibn Khaldūn, *Al-Muqaddimah*, vol. 3, p. 877.
31 See al-Jabiri, *Fikr ibn Khaldūn*, pp. 233ff.
32 Malek Bennabi, *Mushkilat al-Afkār fī al-ʿĀlam al-Islāmī* (Cairo: Maktabat ʿAmmār, 1971), p. 41.
33 Arnold Joseph Toynbee, *A Study of History* (New York: Oxford University Press), 1987.
34 Abū al-Fidā' Ismāʿīl ibn ʿUmar ibn Kathīr, *Al-Bidāyah wa al-Nihāyah*, vol. 7, p. 46.
35 See the discussion on this topic in an article by Faysal al-Qasim in *Al-Sharq*, 9 April, 2006. The author is referencing the exhibition, "1001 Inventions: Discover the Muslim Heritage in Our World". The exhibition has since gone worldwide. For more information, see the official website, http://www.1001inventions.com/.
36 Paul Vallely, "How Islamic Inventors Changed the World," *The Independent*, March 11, 2006. See also *1001 Inventions: The Enduring Legacy of Muslim Civilization*, ed. Salim T.S. al-Hassani, 3rd edn., (Washington: National Geographic, 2012). For further information see also, *Muslim Contributions to World Civilization*, eds., Basheer Ahmed, Syed A. Ahsani, Dilnawaz A. Siddiqui, (UK: IIIT, 2005), and Ahmed Essa, Othman Ali, *Studies in Islamic Civilization: The Muslim Contribution to the Renaissance* (Malta: IIIT, 2010).
37 See Abd al-Hamid al-Najjar, *Fiqh al-Taḥaḍḍur al-Islāmī* (Beirut: Dār al-Gharb al-Islāmī), 1999, pp. 81-122.

CHAPTER 3

1 Recorded by al-Tirmidhī (hadith no. 2517), who judged this saying to be "good" (*ḥasan*), but "unfamiliar" (*gharīb*, meaning that it was related by only two chains of narrators).
2 Al-Māwardī, *Al-Aḥkām al-Sulṭāniyyah wa al-Wilāyah al-Dīniyyah*, p. 5.
3 Ibn Ashur, *Maqāṣid al-Sharīʿah al-Islāmiyyah*, p. 63.
4 See al-Ghazālī, *Al-Mustaṣfā*; Minla Khosrow, *Mir'āt al-Uṣūl fī Sharḥ Mirqāt al-Wuṣūl*, vol. 1, p. 30; and al-Zarkashī, *Al-Baḥr al-Muḥīṭ*, vol. 2, p. 241.
5 Ibn Taymiyyah, *Al-ʿAqīdah al-Wāsiṭiyyah*, p. 93.
6 Al-Shāṭibī, *Al-Iʿtiṣām* (Beirut: Dār al-Kutub al-Ilmiyyah, 1408 AH/1987 CE), vol. 1, p. 222.
7 See Muhammad Khayr Haykal, *Al-Jihād wa al-Qitāl fī al-Siyāsah al Sharʿiyyah*, 3 volumes, (Beirut: Dār al-Bayāriq, 1993), vol. 2, p. 946.
8 Abū al-Qāsim Muḥammad ibn Aḥmad ibn Juzayy al-Kalbī, *Qawānīn al-*

Aḥkām al-Sharʿiyyah wa Masā'il al-Furūʿ al-Fiqhiyyah, p. 165.

9 Muḥammad ʿAlī al-Shawkānī, *Kitāb al-Sayl al-Jarrār al-Mutadaffiq ʿAlā Ḥadā'iq al-Azhār*, vol. 4, p. 529.

10 See al-Ghazālī, *Al-Mustaṣfā*, vol. 1, p. 297; Al-Subkī, *Al-Ibhāj*, vol. 3, p. 190; Al-Rāzī, *Al-Maḥṣūl*, vol. 2, p. 579; and al-Zarkashī, *Al-Baḥr al-Muḥīṭ*, vol. 6, p. 79.

11 Ibn al-Qayyim al-Jawziyyah, *Iʿlām al-Muwaqqiʿīn*, vol. 1, p. 69.

12 Al-Shāṭibī, *Al-Iʿtiṣām*, vol. 2, p. 493.

13 *Ṣaḥīḥ al-Bukhārī*, hadith no. 3610.

14 Ibn al-Qayyim al-Jawziyyah, *Iʿlām al-Muwaqqiʿīn*, vol. 2, p. 236.

15 See Nasir ibn Abd al-Karim al-Aql, *Dirāsāt fī al-Ahwā' wa al-Firaq wa al-Bidaʿ wa Mawqif al-Salaf Minhā* (Riyadh: Markaz al-Dirāsāt wa al-Iʿlām, Dār Ishabīliyā, 1997), vol. 2, p. 119.

16 See Ibn Taymiyyah, *Majmūʿ Fatāwā Shaykh al-Islām Ibn Taymiyyah*, vol. 6, p. 396.

17 Recorded by Aḥmad, hadith no. 12578 and deemed authentic (*ṣaḥīḥ*) by al-Ḥākim. See al-Nisābūrī, *Al-Mustadrak*. A summary of *al-Mustadrak* appears in the footnotes, and al-Dhahabī (hadith no. 2427) agrees with al-Ḥākim's classification.

18 Ibid., vol. 3, p. 77-87; and al-Ṭabarī, *Tārīkh al-Rusul wa al-Mulūk*, vol. 2, p. 647.

19 Jalal al-Din al-Umari, *Al-Amr bi al-Maʿrūf wa al-Nahī ʿan al-Munkar* (Kuwait: 1404 AH/1984 CE), p. 34.

20 *Ṣaḥīḥ Muslim*, hadith no. 78. See also Ibn Taymiyyah, *Majmūʿ Fatāwā Shaykh al-Islām Ibn Taymiyyah*, vol. 28, p. 120.

21 Ibn Taymiyyah, *Majmūʿ Fatāwa Shaykh al-Islām Ibn Taymiyyah*, vol. 20, p. 221.

22 See Ibn Rajab, *Jāmiʿ al-ʿUlūm*, vol. 2, p. 254; Abū al-Ḥusayn Muslim ibn al-Ḥajjāj, *Ṣaḥīḥ Muslim bi Sharḥ al-Imām al-Nawawī* (d. 651 AH/1253 CE), known as *Al-Minhāj: Sharḥ Muslim ibn al-Hajjaj*, vol. 2, p. 23; and ʿAbd al-Raḥmān ibn Abū Bakr ibn Dāwūd, *Al-Kanz al-Akbar fī al-Amr bi al-Maʿrūf wa al-Nahī ʿan al-Munkar*, pp. 225-228.

23 Abū Ḥāmid Muḥammad ibn Muḥammad al-Ghazālī, *Ihyā' ʿUlūm al-Dīn* (Bulaq: al-Maṭbaʿah al-Amīriyyah, 1322 AH/1904 CE), vol. 2, pp. 331-332.

24 Al-Shawkānī, *Kitāb al-Sayl al-Jarrār*, p. 586.

25 Ibn Rajab, *Jāmiʿ al-ʿUlūm*, vol. 2, p. 254.

26 Al-Jaṣṣāṣ, *Aḥkām al-Qur'ān*, vol. 2, p. 619.

27 Ibn al-Qayyim al-Jawziyyah, *Iʿlām al-Muwaqqiʿīn*, vol. 3, pp. 12-13, slightly paraphrased.

28 Ibn Rajab, *Jāmiʿ al-ʿUlūm*, vol. 2, p. 239.

29 An authentic hadith, reported by Abū Dāwūd, hadith no. 4344; and by al-Tirmidhī, hadith no. 2174.

30 Recorded by Abū Dāwūd, hadith no. 4341, and al-Tirmidhī, hadith no. 3058.

31 See Salah al-Sawi, *Al-Thawābit wa al-Mutaghayyirāt fī Masīrat al-ʿAmal al-Islāmī al-Muʿāṣir* (London: al-Muntadā al-Islāmī, 1414 AH/1999 CE), pp. 280-304; and al-Umari, *Al-Amr bi al-Maʿrūf wa al-Nahī ʿan al-Munkar* (Kuwait: 1404 AH/1984 CE), pp. 133-181. The "incident of the Sabbath-breakers" is a reference to a story recorded in *Sūrah al-Aʿrāf* 7:163-166 in which certain people of a certain town had been violating the Sabbath by fishing on this day, since it was only on this day of the week that the fish would come up toward the surface of the water. When some people around them who had been trying to restrain them from this behavior were asked why they were trying to reform sinners destined for God's chastisement, they replied, saying, "In order to be free from blame before Your Sustainer, and that these [transgressors, too,] might become conscious of Him" (*Sūrah al-Aʿrāf* 7:164). When God's chastisement came later upon the wrongdoers, God rescued "those who had tried to prevent the doing of evil" (v. 165).

32 Abū al-Fatḥ Muḥammad ibn ʿAbd al-Karīm al-Shahristānī, *Al-Milal wa al-Niḥal*, vol. 1, p. 31.

33 Muslim ibn al-Ḥajjāj, *Ṣaḥīḥ Muslim bi Sharḥ al-Imām al-Nawawī*, vol. 12, p. 229.

34 *Ṣaḥīḥ Muslim*, 3/1481.

35 *Ṣaḥīḥ al-Bukhārī*, hadith no. 121.

36 *Ṣaḥīḥ al-Bukhārī*, hadith no. 3410.

37 *Ṣaḥīḥ al-Bukhārī*, hadith no. 6673.

38 Abū ʿAbd Allāh Muḥammad ibn Manīʿ ibn Saʿd, *Al-Ṭabaqāt al-Kubrā* (Beirut: Dār al-Kutub al-ʿIlmiyyah, 1996), vol. 7, p. 120.

39 Al-Ashʿath (d. 85 AH/704 CE) was an Umayyad general who led a failed revolt (80-82 AH/699-701 CE) against the governor of Iraq, al-Ḥajjāj ibn Yūsuf (d. 95 AH/714 CE).

40 Abū ʿAbd Allāh Muḥammad ibn Manīʿ ibn Saʿd, *Al-Ṭabaqāt al-Kubrā*, vol. 7, pp. 120-121.

41 *Ṣaḥīḥ al-Bukhārī*, hadith no. 6725; al-Luwayhiq, *Al-Ghulū fī al-Dīn*, pp. 411ff.; and Haykal, *Al-Jihād wa al-Qitāl fī al-Siyāsah al-Sharʿiyyah*, pp. 113-140.

42 Ibn Taymiyyah, *Minhāj al-Sunnah al-Nabawiyyah fī Naqḍ Kalām al-Shīʿah al-Qadariyyah*, ed. Muhammad Rashad Salim, vol. 9, 2nd edn., (Riyadh: Imam Saʿūd Islamic University, 1991 CE), vol. 3, p. 391.

43 The Battle of al-Ḥarrah took place in 63 AH/683 CE between the people of Madinah and an army that had been sent out against them by Umayyad Caliph Yazīd Ibn Muʿāwiyah Ibn Abī Sufyān. The army was sent out because, in response to Yazīd's corrupt rule and his slaying of the Prophet's grandson al-Ḥusayn at the Battle of Karbala in the year 680 CE (10th of Muharram, 61 AH), the people of Madinah had expelled the governor Yazīd had appointed over the city. The ensuing battle resulted in the deaths of a large number of the Prophet's Companions, their sons, and their successors.

44 Ibn Ḥajar al-ʿAsqalānī, *Tahdhīb al-Tahdhīb*, vol. 2, p. 263. Regarding al-Ḥasan al-Baṣrī's position on Ibn al-Ashʿath's uprising, see Ibn Saʿd, *Al-Ṭabaqāt al-Kubrā*, vol. 7, p. 120.

45 Abū Zakariyyā Yaḥyā ibn Sharaf al-Nawawī, *Sharḥ al-Nawawī ʿalā Ṣaḥīḥ Muslim* (Beirut: Dār Iḥyā' al-Turāth al-ʿArabī), 1972, vol.12, p.229.

46 Michael Cook, *Commanding Right and Forbidding Wrong in Islamic Thought* (UK: Cambridge University Press, Reissue edition, 2010).

CHAPTER 4

1 Al-Shāṭibī, *Al-Muwāfaqāt*, vol. 3, pp. 23-24.

2 The principles spoken of here refer to the notions of essentials (*al-ḍarūriyyāt*), needs (*al-ḥājiyyāt*), and enhancements (*al-taḥsīniyyāt*). See al-Shāṭibī, *Al-Muwāfaqāt*, vol. 2, p. 79, footnote.

3 See al-Shāṭibī, *Al-Muwāfaqāt*, vol. 2, p. 82.

4 Ibn Ashur, *Maqāṣid al-Sharīʿah al-Islāmiyyah*, pp. 50-52.

5 See ʿIzz al-Dīn Ibn Zughaybah, *Al-Maqāṣid al-ʿĀmmah li al-Sharīʿah*, p. 78.

6 Ibn Ashur, *Maqāṣid al-Sharīʿah al-Islāmiyyah*, pp. 59-60.

7 See ʿIzz al-Dīn ʿAbd al-Salām, *Qawāʿid al-Aḥkām*, p. 56.

8 Abd al-Wahhab al-Masiri and Fathi al-Turayki, *Al-Ḥadāthah wa mā Baʿda al-Ḥadāthah* (Damascus: Dār al-Fikr, 2003), pp. 36-39.

9 Martin Heidegger, *Nietzsche: Vols. 3 and 4 (vol. 3: The Will to Power as Knowledge and as Metaphysics; vol. 4: Nihilism)*, tr. David Farrell Krell, San Francisco, HarperOne, 1991, p. 203.

10 See al-Masiri and al-Turayki, *Al-Ḥadāthah wa mā Baʿda al-Ḥadāthah*, pp. 12-269; Ridwan Ziyadah, *Ṣadā al-Ḥadāthah* (Beirut: Al-Markaz al-Thaqāfī al-ʿArabī, 2003), pp. 17-98; David Harvey, *The State of Postmodernity: An Enquiry Into the Origins of Social Change* (Hoboken, New Jersey: Wiley-Blackwell, 1991); and Taha Abd al-Rahman, *Rūḥ al-Ḥadāthah* (Beirut: al-Markaz al-Thaqāfī al-ʿArabī), 2006. pp. 77-142.

CHAPTER 5

1 Aḥmad ibn ʿAbd al-Ḥalīm ibn Taymiyyah, *Al-Siyāsah al-Sharʿiyyah fī Iṣlāḥ al-Rāʿī wa al-Raʿiyyah* (Cairo: Maktabah ibn Taymiyyah, 1998), p.186.
2 *Ṣaḥīḥ al-Bukhārī*, hadith no. 2097, and *Ṣaḥīḥ Muslim*, hadith no. 715.
3 *Ṣaḥīḥ al-Bukhārī*, hadith no. 5190, and *Ṣaḥīḥ Muslim*, hadith no. 892.
4 *Musnad Aḥmad*, hadith no. 24899.
5 Narrated and deemed authentic by al-Ḥākim, no. 9/226.
6 *Ṣaḥīḥ al-Bukhārī*, hadith no. 1867.
7 Carl J. Dahlman, Anuja Utz, *India and the Knowledge Economy: Leveraging Strengths and Opportunities*, World Bank Publications, June 2005.
8 Data available at http://data.worldbank.org/data-catalog/GDP-ranking-table.
9 Data available at http://povertydata.worldbank.org/poverty/country/CHN
10 Isam Muhammad Ali Udwan, "Mushkilāt al-ʿĀlam al-Islāmī al-Thaqāfiyyah wa al-Fikriyyah wa al-Dīniyyah fī Fikr Mālik ibn Nabi", Paper presented at the Conference on Islam and Contemporary Challenges, (Jerusalem: Faculty of Uṣūl al-Dīn at the Islamic University, 2007), p.281.
11 Narrated by Aḥmad, hadith no. 11809, and included by al-Haythamī in al-Haythami, *Majmaʿ al-Zawā'id*, vol. 8, p. 291. Al-Haythamī states that the same hadith was narrated by Aḥmad, while al-Bazzār narrated a similar, but abbreviated account, and that the men included in both of Aḥmad's chains of narrators are those associated with the soundest, most authentic hadiths.
12 Ibn Khaldūn, *Al-Muqaddimah*, vol. 1, p. 160.
13 Abd al-Salam al-Harras, "Shurūṭ al-Nahḍah wa Mushkilāt al-Ḥaḍārah", *Majallah Daʿwah al-Ḥaqq*, no.17, (Rabat: Wizārah al-Awqāf wa al-Shu'ūn al-Dīniyyah).
14 *Saḥīḥ al-Bukhārī*, hadith no. 3475, and *Ṣaḥīḥ Muslim*, hadith no. 1888.
15 Ibn Khaldūn, *Al-Muqaddimah*, vol. 1, p. 160.
16 Ibid., vol. 1, pp. 88-99.
17 Narrated by Abū ʿAbd Allāh Muḥammad ibn Ismāʿīl al-Bukhārī in *al-Adab al-Mufrad*, hadith no. 543, and by Abū Dāwūd, hadith no. 5124.
18 Abū al-Qāsim Sulaymān ibn Aḥmad ibn Ayyūb al-Ṭabarānī, *Al-Muʿjam al-Aswaṭ*, hadith no. 2899, and *Ṣaḥīḥ ibn Ḥibbān*, hadith no. 566.
19 *Ṣaḥīḥ Muslim*, hadith no. 2566.
20 *Ṣaḥīḥ Muslim*, hadith no. 54.
21 *Ṣaḥīḥ al-Bukhārī*, hadith no. 4083, and *Ṣaḥīḥ Muslim*, hadith no. 1392.
22 *Ṣaḥīḥ Muslim*, hadith no. 91.

BIBLIOGRAPHY

Abd al-Baqi, Muhammad Fuad, *Al-Muʿjam al-Mufahras li Alfāẓ al-Qur'ān al-Karīm.*

Abd al-Rahman ibn Hasan, ibn Muhammad ibn Abd al-Wahhab, *Fatḥ al-Majīd: Sharḥ Kitāb al-Tawḥīd* (Riyadh: Ri'āsat Idārāt al-Buḥūth al-ʿIlmiyyah wa al-Iftā' wa al-Daʿwah wa al-Irshād, 1403 AH/1982 CE).

Abd al-Rahman, Taha, *Rūḥ al-Ḥadāthah* (Beirut: al-Markaz al-Thaqāfī al-ʿArabī, 2006).

Abu al-Basal, Abd al-Nasir, "Al-Madkhal ilā Fiqh al-Nawāzil," *Abḥāth al-Yarmūk*, year 13, issue no 1, 1997.

Abū Dāwūd, Sulaymān ibn al-Ashʿath al-Sijistānī, *ʿAwn al-Maʿbūd: Sharḥ Sunan Abī Dāwūd.* Commentary by al-Ḥāfiẓ ibn al-Qayyim al-Jawziyyah.

Abū al-Faraj ʿAbd al-Raḥmān ibn ʿAlī ibn al-Jawzī, *Ṣifat al-Ṣafwah.*

______, *Ṣayd al-Khāṭir.*

Abu Sulayman, Abd al-Wahhab ibn Ibrahim, *Manhaj al-Baḥth fī al-Fiqh al-Islāmī: Khaṣā'isuhu wa Naqā'iṣuhu* (Beirut: Dār Ibn Ḥazm, 1996).

Al-Ahdal, Abd Allah Ahmad al-Qadiri, *Al-Islām wa Ḍarūrāt al-Ḥayāh*, (Jeddah: Dar al-Mujtamaʿ, 1406 AH/1986 CE), and the book's 3rd edn.,: (Jeddah: Dār al-Mujtamaʿ, 1422 AH/2001 CE).

Al-Alam, Yusuf Hamid, *Al-Maqāsid al-ʿĀmmah li al-Sharīʿah al-Islāmiyyah* (University Publication Series. 2nd edn., Herndon, Virginia: International Institute of Islamic Thought, 1414 AH/1993 CE).

Al-Albānī, Muḥammad Nāṣir al-Dīn, *Irwā' al-Ghalīl fī Takhrīj Aḥādīth Manār al-Sabīl.*

Al Salman, Mashhur ibn Hasan, ed., *Qawāʿid ibn Rajab.*

Al-Āmidī, Sayf al-Dīn, *Al-Iḥkām fī Uṣūl al-Aḥkām*, ed. Sayyid al-Jamili, 2nd edn., (Beirut: Dār al-Kitāb al-ʿArabī, 1406 AH/1985 CE).

Amir Badshah al-Bukhari, Muhammad Amin, *Taysīr al-Taḥrīr*, 2 vols, (Cairo, Maṭbaʿat Muṣṭafā al-Bābī al-Ḥalabī, 1351 AH/1932 CE).

Al-Anṣārī, ʿAbd al-ʿAlī ibn Muḥammad ibn Muḥammad al-Laknawī, *Fawātiḥ al-Raḥmūt* (Bulaq: al-Maṭbaʿah al-Amīriyyah, 1322 AH/1904 CE).

Al-Anzi, Sad, "Al-Talfīqu fī al-Fatwā," *Majallat al-Sharīʿah wa al-Dirāsāt al-Islāmiyyah*, year 14, no. 38, 1420 AH/1999 CE), pp. 274-305.

Al-Aql, Nasir ibn Abd al-Karim. *Dirāsāt fī al-Ahwā' wa al-Firaq wa al-Bidaʿ wa Mawqif al-Salaf Minhā* (Riyadh: Markaz al-Dirāsāt wa al-Iʿlām, Dār Ishabīliyā, 1997).

_____, *Manāhij Ahl al-Ahwā' wa al-Iftirāq* (Dār al-Waṭan).

Al-Ashqar, Umar, *Khaṣā'iṣ al-Sharīʿah al-Islāmiyyah*, 3rd edn., (Dār al-Nafā'is, 1412 AH/1991 CE).

Al-ʿAṭṭār, Ḥasan ibn Muḥammad, *Hāshiyat al-ʿAṭṭār ʿalā Jamʿ al-Jawāmiʿ* (Beirut: Dār al-Kutub al-ʿIlmiyyah).

Al-Awdah, Salman, *Ḍawābiṭ al-Dirāsāt al-Fiqhiyyah*.

Awwamah, Muhammad, *Ṣafaḥāt fī Adab al-Ra'ī: Adab al-Ikhtilāf fī Masā'il al-ʿIlm* (Jeddah: Dār al-Qiblah li al-Thaqāfah al-Islāmiyyah), and (Beirut: Mu'assasat ʿUlūm al-Qur'ān, 1412 AH/1991 CE).

Al-Azzaz, Badriyyah, *Al-Mar'ah: Mādhā Baʿd al-Suqūṭ?*

Al-Baghawī, Abū Muḥammad al-Ḥusayn ibn Masʿūd, *Maʿālim al-Tanzīl fī al-Tafsīr wa al-Ta'wīl*.

Al-Bājī, Abū al-Walīd Sulaymān ibn Khalaf, *Aḥkām al-Fuṣūl fī Aḥkām al-Uṣūl*, edited with an introduction and indices by Abd al-Majid Turki, (Beirut: Dār al-Gharb al-Islāmī, 1407 AH/1986 CE).

Bakkar, Abd al-Karim, *Tajdīd al-Waʿy: Al-Riḥlah ilā al-Dhāt* (Damascus: Dār al-Qalam, 2000), and (Cairo: Dār al-Taḥrīr, 1980).

_____, *Al-ʿAwlamah: Ṭabīʿātuhā, Wasā'iluhā, Taḥaddiyātuhā, al-Taʿāmul Maʿahā* (Ammān: Dār al-Iʿlām, 1421 AH/2001 CE).

_____, *Madkhal Ilā al-Tanmiyyah al-Mutakāmilah: Ru'yah Islāmiyyah* (Riyadh: Dār al-Muslim, 1418 AH/1997 CE).

_____, *Muqaddimātun li al-Nuhūḍ bi al-ʿAmal al-Daʿwī* (Dār al-Muslim, 1417 AH/1996 CE).

Al-Bayḍāwī, Abū Saʿīd ʿAbd Allāh ibn ʿUmar, *Tafsīr al-Qāḍī al-Bayḍāwī: Tafsīr Anwār al- Tanzīl wa Asrār al-Ta'wīl*.

Al-Bayhaqī, Abū Bakr Aḥmad ibn al-Ḥusayn, *Al-Sunan al-Kubrā*.

_____, *Shuʿab al-Īmān*.

Bazmul, Muhammad, *Taghayyur al-Fatwā* (Al-Thuqbah: Dār al-Hijrah, 1415 AH/1994 CE).

Bennabi, Malek, *Mushkilat al-Afkār fī al-ʿĀlam al-Islāmī* (Cairo: Maktabat ʿAmmār, 1971).

Al-Buhusayn, Yaqub Abd al-Wahhab, *Rafʿ al-Ḥaraj fī al-Sharīʿah al-Islāmiyyah: Dirāsah Uṣūliyyah Ta'ṣīliyyah*, 2nd. edn, (Dār al-Nashr al-Dawlī, 1416 AH/1995 CE).

Al-Bukhārī, Abū ʿAbd Allāh Muḥammad ibn Ismāʿīl, *Al-Adab al-Mufrad.*

Al-Bukhārī, ʿAlā' al-Dīn ʿAbd al-ʿAzīz ibn Aḥmad, *Kashf al-Asrār ʿan Uṣūl Fakhr al-Islām al-Bazdawī* (Beirut: Dār al-Kitāb al-ʿArabī, 1414 AH/1993 CE).

Al-Burnu, Muhammad Sidqi, *Al-Wajīz fī al-Qawāʿid al-Fiqhiyyah* (Beirut: Mu'assasat al-Risālah, 1416 AH/1995 CE).

Al-Buti, Muhammad Said Ramadan, *Ḍawābiṭ al-Maṣlaḥah fī al-Sharīʿah al-Islāmiyyah*, 6th edn., (Mu'assasat al-Risālah, 1413 AH/1992 CE).

Cook, Michael, *Commanding Right and Forbidding Wrong in Islamic Thought* (UK: Cambridge University Press, Reissue edition, 2010).

Dahlman, Carl J., Anuja Utz, *India and the Knowledge Economy: Leveraging Strengths and Opportunities*, World Bank Publications, June 2005.

Al-Dārimī, Abū Muḥammad ʿAbd Allāh ibn ʿAbd al-Raḥmān, *Sunan al-Dārimī.*

Al-Dasuqi, Muhammad, *Al-Ijtihād wa al-Taqlīd fī al-Sharīʿah al-Islāmiyyah* (Doha: Dār al-Thaqāfah, 1987).

Durant, Will, *The Story of Civilization*, 11 vols., (New York: MJF Books, 1993).

Farhat, Muhammad Nur, *Al-Mujtamaʿ ww al al-Sharīʿah wa al-Qānūn* (Cairo: Dār al-Hilāl, 1986).

Al-Fasi, Allal, *Maqāṣid al-Sharīʿah al-Islāmiyyah wa Makārimuhā*, 5th edn., (Dār al-Gharb al-Islāmī, 1993).

al-Fawzan, Salih ibn Fawzan ibn Abd Allah, *Al-Irshād ilā Ṣaḥīḥ al-Iʿtiqād wa al-Radd ʿalā Ahl al-Shirk wa al-Ilḥād* (Riyadh: Al-Imām Muḥammad ibn Saʿūd Islamic University, 1411 AH/1990 CE).

Al-Fayrūz Ābādī, Abū al-Ṭāhir Muḥammad ibn Yaʿqūb, *Al-Qāmūs al-Muḥīṭ*, 2nd edn., (Mu'assasat al-Risālah, 1407 AH/1987 CE).

Al-Fayyumī, Aḥmad ibn Muḥammad ibn ʿAlī, *Al-Miṣbāḥ al-Munīr* (Beirut: Maktabat Lubnān, 1990).

Al-Ghamidi, Said ibn Nasir, *Zaghal al-Duʿāh* (Jeddah: Dār al-Andalus al-Khaḍrā', 1416 AH/1995 CE).

Al-Ghazālī, Abū Ḥāmid Muḥammad ibn Muḥammad, *Iḥyā' ʿUlūm al-Dīn.*

______, *Shifā' al-ʿGhalīl fī Bayān al-Shabah wa al-Makhīl wa Masālik al-Taʿlīl.*

______, *al-Mustaṣfā min ʿIlm al-Uṣūl* (Bulaq: al-Maṭbaʿah al-Amīriyyah, 1322 AH/1904 CE).

Al-Ghazali, Muhammad, *Al-Sunnah al-Nabawiyyah Bayna Ahl al-Fiqh…wa Ahl al-Ḥadīth*.

Al-Ghutaymil, Abd Allah, "Taghayyur al-Fatwā: Mafhūmuhu wa Ḍawābiṭuhu wa Taṭbīqātuhu," *Majallat al-Buḥūth al-Fiqhiyyah al-Muᶜāṣirah*, no. 35, 1418 AH/1997 CE, pp. 21-22.

Al-Hajawī, Muḥammad ibn al-Ḥasan, *Al-Fikr al-Sāmī fī Tārīkh al-Fiqh al-Islāmī* (Beirut, Dār al-Kutub al-ᶜIlmiyyah, 1416 AH/1995 CE).

Al-Ḥājj, Muḥammad ibn Amīr, *Al-Taqrīr wa al-Taḥbīr: Sharḥ ibn Amīr al-Ḥājj* (Bulaq: al-Maṭbaᶜah al-Amīriyyah, 1416 AH/1995 CE).

Al-Harras, Abd al-Salam , "Shurūṭ al-Nahḍah wa Mushkilāt al-Ḥaḍārah", *Majallah Daᶜwah al-Ḥaqq*, no.17, (Rabat: Wizārah al-Awqāf wa al-Shu'ūn al-Dīniyyah).

Harvey, David, *The State of Postmodernity: An Enquiry Into the Origins of Social Change* (Hoboken, New Jersey: Wiley-Blackwell, 1991).

Hassan, Husayn Hamid Hassan, *Naḍariyat al-Maṣlaḥah fī al-Fiqh al-Islāmī* (Maktabat al-Mutanabbī, 1918 CE).

Haykal, Muhammad Khayr, *Al-Jihād wa al-Qitāl fī al-Siyāsah al-Sharᶜiyyah*. 3 vols., (Beirut: Dār al-Bayāriq, 1993).

Al-Haythami, Nur al-Din Ali, *Majmaᶜ al-Zawā'id wa Manbaᶜ al-Fawā'id* (Beirut: Dār al-Kutub al-ᶜIlmiyyah, 1408 AH/1987 CE).

Hawwā, Said, *Fuṣūl fī al-Imrah wa al-Amīr*, 2nd edn., (Cairo: Dār al-Salām, 1403 AH/1983 CE).

Heidegger, Martin, *Nietzsche: Vols. 3 and 4 (vol. 3: The Will to Power as Knowledge and as Metaphysics; vol. 4: Nihilism)*, tr. David Farrell Krell, San Francisco, HarperOne, 1991, p. 203.

Al-Hijjāwī, Sharaf al-Dīn Abū al-Najā Mūsā ibn Aḥmad, *Al-Iqnāᶜ*.

Al-Hikmi, Ali Abbas, *Uṣūl al-Fatwā wa Taṭbīq al-Aḥkām al-Sharᶜiyyah fī Bilād Ghayr al-Muslimīn*.

Al-Hilali, Majdi, *Fiqh al-Awlawiyāt fī al-Islām* (Dār al-Tawzīᶜ, 1414 AH/1993 CE).

Al-Ḥiṣnī, Taqī al-Dīn Abū Bakr Abū Muḥammad, *Kitāb al-Qawāᶜid*.

Huwaydi, Fahmi, *Tazyīf al-Waᶜy*, 3rd edn., (Dār al-Shurūq: 1420 AH/1999 CE).

Ibn ᶜAbd al-Barr, Abū ᶜUmar Yūsuf ibn ᶜAbd Allāh, *Jāmiᶜ Bayān al-ᶜIlm wa Faḍlihi* (Al-Dammam: Dār ibn al-Jawzī, 1994).

______, *al-Kāfī*.

Ibn ᶜAbd al-Salām, ᶜIzz al-Dīn ᶜAbd al-ᶜAzīz, *Qawāᶜid al-Aḥkām fī Maṣāliḥ al-Anām* (Dār al-Ṭibāᶜ, 1413 AH/1992 CE).

______, *Mukhtaṣar al-Fawā'id fī Aḥkām al-Maqāṣid al-Maᶜrūf bi al-*

Qawā'id al-Ṣughrā. Introduced, edited and annotated by Salih ibn Abd al-Aziz ibn Ibrahim al-Mansur, (Riyadh: Dār al-Furqān, 1417 AH/1997 CE).

Ibn Abī 'Āṣim, Abū Bakr al-Shaybānī, *Al-Zuhd*, ed. Abd al-Ali Abd al-Hamid Hamid, (Cairo: Dār al-Rayyān li al-Turāth, 1988).

Ibn 'Ābidīn, Muḥammad Amīn *Majmū'at Rasā'il ibn 'Ābidīn*, 2 vols., (Beirut: 'Ālam al-Kutub, n.d.).

Ibn Ashur, Muhammad al-Tahir, *Al-Taḥrīr wa al-Tanwīr: Al-Muqaddimāt wa Tafsīr Sūrah al-Fātiḥah wa Juz' 'Amma*.

_____, *Maqāṣid al-Sharī'ah al-Islāmiyyah* (Tunis: Al-Sharikah al-Tūnisiyah li al-Nashr, 1978).

Ibn al-Athīr, 'Izz al-Dīn, *Al-Kāmil fī al-Tārīkh*.

Ibn Burhān, Abū al-Fatḥ Aḥmad ibn 'Alī, *Al-Wuṣūl ilā al-Uṣūl*, 2 vols., edited by Abd al-Hamid Ali Abu Zunayd, (Riyadh: Maktabat al-Ma'ārif, 1404 AH/1983 CE).

Ibn Dāwūd, 'Abd al-Raḥmān ibn Abū Bakr, *Al-Kanz al-Akbar fī al-Amr bi al-Ma'rūf wa al-Nahī 'an al-Munkar*.

Ibn Farḥūn, Burhān al-Dīn Ibrāhīm ibn 'Alī, *Tabṣirat al-Ḥukkām fī Uṣūl al-Aqḍiyah wa Manāhij al-Aḥkām*.

Ibn Fāris, Abū al-Ḥusayn Aḥmad ibn Zakariyyā, *Mu'jam Maqāyīs al-Lughah*, ed., Abd al-Salam Muhammad Harun, (Dār al-Jīl, 1411 AH/1990 CE).

Ibn al-Hammam, Kamal al-Din Muhammad ibn Abd al-Wahid. *Sharḥ Fatḥ al-Qadīr* (Beirut: Dār al-Fikr, 1998).

Ibn Ḥanbal, Aḥmad ibn Muḥammad, *Kitāb al-Zuhd*.

_____, *Musnad al-Imām Aḥmad ibn Ḥanbal*.

Ibn Ḥajar al-'Asqalānī, *Taqrīb al-Tahdhīb*.

_____, *Talkhīṣ al-Ḥabīr fī Takhrīj Aḥādīth al-Rāfi'ī al-Kabīr*, Compiled, arranged, and edited by Abd Allah Hashim Yamani al-Madani, (1384AH/1964 CE).

_____, *Tahdhīb al-Tahdhīb*.

_____, *Fatḥ al-Bārī Sharḥ Ṣaḥīḥ al-Bukhārī* (al-Maktabah al-Salafiyyah, 1407 AH/1986 CE).

Ibn Ḥazm, Abū Muḥammad 'Alī Aḥmad, *Marātib al-Ijmā' fī al-'Ibādāt wa al-Mu'āmalāt wa al-I'tiqādāt*.

Ibn Hamid, Salih ibn Abd Allah, *Raf' al-Ḥaraj fī al-Sharī'ah al-Islāmiyyah: Ḍawābiṭuhu wa Taṭbīqātuhu* (Makkah al-Mukarramah: Umm al-Qurā University, 1403 AH/1983 CE).

Ibn al-Jawzī, Abū al-Maḥāsin Yūsuf ibn 'Abd al-Raḥmān, *Al-Īḍāḥ fī Qawānīn al-Iṣṭilāḥ fī al-Jadal al-Uṣūlī al-Fiqhī*, Edited, with commentary and introduction, by Fahd ibn Muhammad al-Sadhan, (Riyadh: Maktabat al-ᶜUbaykān, 1412 AH/1991 CE).

Ibn Juzay al-Kalbī, *Taqrīb al-Wuṣūl Ilā ᶜIlm al-Wuṣūl*, ed., Muhammad al-Mukhtar al-Shanqiti, (Maktabat ibn Taymiyyah, 1414 AH/1993 CE).

_____, *Qawānīn al-Aḥkām al-Sharᶜiyyah wa Masā'il al-Furūᶜ al-Fiqhiyyah*.

Ibn Kathīr, Abū al-Fidā' Ismāᶜīl ibn ᶜUmar, *Al-Bidāyah wa al-Nihāyah*.

_____, *Tafsīr al-Qur'ān al-ᶜAẓīm* (Dār Ṭībah, 1418 AH/1997 CE).

Al-Kaylani, Abd Allah, *Ijtihād ᶜUmar ibn al-Khaṭṭāb fī Arḍ al-Sawād wa Ṣilatuhū bi al-Siyāsah al-Iqtiṣādiyyah al-Sharᶜiyyah* (Amman: Al-Dār al-Athariyyah, 2008).

Ibn Khaldūn, Abū Zayd ᶜAbd al-Raḥmān ibn Muḥammad, *Al-Muqaddimah*.

Ibn Manṣūr, Abū al-Faḍl Muḥammad ibn Makram, *Lisān al-ᶜArab* (Damascus: Dār al-Fikr, 1410 AH/1989 CE).

Ibn al-Mubārak, Abū ᶜAbd al-Raḥmān ᶜAbd Allāh, *Al-Zuhd wa al-Raqā'iq*, ed., Habib al-Rahman al-Azami, (Makkah al-Mukarramah: Dār al-Bāz, n.d.).

Ibn Mufliḥ, Ibrāhīm ibn Muḥammad, *Al-Mubdiᶜ fī Sharḥ al-Muqniᶜ*.

Ibn al-Najjār, Taqī al-Dīn Muḥammad Aḥmad al-Fattūḥī, *Sharḥ al-Kawkab al-Munīr*, also known as *Mukhtaṣar al-Taḥrīr*, or *al-Mukhtabar al-Mubtakir Sharḥ al-Mukhtaṣar fī Uṣūl al-Fiqh*, ed., Muhammad al-Zuhayli and Nazih Hammad, 2nd edn., (Makkah: Umm al-Qurā University, 1413 AH/1992 CE).

Ibn Nujaym, Zayn al-Dīn ibn Ibrāhīm, *Al-Ashbāh wa al-Naẓā'ir*.

Ibn Qayyim al-Jawziyyah, Abū ᶜAbd Allāh Muḥammad ibn Abū Bakr, *Shifā' al-ᶜAlīl fī Masā'il al-Qaḍā' wa al-Qadar wa al-Ḥikmah wa al-Taᶜlīl*.

_____, *Ighāthat al-Lahfān min Maṣā'id al-Shayṭān*.

_____, *Iᶜlām al-Muwaqqiᶜīn ᶜan Rabb al-ᶜĀlamīn* (Beirut: Dār al-Kutub al-ᶜIlmiyyah, 1408 AH/1987 CE, and also 1991).

_____, *Al-Kalām ᶜAlā Mas'alat al-Samāᶜ*, ed., Rashīd ibn ᶜAbd al-ᶜAzīz al-Ḥamd, (Riyadh, Dār al-ᶜĀṣimah, 1409 AH/1988 CE).

_____, *Madārij al-Sālikīn bayna Manāzil Iyyāka Naᶜbudu wa Iyyāka Nastaᶜīn* (Beirut, Dār al-Kutub al-ᶜIlmiyyah, n.d.).

_____, *Miftāḥ Dār al-Saᶜādah Wa Manshūr Wilāyat al-ᶜIlm wa al-Irādah*.

_____, *Al-Ṭuruq al-Ḥukmiyyah fī al-Siyāsah al-Sharᶜiyyah*.

Ibn Qudāmah al-Maqdisī, Abū Muḥammad ᶜAbd Allāh ibn Aḥmad, *Rawḍat al-Nāḍir wa Jannat al-Munāḍir fī Uṣūl al-Fiqh ᶜalā Madhhab al-Imām Aḥmad ibn Ḥanbal*, Edited and annotated by Abd al-Karim ibn Ali ibn

Muhammad al-Namlah, 3rd edn., (Riyadh: Maktabat al-Rushd, 1415 AH/1993 CE).

Ibn Rajab, Abū al-Faraj ʿAbd al-Raḥmān ibn Aḥmad, *Jāmiʿ al-ʿUlūm wa al-Ḥikam fī Sharḥ Khamsīn Ḥadīth min Jawāmiʿ al-Kalim*, ed., Shuayb al-Arnaut and Ibrahim Bahis, 2nd edn., (Oman: Mu'assasat al-Risālah, 1413 AH/1992 CE).

Ibn Saʿd, Abū ʿAbd Allāh Muḥammad ibn Manīʿ, *Al-Ṭabaqāt al-Kubrā*, (Beirut: Dār al-Kutub al-ʿIlmiyyah, 1996).

Ibn al-Ṣalāḥ, Abū ʿAmrū ʿUthmān ibn ʿAbd al-Raḥmān, *Adab al-Muftī wa al-Mustaftī*.

Ibn al-Sirrī, Hunād, *Al-Zuhd*.

Ibn Taymiyyah, Aḥmad ibn ʿAbd al-Ḥalīm, *Al-Siyāsah al-Sharʿiyyah fī Iṣlāḥ al-Rāʿī wa al-Raʿiyyah* (Cairo: Maktabah ibn Taymiyyah, 1998).

Ibn Taymiyyah al-Ḥarrānī, Abū al-ʿAbbās Aḥmad ibn ʿAbd al-Halīm, Majd al-Dīn Abū al-Barakāt ʿAbd al-Salām ibn ʿAbd Allāh ibn al-Khiḍr and Shihāb al-Dīn Abū al-Maḥāsin ʿAbd al-Ḥalīm, *Al-Musawwadah fī Uṣūl al-Fiqh*.

Ibn Taymiyyah al-Ḥarrānī, Abū al-ʿAbbās Aḥmad ibn ʿAbd al-Ḥalīm, *Iqtiḍā' al-Ṣirāṭ al-Mustaqīm Mukhālafāt Aṣḥāb al-Jaḥīm*, ed., Nasir al-Aql, 3rd edn., (Riyadh: Maktabat al-Rushd, 1414 AH/1993 CE).

______, *Al-ʿAqīdah al-Wāsiṭiyyah*, Commentary by Salih ibn Fawzan ibn Abd Allah al-Fawzan.

______, *Al-Fatāwā al-Kubrā*.

______, *Al-Qawāʿid al-Nūrāniyyah al-Fiqhiyyah* (Beirut: Dār al-Kutub al-ʿIlmiyyah, 1414 AH/1993 CE).

______, *Majmūʿ Fatāwā Shaykh al-Islām Aḥmad ibn Taymiyyah*, Compiled and arranged by Abd al-Rahman ibn Muhammad ibn Qasim al-Asimi al-Najdi al-Hanbali with assistance from his son Muhammad, (Riyadh: Maṭābiʿ al-Riyāḍ, 1381-1383 AH/1961-1963 CE).

______, *Minhāj al-Sunnah al-Nabawiyyah fī Naqḍ Kalām al-Shīʿah al-Qadariyah*, ed., Muhammad Rashad Salim, vol. 9, 2nd edn., (Riyadh: Imam Saʿūd Islamic University, 1991 CE).

Ibn Zughaybah, ʿIzz al-Dīn, *Al-Maqāṣid al-ʿĀmmah li al-Sharīʿah*.

Al-Iṣbahānī, Abū Nuʿaym Aḥmad ibn ʿAbd Allāh, *Ḥilyat al-Awliyā' wa Ṭabaqāt al-Aṣfiyā'*.

Al-Iṣfahānī, Shams al-Dīn Abū ʿAbd Allāh Muḥammad ibn Maḥmūd, *Bayān al-Mukhtaṣar: Sharḥ Mukhtaṣar ibn al-Ḥājib*.

_____, *Sharḥ al-Minhāj li al-Bayḍāwī fī ʿIlm al-Uṣūl*, ed., with an introduction and commentary by Abd al-Karm ibn Ali ibn Muhammad al-Namlah, (Riyadh, Maktabat al-Rushd, 1989).

Al-Isnawī, Jamāl al-Dīn, *Nihāyat al-Sūl fī Sharḥ Minhāj al-Wuṣūl*, 4 vols., (Beirut: ʿĀlam al-Kutub, n.d.).

Al-Jabiri, Muhammad Abid, *Fikr ibn Khaldūn: Al-ʿAṣabiyyah wa al-Dawlah: Maʿālim Naḍariyyah Khaldūniyyah fī al-Tārīkh al-Islāmī*, 7th edn., (Beirut: Markaz Dirāsāt al-Waḥdah al-ʿArabiyyah, 2001).

Al-Jaṣṣāṣ, Abū Bakr Aḥmad ibn ʿAlī, *Aḥkām al-Qur'ān* (Beirut: Dār al-Kutub al-ʿIlmiyyah, 1415 AH/1994 CE).

Jumah, Adnan Muhammad, *Rafʿ al-Ḥaraj fī al-Sharīʿah al-Islāmiyyah* (Damascus: Dār al-Imām al-Jārī, 1979).

Al-Jurjānī, ʿAlī ibn Muḥammad, *Al-Taʿrīfāt*.

Al-Juwaynī, Abū al-Maʿālī ʿAbd al-Malik ibn ʿAbd Allāh, *Al-Burhān fī Uṣūl al-Fiqh*.

_____, *Al-Kifāyah fī al-Jadal*, Introduction and commentary by Husayn Mahmud (Cairo: Maktabat al-Kulliyāt al-Azhariyyah, 1399 AH/1979 CE).

Al-Kāsānī, ʿAlā' al-Dīn Abū Bakr ibn Masʿūd, *Badā'iʿ al-Ṣāniʿ*.

Al-Khadimi, Nur al-Din Mukhtar, *Al-Ijitihād al-Maqāṣidī: Hujiyyatuhu, Ḍawābiṭuhu, Majālātuhu* (Kitab al-Ummah no. 65, 1419 AH/1998 CE).

Al-Khaṭīb al-Baghdādī, Abū Bakr Aḥmad ibn ʿAlī, *Al-Faqīh wa al-Mutafaqqih*, ed., Abu Abd al-Rahman Adil ibn Yusuf al-Gharazi, 2 vols., (Dammam: Dār ibn al-Jawzī, 1417 AH/1996 CE).

Khosrow, Minla, *Mir'āt al-Uṣūl fī Sharḥ Mirqāt al-Wuṣūl*.

Al-Laknawī, Abd al-ʿAlī Muḥammad ibn Niẓām al-Dīn, *Fawātiḥ al-Raḥamūt bi Sharḥ Muslim al-Thubūt*, 2 vols., ed. Abd Allah Mahmud Umar, (Beirut: Dār al-Kutub al-ʿIlmiyyah, 2002).

Linton, Ralph, *Tree of Culture* (Shajarat al-Ḥaḍārah), translated by Ahmad Fakhri, (Cairo: Maktabat al-Anjalū-Maṣriyah, n.d.), vol. 1.

Al-Luwayhiq, Abd al-Rahman, *Al-Ghulū fī al-Dīn fī Ḥayāt al-Muslimīn al-Muʿāṣirah: Dirāsah ʿIlmiyyah ḥawla Maẓāhir al-Ghulū wa Mafāhīm al-Taṭarruf wa al-Uṣūliyyah* (Beirut: Mu'assasat al-Risālah, 1992).

Al-Maḥallī, Jalāl al-Dīn Muḥammad ibn Aḥmad, *Sharḥ Jamʿ al-Jawāmiʿ*.

Mahyub, Abd al-Hamid, *Aḥkām al-Fatwā wa al-Istiftā'* (Cairo: Dār al-Kitāb al-Jāmiʿī, 1404 AH/1984 CE).

Majallat Majmaʿ al-Fiqh al-Islāmī, year 1, no. 8. (1988).

Majmaʿ al-Lughah al-ʿArabiyyah, *Al-Muʿjam al-Wajīz* (Cairo: Dār al-Taḥrīr, 1980).

Al-Masiri, Abd al-Wahhab and Fathi al-Turayki, *Al-Ḥadāthah wa mā Baᶜda al-Ḥadāthah* (Damascus: Dār al-Fikr, 2003).

Al-Māwardī, Abū al-Ḥasan ᶜAlī ibn Muḥammad, *Al-Aḥkām al-Sulṭāniyyah wa al-Wilāyāh al-Dīniyyah*.

_____, *Al-Nukat wa al-ᶜUyūn: Tafsīr al-Māwardī*.

Al-Mazid, Salih, *Fiqh al-A'immah al-Arbaᶜah Bayna al-Zāhidīna fīhi wa al-Mutaᶜaṣṣibīna lahu*.

Al-Mujtamaᶜ, no 1321, (1996).

Al-Munāwī, ᶜAbd al-Ra'ūf Muḥammad ibn ᶜAlī, *Fayḍ al-Qadīr: Sharḥ al-Jāmiᶜ al-Ṣaghīr min Aḥādīth al-Bashīr al-Nadhīr*.

Muslim ibn al-Ḥajjāj, Abū al-Ḥusayn, *Ṣaḥīḥ Muslim*, ed., Fuad Abd al-Baqi, 2nd edn., (Dār Iḥyā' al-Turāth al-ᶜArabī, 1372 AH/1962 CE).

_____, *Ṣaḥīḥ Muslim bi Sharḥ al-Imām al-Nawawī*, known as *Al-Minhāj: Sharḥ Ṣaḥīḥ Muslim ibn al-Ḥajjāj*.

Al-Musnad, Muhammad, compiler and arranger, *Fatāwā al-Ḥajj wa al-ᶜUmrah wa al-Ziyārah*.

Al-Nafisah, Abd al-Rahman, "Risālatun fī Fiqh al-Ḥajj wa al-ᶜUmrah," *Majallat al-Buḥūth al-Fiqhiyyah al-Muᶜāṣirah*, no 33, 1416 AH/1995 CE.

Al-Najjar, Abd al-Hamid, *Fiqh al-Taḥaḍḍur al-Islāmī* (Beirut: Dār al-Gharb al-Islāmī, 1999).

Al-Nasafī, Abū al-Barakāt ᶜAbd Allāh ibn Aḥmad, *Kashf al-Asrār: Sharḥ al-Muṣannif ᶜalā al-Manār*.

Al-Nawawī, Abū Zakariyyā Yaḥyā ibn Sharaf, *Tahdhīb al-Asmā' wa al-Lughāt* (Dār al Fikr, 1416 AH/1995 CE).

_____, *Al-Majmūᶜ: Sharḥ al-Muhadhdhab*.

_____, *Sharḥ al-Nawawī ᶜalā Ṣaḥīḥ Muslim* (Beirut: Dār Iḥyā' al-Turāth al-ᶜArabī), 1972.

Al-Nisābūrī, al-Ḥākim Abū ᶜAbd Allāh Muḥammad ibn ᶜAbd Allāh, *Al-Mustadrak ᶜalā al-Ṣaḥīḥayn fī al-Ḥadīth*.

Al-Qāḍī ᶜIyāḍ, Abū al-Faḍl ᶜIyāḍ ibn Mūsā, *Tartīb al-Madārik wa Taqrīb al-Masālik li Maᶜrifat Aᶜlām Madhhab Mālik*, ed., Said Aghrab, 3rd edn., (Rabat: Ministry of Religious Endowments and Islamic Affairs, 1403 AH/1983 CE).

Al-Qahtani, Musfir ibn Ali, *Fiqh al-Muwāzanāt* (Dār al-Dhakhā'ir, 1420 AH/1999 CE).

Al-Qāqūnī, Abū ᶜAbd Allāh Muḥammad Mufliḥ, *Al-Ādāb al-Sharᶜiyyah*.

Al-Qaradawi, Yusuf, *Al-Ijtihād al-Muᶜāṣir bayna al-Inḍibāṭ wa al-Infirāṭ* (Cairo: Dār at-Tawzīᶜ wa al-Nashr al-Islāmiyyah, 1414 AH/1994 CE).

_____, *Al-Ijtihād fī al-Sharīʿah al-Islāmiyyah: Maʿa Naḍarāt Taḥlīliyyah fī al-Ijtihād al-Muʿāṣir* (Kuwait: Dār al-Qalam, 1985).

_____, *Al-Siyāsah al-Sharʿiyyah fī Ḍaw' Nuṣūṣ al-Sharīʿah wa Maqāṣidiha: Naḥwa Waḥdah Fikriyyah li al-ʿĀmilīna li al-Islām* (Cairo: Maktabat Wahbah, 1419 AH/1998 CE).

_____, *Al-Fatwā bayna al-Inḍibāṭ wa al-Tasayyub* (Cairo: Dār al-Ṣaḥwah, 1988).

_____, *Markaz al-Mar'ah fī al-Ḥayāt al-Islāmiyyah*.

_____, *Al-Muslimūn wa al-ʿAwlamah* (Cairo: Dār al-Tawzīʿ wa al-Nashr al-Islāmiyyah, 1421 AH/2000 CE).

Al-Qarn, Awad, *Al-Mukhtaṣar al-Wajīz fī Maqāṣid al-Tashrīʿ* (Jeddah: Dār al-Andalus al-Khaḍrā', 1419 AH/1998 CE).

Al-Qarrāfī, Abū al-ʿAbbās Aḥmad ibn Idrīs, *Al-Iḥkām fī Tamyīz al-Fatāwā ʿan al-Aḥkām wa Taṣarrufāt al-Qāḍī wa al-lmām*.

_____, *Sharḥ Tanqīḥ al-Fuṣūl*, 2nd edn., (al-Maktabah al-Azhariyyah, 1414 AH/1993 CE).

_____, *Al-Furūq*.

Al-Qasimi, Muhammad ibn Muhammad, *Al-Fatwā fī al-Islām*.

Al-Rabiah, Abd al-Aziz ibn Abd al-Rahman ibn Ali. *Al-Sabab ʿinda al-Uṣūliyīn*, 3 vols., (Riyadh: Imam Muḥammad ibn Saʿūd Islamic University, 1980 CE).

_____, *Al-Muftī fī al-Sharīʿah al-Islāmiyyah*.

Al-Raysuni, Ahmad, *Al-Taʿaddud al-Tanẓīmī fī al-Ḥarakah al-Islāmiyyah* (Maṭbūʿāt al-Jamʿiyyah al-Islāmiyyah, 1416 AH/1995 CE).

_____, *Naḍariyyat al-Maqāṣid ʿInda al-Imām al-Shāṭibī* (University Publications Series, no. 1, 2nd edn., (Virginia: International Institute of Islamic Thought, 1412 AH/1991 CE).

_____, *Al-Muftī fī al-Sharī'ah al-Islāmiyyah*.

Al-Rāzī, Fakhr al-Dīn Muḥammad ibn ʿUmar, *Al-Kāshif ʿan Uṣūl al-Dalā'il wa Fuṣūl al-ʿIlal*.

_____, *Al-Maḥṣūl fī ʿIlm Uṣūl al-Fiqh* (Beirut: Dār al-Kutub al-ʿIlmiyyah, 1408 AH/1987 CE).

Al-Rāzī, Muḥammad ibn Abū Bakr, *Mukhtār al-Ṣiḥāḥ*.

Riyad, Muhammad Riyad, *Uṣūl al-Fatwā wa al-Qaḍā' fī al-Madhhab al-Mālikī*.

Al-Rummani, Zayd. *Maqāṣid al-Sharīʿah al-lslāmiyyah* (Dār al-Ghayth, 1415 AH/1994 CE).

Al-Sadlan, Salih ibn Ghanim, *Wujūb Taṭbīq al-Sharīʿah al-Islāmiyyah fī Kulli ʿAṣr* (Riyadh, Dār Balansiyah, 1417 AH/1997 CE).

Al-Salus, Alī Ahmad, *Al-Iqtiṣād al-Islāmī wa al-Qaḍāyā al-Fiqhiyyah al-Muᶜāṣirah* (Beirut: Mu'assasat al-Rayyān, 1996).

Al-Sarkhasī, Abū Bakr Muḥammad ibn Aḥmad, *Al-Mabsūṭ*.

Al-Sawi, Salah, *Al-Thawābit wa al-Mutaghayyirāt fī Masīrat al-ᶜAmal al-Islāmī al-Muᶜāṣir* (London: Al-Muntadā al-Islāmī, 1414 AH/1999 CE).

Al-Shāfiᶜī, Muḥammad ibn Idrīs, *Al-Risālah*.

Shakir, Munib Mahmud, *Al-ᶜAmal bi al-Iḥtiyāṭ fī al-Fiqh al-Islāmī* (Riyadh: Dār al-Nafā'is, 1418 AH/1997 CE).

Al-Shahristānī, Abū al-Fatḥ Muḥammad ibn ᶜAbd al-Karīm, *Al-Milal wa al-Niḥal*.

Al-Shalabi, Muhammad Mustafa, *Uṣūl al-Fiqh al-Islāmī*, 3rd edn., (Beirut, Dār al-Nahḍah al-ᶜArabiyyah, 1406 AH/1986 CE).

_____, *Taᶜlīl al-Aḥkām: ᶜArḍ wa Taḥlīl li Ṭarīqat al-Taᶜlīl wa Taṭawwurātihā fī ᶜUṣūr al-Ijtihād wa al-Taqlīd*.

Al-Shanqiti, Muhammad al-Amin, *Aḍwā' al-Bayān fī Īḍāḥ al-Qur'ān*.

Al-Sharafi, Abd al-Majid al-Susuwah, *Al-Ijitihād al-Jamāᶜī fī al-Tashrīᶜ al-Islāmī* (1418 AH/1997 CE).

Al-Sharbīnī, Shams al-Dīn Muḥammad ibn Aḥmad, *Mughnī al-Muḥtāj ilā Maᶜrifat Maᶜānī Alfāẓ al-Minhāj*.

Al-Shāṭibī, Abū Isḥāq Ibrāhīm ibn Mūsā ibn Muḥammad al-Lakhmī, *Al-Muwāfaqāt*, Introduction by Bakr ibn Abd Allah Abu Zayd, text arrangement, introduction, commentary and sourcing of hadiths by Abu Ubaydah Mashhur ibn Hasan Al Salman, (Khobar: Dār ibn ᶜAffān, 1417 AH/1997 CE).

_____, *Al-Fatāwā*, Compiled and edited by Muhammad Abu al-Ajfan.

Al-Shawkānī, Muḥammad ibn ᶜAlī, *Irshād al-Fuḥūl ilā Taḥqīq al-Ḥaqq min ᶜIlm al-Uṣūl* (Nizār al-Bāz, 1417 AH/1996 CE).

_____, *Kitāb al-Sayl al-Jarrār al-Mutadaffiq ᶜalā Ḥadā'iq al-Azhār*.

Al-Shaykh, Abd al-Sattar, *ᶜUmar ibn ᶜAbd al-ᶜAzīz: Khāmis al-Khulafā' al-Rāshidīn* (Damascus: Dār al-Qalam, 1412 AH/1992 CE).

Al-Subkī, Tāj al-Dīn Abū al-Naṣr ᶜAbd al-Wahhāb ibn ᶜAlī, *Al-Ibhāj fī Sharḥ al-Minhāj*, being a commentary on al-Bayḍāwī's *Minhāj al-Wuṣūl ilā ᶜIlm al-Uṣūl*.

Al-Suyūṭī, Jalāl al-Dīn ᶜAbd al-Raḥmān ibn Abū Bakr, *Al-Ashbāh wa al-Naẓā'ir* (Beirut: Dār al-Kitāb al-ᶜArabī, 1407 AH/1986 CE).

_____, *Tārīkh al-Khulafā'* (Beirut, Dār al-Kutub al-ᶜIlmiyyah).

_____, *Ṣaḥīḥ al-Jāmiᶜ al-Ṣaghīr wa Ziyādatuhu* (*al-Fatḥ al-Kabīr*), ed., Muhammad Nasir al-Din al-Albani.

Al-Ṭabarānī, ʿAbd al-Qāsim Sulaymān ibn Aḥmad ibn Ayyūb, *Al-Muʿjam al-Awsaṭ*.

Al-Ṭabarī, Abū Jaʿfar Muḥammad ibn Jarīr, *Tārīkh al-Rusul wa al-Mulūk*.

Al-Tarturi, Husayn, "Fiqh al-Wāqiʿ: Dirāsah Uṣūliyyah Fiqhiyyah," *Majallat al-Buḥūth al-Fiqhiyyah al-Muʿāṣirah*, no. 34 (1418 AH/1997 CE), pp. 71-114.

_____, *Tafsīr al-Ṭabarī: Jāmiʿ al-Bayān ʿan Ta'wīl Āy al-Qurʿān*.

Toynbee, Arnold Joseph, *A Study of History* (New York: Oxford University Press), 1987.

Al-Ṭūfī, Sulaymān ibn ʿAbd al-Qawī, *Al-Bulbul fī Uṣūl al-Fiqh*, being an abridged version of *Rawḍat al-Nāẓir* by al-Muwaffaq ibn Qudāmah, 2nd edn., (Riyadh: Maktabat al-Imām al-Shāfiʿī, 1410 AH/1989-1990 CE).

Al-Turki, Abd Allah ibn Abd al-Muhsin, *Uṣūl Madhhab al-Imām Aḥmad: Dirāsah Uṣūliyyah Muqāranah*, 3rd edn., (Beirut: Mu'assasat al-Risālah, 1410 AH/1989 CE).

Al-Tuwayjiri, Hammud, *Taghlīẓ al-Malāmʿalā al-Mutasarriʿīn ilā al-Futyā wa Taghyīr al-Aḥkām*.

Al-Ubaydi, Hamadi, *Al-Shāṭibī wa Maqāṣid al-Sharīʿah*.

Al-Umari, Jalal al-Din, *Al-Amr bi al-Maʿrūf wa al-Nahī ʿan al-Munkar* (Kuwait: 1404 AH/1984 CE).

Uthaymin, Shaykh Muhammad ibn Salih, *Al-Sharḥ al-Mumtiʿ ʿalā Zād al-Mustaqniʿ*, Compiled and arranged by Sulayman ibn Abd Allah ibn Hammud Abu al-Khayl and Khalid ibn Ali ibn Muhammad al-Mushayqih, (Riyadh: Mu'assasat Āsām li al-Nashr, 1995-1997).

Vallely, Paul, "How Islamic Inventors Changed the World," *The Independent*, March 11, 2006. See also *1001 Inventions: The Enduring Legacy of Muslim Civilization*, ed. Salim T.S. al-Hassani, 3rd edn., (Washington: National Geographic, 2012).

Wakīʿ ibn al-Jarrāḥ, *Al-Zuhd*.

Al-Wakili, Muhammad, *Fiqh al-Awlawiyyāt: Dirāsah fī al-Ḍawābiṭ* (Herndon, Virginia: International Institute of Islamic Thought, 1416 AH/1995 CE).

Al-Yubi, Muhammad Sad, *Maqāṣid al-Sharīʿah al-Islāmiyyah wa ʿAlāqatuhā bi al-Adillah al-Sharʿiyyah* (Riyadh: Dār al-Hijrah li al-Nashr wa al-Tawzīʿ, 1418 AH/1997 CE).

Al-Zarkashī, Badr al-Dīn Abū ʿAbd Allāh Muḥammad, *Al-Baḥr al-Muḥīt fī Uṣūl al-Fiqh*, ed., Abd al-Qadir Abd Allah al-Ani. Revised by Umar Sulayman al-Ashqar. 6 vols, 2nd edn., (Kuwait: Ministry of Endowments and Islamic Affairs, 1413 AH/1992 CE).

_____, *Al-Manthūr fī al-Qawāʿid.*

_____, *Tashnīf al-Masāmiʿ bi Jamʿ al-Jawāmiʿ li Tāj al-Dīn al-Subkī.*

Al-Zarqa, Ahmad, *Sharḥ al-Qawāʿid al-Fiqhiyyah* (Damascus: Dār al-Qalam, 1409 AH/1989 CE).

_____, *Al-Istiṣlāḥ wa al-Maṣāliḥ al-Mursalah fī al-Sharīʿah al-Islāmiyyah wa Uṣūl Fiqhihā: Dirāsah Muqāranah fī al-Madhāhib al-Fiqhiyyah al-Thamāniyah, maʿa Muqaddimah Tamhīdiyyah Mūjazah ʿan al-Maṣādir al-Fiqhiyyah al-Arbaʿah wa al-Istiḥsān* (Damascus: Dār al-Qalam, 1988 CE).

_____, *Al-Madkhal al-Fiqhī al-ʿĀmm*, 10th edn., (Dār al-Fikr, 1387 AH/1967 CE).

Zaydan, Abd al-Karim, *Al-Wajīz fī Uṣūl al-Fiqh* (Dār al-Tawzīʿ, 1414 AH/1993 CE).

Al-Zaylaʿī, ʿUthmān ibn ʿAlī, *Tabyīn al-Ḥaqā'iq fī Sharḥ Kanz al-Raqā'iq* (Bulaq: Al-Maṭbaʿah al-Amīriyyah, 1315 AH/1897 CE).

Ziyadah, Ridwan, *Ṣadā al-Ḥadāthah* (Beirut: al-Markaz al-Thaqāfī al-ʿArabī, 2003).

Al-Zuhayli, Wahbah Mustafa, *Uṣūl al-Fiqh al-Islāmī* (Damascus: Dār al-Fikr, 1406 AH/1985 CE).

_____, *Al-Fiqh al-Islāmī wa Adillatuhu: al-Shāmil li al-Adillah al-Sharʿiyyah wa al-Ārā' al-Madhhabiyyah wa Ahamm al-Naẓariyyāt al-Fiqhiyyah wa Taḥqīq al-Aḥādīth al-Nabawiyyah wa Takhrījuhā wa Fahrasah Alifbā'iyyah li al-Mawḍūʿāt wa Ahamm al-Masā'il al-Fiqhiyyah.*

GLOSSARY OF TERMS

Ḥasan: Translated usually as "good", a hadith classed as *ḥasan* is a hadith one of whose narrators fails to meet the standards of moral excellence required for it to be classed as *ṣaḥīḥ*, or authentic. (See the entry for *ṣaḥīḥ* below.)

Iftā': The process of formulating and issuing Islamic legal rulings (*fatāwā*, singular, *fatwā*).

Ijtihād: The effort exerted by a suitably qualified scholar of jurisprudence to arrive at an accurate conceptualization of the divine will based on Muslim legal sources (the Qur'an, the Hadith, analogical deduction and consensus) and the means by which to apply this will in a given age and under given circumstances; as such, *ijtihād* is the effort exerted to derive a legal ruling from Muslim legal sources, and to reach certainty on questions of an ambiguous nature.

Istidlāl: The search for textual evidence on the basis of which one may arrive at a ruling on this or that question or situation.

Istiḥsān, or juristic preference: A decision to refrain from applying to a given situation the same ruling which has been applied to analogous situations in favor of another ruling which is more in keeping with the aims of Islamic Law. In other words, juristic preference involves giving human interests and *maqāṣid al-sharīʿah* priority over the results of *qiyās*, or analogical deduction.

Istiṣlāḥ, or reasoning based on unrestricted interests: The practice of issuing a legal ruling concerning a case which is not mentioned explicitly in any authoritative Islamic legal text and on which there is no consensus, based on consideration for an unrestricted interest (see below, *al-maṣāliḥ al-mursalah*).

Kharijites (Arabic, *al-Khawāriji*; literally, "those who went out"): The Kharijites were a group of Muslims who, after initially supporting the authority of the Prophet's cousin and son-in-law ʿAlī ibn Abī Ṭālib, later rejected his leadership. The Kharijites, who first emerged in the late seventh century in today's southern Iraq, developed extreme doctrines that further set them apart from both mainstream Sunnite and Shiite Muslims. In particular, the Kharijites were prone to declare other Muslims to be unbelievers.

Al-Maṣāliḥ al-Mursalah (singular, *maṣlaḥah mursalah*), or unrestricted interests (sometimes referred to also as public interests): Interests which are not explicitly identified by any text in the Qur'an or the Sunnah but which are generally agreed upon based on circumstances that arise in human society. Examples of unrestricted interests include the paving of roads, the setting up of administrative offices to handle public needs, the use of traffic signals, the construction of sewers and waste disposal facilities, vaccination against disease, etc.

Muʿtazilah (Arabic, *al-muʿtazilah*, or "those who have separated themselves", a term by which they were known by their opponents): Adherents of a school of scholastic theology which flourished in the Iraqi cities of Basra and Baghdad during the second-fourth AH/eighth–tenth centuries CE (the Umayyad and Abbasid eras). This school is best known for its assertion that, because of God's perfect unity and eternal nature, the Qur'an must have been created, as nothing could be co-eternal with God. The school's adherents also held that God's commands are accessible to rational thought and inquiry, and that human reason is the final arbiter in distinguishing right from wrong.

Mujtahid: Someone who engages in *ijtihād*. (See *ijtihād*.)

Sadd al-dharāʾiʿ (literally, "the blocking of pretexts"): The prohibition of anything which has the potential of leading to that which is forbidden by Islamic law.

Ṣaḥīḥ: A hadith or tradition classified as *ṣaḥīḥ*, or "sound", is traceable back to the Prophet through a chain of narrators all of whom are known to have been pious and trustworthy.

Unrestricted interests: See entry for *al-maṣāliḥ al-mursalah* above.

Uṣūl al-Fiqh: The principles of Islamic jurisprudence.

Ẓahirīs: Followers of an Islamic legal and theological school that insisted on strict adherence to the literal text (*ẓāhir*) of the Qur'an and the Sunnah as the only source of Muslim law. The Ẓahirīs rejected analogical deduction (*qiyās*) as a source of juristic rulings and looked askance at consensus (*ijmāʿ*).

Zaydis: A Muslim sect that emerged out of Shiite Islam, and who take their name from Zayd ibn ʿAlī (d. 123 AH/740 CE). In matters of theology, the Zaydis are close to the Muʿtazilite school, and of the Shiites, the Zaydis are most similar to Sunnis in their doctrines and juristic opinions.